The Method(s) of Phenomenology

Maren Wehrle

The Method(s) of Phenomenology

An Introduction

Maren Wehrle
Erasmus School of Philosophy
Erasmus University
Rotterdam, The Netherlands

ISBN 978-3-662-71776-9   ISBN 978-3-662-71777-6   (eBook)
https://doi.org/10.1007/978-3-662-71777-6

Translation from the German language edition: "Phänomenologie. Eine Einführung" by Maren Wehrle, © Springer-Verlag GmbH Deutschland, ein Teil von Springer Nature 2022. Published by J.B. Metzler. All Rights Reserved.

This book is a translation of the original German edition "Phänomenologie. Eine Einführung" by Maren Wehrle, published by Springer-Verlag GmbH, DE in 2022. The translation was done with the help of an artificial intelligence machine translation tool. A subsequent human revision was done primarily in terms of content, so that the book will read stylistically differently from a conventional translation. Springer Nature works continuously to further the development of tools for the production of books and on the related technologies to support the authors.

Editorial Contact: Franziska Remeika

This Palgrave Macmillan imprint is published by the registered company Springer-Verlag GmbH, DE, part of Springer Nature.
The registered company address is: Heidelberger Platz 3, 14197 Berlin, Germany

If disposing of this product, please recycle the paper.

Preface: To the Things and Back

This book sets out to clarify what the famous phenomenological imperative 'to the things themselves' means in theory and practice. The focus is less on the question of what phenomenology *is* and more on what we actually *do* when we practise phenomenology. This is not, therefore, an introduction to the historical texts or figures of phenomenology but an attempt to present its method(s) in a unified way. All phenomenology, whether classical or critical, theoretical or applied, according to the guiding thesis of this introduction, attempts to describe without prejudice (► Chap. 2, ► Sect. 2.1), to determine the general (► Chap. 2, ► Sect. 2.2), or to inquire into the conditions (► Chap. 2, ► Sect. 2.3). True to the motto 'to the things themselves', the method(s) of phenomenology is not simply defined schematically or abstractly but illustrated and discussed using concrete examples.

First, the introductory chapter 'To the Things Themselves?' considers what things or objects actually *are* for phenomenology, and what it means to want to come to these things 'themselves' (► Chap. 1). This is followed by a first overview of (the) phenomenological method(s), starting from Edmund Husserl (► Chap. 1, ► Sect. 1.3).

The second chapter 'Methods of Phenomenology' gives examples of description, eidetic variation, and transcendental questions to show the extent to which these methods depend on each other or can be applied independently of each other (► Chap. 2). Finally, it presents criticisms, further developments, and changes in these methods after and beyond Husserl (► Chap. 2, ► Sect. 2.4).

The third and final chapter 'Phenomenology in Action' is dedicated to contemporary problems (► Chap. 3, ► Sect. 3.1) and interdisciplinary applications of phenomenology, either within philosophy (► Chap. 3, ► Sect. 3.2) or in other disciplines (► Chap. 3, ► Sect. 3.3). Phenomenology, as this introduction concludes, was, and is, primarily a method, or rather, a methodological project, and thus a method in progress (► Chap. 3, ► Sect. 3.4). This is what makes it so adaptable for use on contemporary questions and in disciplines outside of philosophy. The intention and practice of phenomenology is to describe and understand the world and its various 'things' as well as possible. In doing so, it must constantly re-examine whether its methods are doing justice to these 'things'.

Once these 'things' have been arrived at, phenomenology must not stop there but must continue to critically monitor its approach. Complacency and dogmatism are the pitfalls that every phenomenological method must avoid. Therefore, we must not only get to the things, but also get back, as Hans Blumenberg puts it in his book *To the Things and Back* (2002). Blumenberg's playful criticism of Husserl's plea 'back to the things themselves' points out that a philosophy of experience can never be unmediated and pure. We always grasp experience through the detour of concepts, metaphors, and symbols. The directness demanded by the credo 'to the things' can thus, according to Blumenberg, only be achieved in and through indirectness.

Husserl himself saw this problem but tried to circumvent it pragmatically. Since we cannot philosophize and reflect in any other way than linguistically, we have no choice but to work with what we have. This is no reason for phenomenology to simply abandon the task of describing and clarifying reality or merely revert to analysing already existing concepts and terms. However, language must be used carefully and constantly tested and refined in the course of description. This explains Husserl's searching, creative, and sometimes cumbersome use of technical terms, such as 'kept-in-grip' (*Noch-im-Griff-behalten*), 'intending-beyond-itself' (*Über-sich-hinaus-meinen*), 'co-perceive' (*Mit-wahrnehmen*), 'sensings' (*Empfindnisse*), or the use of mathematical terms such as 'pairing' (*Paarung*), 'index', 'continuum', and 'variation'.

It is therefore the task of all phenomenology to continually subject language, as a historical-cultural means of description, to critical reflection and to remain aware of its influence and the necessary indirectness of every description. This can only succeed, like phenomenology itself, with intersubjective cooperation, in which different perspectives merge into a shared objectivity and mutually correct or confirm each other. In Husserl's phenomenology—and indeed in *all* phenomenology—it becomes apparent that the path to the things themselves (objectivity) leads us back to an experiencing subjectivity, but ultimately to the insight that neither the ready-made world nor the absolute subject is at the beginning. Rather, it is a practical, historical, and discursive intersubjectivity, which constantly and, for the most part, inconspicuously gives, updates, or shifts meaning.

At the same time, the statement also points to the irreducibility and transcendence of the 'things' and the world, to which we are constantly thrown back. It is a world whose meaning we cannot arbitrarily construct, but always only find and interpret. The hopefully unbiased description, the determination of the general, or the inquiry into the conditions is always tied to a real, factual, and thus resistant world. This world with all its 'things' is what stands at the beginning and end of every phenomenological description, as its guide as well as its goal. It is a world that we can neither create, possess as an object, nor fully grasp, but which is always one step ahead of our descriptions, determinations, and explanations, just as we ourselves are when we attempt to describe this world of which we are already a part.

Introductory Literature

- Bernet, Rudolf, Iso Kern, and Eduard Marbach. 1993. *An Introduction to Husserlian Phenomenology*. Northwestern University Studies in Phenomenology and Existential Philosophy. Evanston, IL: Northwestern University Press.
- Blumenberg, Hans. 2002. *Zu den Sachen und zurück*. Frankfurt a.M.: Suhrkamp.
- Card, Claudia, ed. 2003. *The Cambridge Companion to Simone de Beauvoir*. Cambridge, UK: Cambridge University Press.
- Carman, Taylor, and Mark B.N. Hansen, eds. 2005. *The Cambridge Companion to Merleau-Ponty*. Cambridge, UK: Cambridge University Press.

- Churchill, Steven, and Jack Reynolds, eds. 2013. *Jean-Paul Sartre: Key Concepts*. Slough, UK: Acumen Publishing.
- Critchley, Simon, and Robert Bernasconi, eds. 2002. *The Cambridge Companion to Levinas*. Cambridge, UK: Cambridge University Press.
- De Santis, Daniele, Burt C. Hopkins, and Claudio Majolino, eds. 2020. *The Routledge Handbook of Phenomenology and Phenomenological Philosophy*. New York: Routledge.
- Diprose, Rosalyn, and Jack Reynolds, eds. 2008. *Merleau-Ponty: Key Concepts*. Slough, UK: Acumen Publishing.
- Gallagher, Shaun. 2022. *Phenomenology*, 2nd edition. London: Palgrave Macmillan.
- Guignon, Charles, ed. 2006. *The Cambridge Companion to Heidegger*. Cambridge, UK: Cambridge University Press.
- Howells, Christina, ed. 1992. *The Cambridge Companion to Sartre*. Cambridge, UK: Cambridge University Press.
- Inwood, Michael. 1997. *Heidegger: A Very Short Introduction*. Oxford: Oxford University Press.
- Jacobs, Hanne, ed. 2022. *The Husserlian Mind*. Routledge Philosophical Minds. London: Routledge.
- Luft, Sebastian, and Søren Overgaard, eds. 2012. *The Routledge Companion to Phenomenology*. New York: Routledge.
- Moran, Dermot. 1999. *Introduction to Phenomenology*. New York: Routledge.
- Moran, Dermot. 2005. *Edmund Husserl: Founder of Phenomenology*. Cambridge, UK: Polity Press.
- Polt, Richard. 1999. *Heidegger: An Introduction*. New York: Routledge.
- Sokolowski, Robert. 2000. *Introduction to Phenomenology*. Cambridge, UK: Cambridge University Press.
- Spiegelberg, Herbert. (1960) 1994. *The Phenomenological Movement. A Historical Introduction*, 3rd revised and enlarged edition. Dordrecht: Springer.
- Trawny, Peter. 2019. *Heidegger: A Critical Introduction*. Trans. Rodrigo Therezo. Cambridge, UK: Polity Press.
- Zahavi, Dan. 2003. *Husserl's Phenomenology*. Stanford: Stanford University Press.
- Zahavi, Dan, ed. 2012. *The Oxford Handbook of Contemporary Phenomenology*. Oxford: Oxford University Press.
- Zahavi, Dan, ed. 2018. *The Oxford Handbook of the History of Phenomenology*. Oxford: Oxford University Press.
- Zahavi, Dan. (2018) 2025. *Phenomenology: The Basics*, 2nd edition. New York: Routledge.

Maren Wehrle
Rotterdam, The Netherlands

Acknowledgement

A book may be written by one author, but it does not write itself, or rather only in critical intersubjective exchange with others. I would like to take this opportunity to thank my dear phenomenological friends and colleagues Thomas Vongehr, Thiemo Breyer, Diego D' Angelo, and Julia Jansen for their helpful advice and critical comments on the original German version, as well as Michael Schnegg for his anthropological and ethnological expertise that lead to a revised section on phenomenological anthropology and ethnography.

This book is an (instantly) automatically translated, revised, updated, and slightly expanded version of an introduction to phenomenology published in German in 2022 (in the series: Methods of Philosophy) by J.B. Metzler Verlag Berlin. In this context, I would especially like to express my thanks to Jeremy Hovda, who not only managed to bring an awkward and often misleading AI translation in form and content into a melodious English that is adequate to the philosophical content, but also contributed significantly to the clarity, readability, and content adequacy of this book with his philosophical expertise.

Last but not least, I would like to express my thanks to my beloved Michel and our little daughter Emma for always bringing me back down to earth and reminding me to devote myself to things and people instead of just indulging in ivory tower of theories.

Contents

Introduction: To the Things Themselves?

Contents

1

The guiding principle of phenomenology, founded in the twentieth century by Edmund Husserl, was 'back to the things themselves' (Husserl LI1, p. 168/Hua XIX/1, p. 10). This was felt as a real liberation within philosophy after the age of German Idealism (epitomized by Kant, Fichte, Schelling, and Hegel), in which the knowing subject, reason, or absolute spirit were central. Finally, the world and things, as well as experience, could again take center stage instead of a critique of knowledge (epistemology), dialectics, or metaphysical speculation. As Husserl emphasizes in the preface to the second edition of the *Logical Investigations* (1900 first edition, 1913 second edition), one must not rely on already established concepts, theories, or methods, but must return to the "immediately envisaged and seized things themselves", leaving the "last word to these things themselves and to one's work upon such things" (LI1, p. 4/Hua XVIII, p. 9). Against any metaphysical speculation, but also against the view of philosophy as mere analysis of concepts, a plea is made here for a return to, and revaluation of, intuition (sense experience): "Away with the hollow word analyses. We must question the things themselves. Back to experience, to intuition, which alone can give sense and reasonable right to our words" (Hua XXV, p. 21, automatic translation, edited).

But what are these 'things' that Husserl speaks of? And why are they philosophically relevant? These are the basic questions of phenomenology. An initial consideration reveals the necessarily circular structure of experience and knowledge. Both science and everyday experience always start from certain 'things', e.g., natural science from nature or experience from the house perceived over there. These things are taken for granted, although at the beginning of each investigation or experience it is not yet clear what these 'things' are in detail or how to determine them (more fully). Phenomenology makes us aware that we always deal with things that are already somehow determined, i.e., perceived as something specific. It wants to find out how it is possible that we experience individual things, as well as the world as a whole, as meaningful.

As the name 'phenomenology' already suggests, the things are treated as phenomena.

> **Definition**
>
> 'Phenomena' (gr. *phainomena*) are the things in their current and possible appearance for us, i.e., not the 'things' as they are in or of themselves (the noumenon, or 'thing in-itself', in Kant's sense). The slogan 'to the things themselves' thus seems a little misleading, as it is not about determining things independently of our subjective experience but about the things as they appear to us in experience. Phenomenology is therefore the description of how something appears to us and the attempt to clarify why something appears to us in this way and not otherwise.

■■ Meticulous Description

What defines the method of this new 'science of phenomena' is description: "The true method follows the nature of the things to be investigated, not our prejudices and models" (Husserl, Hua XXV, p. 26, automatic translation, edited). The work on phenomena must therefore not allow for prior assumptions or established philosophical methods such as deduction, argumentation, dialectics, or causal explanation. It is first and foremost a meticulous description of what appears to us, and only within the limits of the given appearance. For example, a house always appears to us within perception from a certain perspective, such as the view from the front. That is, the 'thing', house, is only partially and incompletely given to us in the various appearances of it. This 'how' of the way of appearing not only says something about how bodily subjects perceive (namely, perspectivally), but also something about the thing, 'house', as a physically extended object. In contrast to the psyche or psychic experiences, which have neither a fixed position nor an extension, we can see and touch the house, we can walk around it and look at it more closely. Yet we can never perceive all its aspects at once, which is why perception remains incomplete.

The required turn to what appears to us is thus supposed to bring us closer to the 'nature' or 'essence' of things. The appearing 'things' are thus the starting point of phenomenological description and analysis, but also its goal. But how do we get to the things themselves, if they are only given to us incompletely and relatively in subjective experience? Why does Husserl start his search for the essence of things and the world with the experiencing subject? And what are the 'things' of philosophy?

1.1　Back to the Matter of Philosophy

■ ■ **Fundamental Questions and Problems**

'Back to the things themselves' is first and foremost a call for philosophy to care more about the 'things' than about itself. Instead of losing itself in the exegesis of old philosophies or internal debates, understanding itself as a worldview (among many other worldviews), or merely presenting itself as a handmaid of the natural sciences, philosophy, according to Husserl, should again have the courage to return to the fundamental questions and problems with which it had begun. These include questions regarding the status of being and the objectivity of the world. In this respect, 'to the things themselves' is the formulation of a program or a call for philosophy to become aware again of its role vis-à-vis the other sciences and to redefine its proper subject area, its methods, and its aims. In the tradition of René Descartes, Husserl calls for starting all over again to find a secure foundation and methods in order to be able to make true and grounded statements about the world.

A necessary first step is to devote oneself to what is given to us and to ask how and why it is, or can be, given to us in this way (and not otherwise). In doing so, we must distance ourselves from all preconceptions, interests, and convictions regarding what we experience. This is intended to enable us to focus entirely on the 'how', i.e., on how things appear.

■ ■ **Correlation of Subject and World**

Philosophically, we can go one step further: We can bracket the seemingly self-evident belief that the things we deal with daily and the world in which we live

1

actually exist. In other words, we can set the belief aside for the time being or place it 'in brackets', as Husserl puts it. This achieves two things: first, it turns the belief itself into a topic, and second, it suspends the validity of the belief (▸ Chap. 2, ▸ Sect. 2.3, Epoché). This suspension of the usual or natural attitude (*natürliche Einstellung*) (in which we simply live in the world) is intended to enable us to direct our attention to the relation between us, as experiencing subject, and the appearing things, in order to clarify this necessary correlation of subject and world.

What can we really know with certainty about the world around us, without having to rely on any presuppositions or methodical procedures such as deduction (derivation from a basic assumption)? Why are we usually so sure of things and the world that we don't even think of doubting their existence? Phenomenology attempts to rediscover this "naive contact with the world in order to finally raise it to a philosophical status" (Merleau-Ponty 2012, p. lxx). In doing so, it only suspends the "affirmations of the natural attitude" to make them visible and understand them (ibid.). These affirmations include both our implicit belief that everything we experience is really there and all the implicit expectations we bring to the world: e.g., that the sun will rise again tomorrow, that a house has a backside and not just a front, or that people will behave in a certain way.

In the 1960s, Michel Foucault criticized these methodological principles of phenomenology by pointing out that there is always 'order', and that this order is historically contingent. However, had Husserl still been alive, he likely would have replied that the existence of a historically contingent order already presupposes that there is something like a world full of things that can be experienced by everyone, i.e., there is objectivity and generality. Only when this is the case, can the world appear as ordered in historically contingent ways. In this context, Husserl refers to the world in a minimal and objective sense, i.e., a world that is given and accessible to everyone. He points to the fact that we can always return to things or ideas we have once perceived. Furthermore, there are general statements or truths that everyone can verify at any time, such as the statement $2 + 2 = 4$. How can this be when each individual subject only experiences this world from their 'subjective' perspective, through their psychological acts, or within their social and historical situation?

▪▪ Subjective Access to Objectivity

Instead of separating subjectivity and objectivity, relativity and generality, and leaving one to the humanities and social sciences and the other to the natural sciences, Husserl emphasizes that subjectivity and objectivity are genuinely philosophical topics that are necessarily related in content. As philosophers, we are therefore not allowed to simply presuppose the objective world or nature, nor are we allowed to retreat to a merely subjective or relative experience, only to practice introspection or compare various historically relative worldviews, without any claim to objectivity or generality. Instead, we must try to understand how we can achieve objectivity, generality, and evidence despite our subjective access.

According to Husserl, we can only do this from a genuinely philosophical perspective in which we distance ourselves not only from the world but also from ourselves as concrete acting subjects. We must then view the relation of subject and world from a reflective distance.

Starting from a description of the 'how' of the appearing, phenomenology seeks the general in the concrete and objectivity in the subjectively appearing. This is why Husserl calls phenomenology an 'essence viewing' (*Wesensschau*) or 'eidetic insight' (gr. eidos: 'essence'; ▶ Chap. 2, ▶ Sect. 2.2). However, these essences are not to be sought in a 'heaven of ideas' but must somehow be experienceable based on that which concretely appears. And, they must be experienceable in the same way for everyone, since they determine why something can be this way and not otherwise.

■■ Intentionality

The essence of a thing includes only that without which it cannot be determined as this thing. Thus, a table can have different sizes, shapes, or colors, but must always be something at which one can sit, on which one can place something, etc. Similarly, there are countless different forms of consciousness, but every consciousness qua general essence must always be consciousness of something. A consciousness completely without some kind of content or subject matter is—at least for Husserl—inconceivable. This content of consciousness might sometimes be vague and indeterminate, or consciousness might have itself as its own content, but the directionality of the act of consciousness towards a content of some kind remains. Therefore, intentionality is part of the essence of consciousness.

> **Definition**
>
> 'Intentionality' is a concept that Husserl adopts from his teacher Franz Brentano (1838–1917), although it originally goes back to medieval-scholastic philosophy. Generally, intentionality refers to the ability to refer to something, such as actual or imagined objects, states of affairs, etc. Husserl adopts this terminology but understands intentionality not only as the basic structure of every (real or existing) psychic phenomenon, but as the necessary essence of every conceivable consciousness or experience. Consciousness is therefore always consciousness *of* something, i.e., intentionally directed at something. We can distinguish between the intentional act, i.e., the way we are directed at something (e.g., through thinking, remembering, perceiving, etc.), and the intentional content or object of consciousness (e.g., an idea, memory, perception, etc.) (cf. Ströker 1984; Zahavi 2008; Merz et al. 2009).

As philosophers, we are therefore not interested in how we personally experience something, any more than the readers of this book are interested in how I, Maren Wehrle, am currently experiencing the heat in Freiburg while writing this introduction. Rather, the aim is to describe how any possible subject can have an objective consciousness of the world and things. What properties, characteristics, and cognitive structures must consciousness have to enable such an experience?

1

▪▪ The Givenness of the Psyche

According to Husserl, such philosophical clarification must necessarily precede the concrete and factually focused questions of the individual scientific disciplines. Before we investigate a part of reality, such as botany or the human psyche, using appropriate methods, one must clarify how the corresponding things, i.e., plants or the psyche, are given to us. One must first determine what constitutes the experience of the object of investigation, that is, how it can appear to us, and how we, as experiencing subjects, relate to this object of investigation. And so, Husserl emphasizes in his essay 'Philosophy as a Rigorous Science' from 1910/1911 that the psyche as a subject matter of psychology should not be investigated in the same way as other natural or physical 'things'. The essence of psychic 'things' is therefore fundamentally different from physical 'things', just as ideal objects differ from material objects, or natural objects from cultural objects. A logical truth or a psychological state, unlike material objects, has no extension, color, or size.

Husserl, who was both an accomplished mathematician and a student of the psychologist Franz Brentano, dealt critically with the emerging empirical psychology of his time. Psychological laboratories in that day tried to precisely measure psychological phenomena according to the model of the empirical sciences using quantitative methods combined with 'introspection'. However, as Husserl was quick to note, this fails to account for the fact that psychic things are fundamentally different in nature from physical things and therefore cannot be determined with the same methods. So how can psychological states or disorders be described in a general way (i.e., in a way that is valid not only for the given individual patient), but also in their specificity and with respect to their concrete context? And what is the relation here between the object of investigation and the one who investigates? Isn't the psyche of the investigator the prerequisite for the psyche of the patient to function as an object of investigation in the first place?

> ### ❯ For further study
> #### Intentionality in contrast to Brentano
> Contrary to Brentano, Husserl does not understand intentionality as an internal relationship between an act of consciousness and an immanent object. If acts only referred to immanent presentations of things and not to the things themselves, then we could only judge our presentations but never the things presented in them (Husserl, Hua XXII, p. 134). Such a distinction between an immanent object and an external, real thing might seem to have its advantages, for example, in explaining why one can imagine something (e.g., a unicorn) that does not exist or is absurd. However, this distinction would also entail that these absurd objects must somehow be contained as real components in the presentation itself. For Husserl, it is therefore nonsensical to distinguish between the intentional object of a presentation on the one hand, and the actual object on the other: the intentional object of the presentation is the same as its "actual object, and on occasion as its external object" (LI2, p. 127/Hua XIX/1, p. 439). For example, in imagining a unicorn, it is the presentation itself to which the intentionality refers, but in perceiving an object, it is the external or transcendent object.

■ ■ **Transcendental Phenomenology**

Philosophically considered, the subject being investigated already presupposes an investigating subject and thus also a psyche. So, in philosophical reflection, we are actually dealing with two subjects: first, the subject as subject (reflecting) and, second, the subject as object (of reflection). Husserl refers to the first, reflecting subject with Immanuel Kant as the transcendental subject, the second as the empirical subject. It is the task of transcendental phenomenology to determine the generally necessary structures and achievements of the transcendental subject, i.e., the structures of consciousness that constitute the conditions of the possibility of experience (of the world). Husserl refers to this as the genuinely philosophical aspect of phenomenology.

Such transcendental problems are not addressed by the natural sciences. The epistemological dependence of science, not only on individual concrete scientists and their subjective interests, but on any possible consciousness, capable of perceiving and investigating things as well as itself, does not really come into view in the empirical sciences themselves. Taking it up as a subject of inquiry would unnecessarily expand their subject area and complicate their orientation.

The questions of what subjectivity and objectivity mean, and what role their interrelatedness plays for science, are therefore questions proper to philosophy. To get to the 'things themselves' one must take a detour through philosophy. All things are accessible to us only through our conscious experience of them, be it direct experience or experience extended and filtered through scientific measurements or methods. Such a dependency on someone or something that sees, experiences, measures, registers, and interprets, always remains. Therefore, it is a genuine task of philosophy to precisely describe this experience (i.e., the necessary correlation of being and consciousness) and critically question it, so that we do not prematurely conclude from our merely subjective perspective that something is objective or general.

1.2 The 'Things' as Intentional Objects: Neither Thing-in-itself nor Sense Datum

■ ■ **Correlation of Being and Consciousness**

From a phenomenological perspective, factuality or objectivity cannot be separated from its experience. In other words, being and consciousness cannot be separated from each other but are necessarily correlated. To be able to make true, or as Husserl puts it, 'evident' (i.e., proven, comprehensible, or legitimate) statements about the world, this world must be accessible to us in some way, i.e., it must be experienceable. Any philosophy, be it epistemology, ontology, or metaphysics, must therefore begin with intuition or sense experience.

Phenomenologically, there is no separation between a world-in-itself on one side and subjective appearances or representations of it on the other: The world we experience is the only one there is. If this were not the case, it would lead to a doubling of the world in which the external world would stand over and against an internal representation of it. This would in turn bring about a tripling of the subject: First, the subject, along with its body, would be an actual part of the world; second, it would be given as an internal representation of the same; and third, it would be the transcendental starting point to whom the representation is given. In such a scenario, one would not have the ability to verify whether the internal representation of the world actually corresponds to the external world (since one has access only to the former), or whether all subjects (each with an individual internal representation of the world) experience one and the same (shared) world.

Therefore, the things of phenomenology can neither be things-in-themselves somehow lying behind appearances, nor can they be mere internal images, simulations, or representations of a world not directly accessible to us. On the contrary, Husserl holds that the things in our experience present themselves as they are.

However, this should not be understood as a form of naive realism, empiricism, or naturalism, in which things are either directly present to our consciousness or causally deposit their physiological imprints there. While Husserl does describe phenomenology as the only true empiricism, what he means by this is far removed from empiricism in the above senses. If the things were actually (in Husserl's words, '*reell*') present in consciousness, there could be no talk of transcendence—and thus of objectivity—of things, e.g., in external perception. The perceived thing would be completely limited to its causal effects, i.e., sensual empirical impact. It would not only be nonsensical to think that a perceived tree is actually in consciousness, but it would also be fundamentally contradictory, since an actual thing, i.e., a thing that is external to consciousness (or, in Husserl's words, 'transcendent'), can never be completely given in consciousness.

As Husserl says, "with an absolutely unconditional universality and necessity it is the case that a physical thing cannot be given in any possible perception, in any possible consciousness, as something really inherently immanent" (CW II, p. 89/ Hua III/1, p. 87). With this, he wants to express that the perception of an external thing, like a house, can never be given in the same way as, for example, a pain, which is immediately 'given from within'. The perception of the house can never be immanent in the same way as a pain. While the act of perception very much belongs to consciousness in a real (actual) sense, this does not apply to the perceived object, which is only intentionally in consciousness. Furthermore, in the perception of a thing, we never have all aspects, sides, etc., given at once or simultaneously, as we do with pain. The house necessarily appears in perspectives. This applies not only to my current perception but to any conceivable perception at all. This is, as Husserl calls it, not a factual, but an eidetic statement, i.e., it describes an essential and necessary characteristic of any conceivable consciousness. Here, an essential onto-logical difference (i.e., a difference concerning how something is) between 'being as consciousness' and 'being as reality' is revealed.

Definition

'**Real**' (*reell*) refers to the mode of being of (natural) things or the world of things; something 'real' is something that belongs to empirical or actual reality. The idea of a house is not a real part of consciousness in this sense but is only '**intentionally**' given in consciousness, i.e., as an object to which consciousness is directed or which it intends or perceives as something (as a house). Husserl makes a distinction between what consciousness intentionally directs itself towards (house, number, object), and what is '**reell**' (really, inherently immanent), i.e., actually belongs to consciousness, such as the sensory basis of perception or sensations in general. The intentional object, which Husserl later calls the '**noema**' (cf. CW II/Hua III/1; Staiti 2015), is neither to be equated with the real object, nor with a mental representation: it denotes the synthesis of subjective and objective moments of perception, which allows objects and the world as such to appear to us.

What we experience, i.e., perceive, remember, imagine, or think, cannot be reduced to sense data or psychological states. Instead, every form of consciousness is objective (*gegenständlich*), i.e., we do not experience sensual stimuli, but 'things', such as a beautiful flower, a house, or more abstractly, a fact or thought. Although the perception of something like a house must indeed have a sensual basis, which distinguishes it from thinking or imagining the same house, the perception of the house cannot be reduced to this sensation or the content of the sensation. The 'house' itself, as the thing that perception aims at, or in Husserl's words, that is 'meant' in perception, is not really in consciousness. However, it must be experienceable in consciousness, and experienceable as something that is transcendent to consciousness (i.e., found outside of it). So, one must somehow be able to experience that the tree is 'out there' and does not completely dissolve in our consciousness of it. Instead of speculatively assuming the existence of a 'thing-in-itself' that cannot be perceived by us, as Immanuel Kant does, Husserl locates the 'real' or 'objective' within perception, precisely because the 'thing' eludes us, by going beyond the current perspective and givenness. We always intend more (e.g., the house as a whole) than what is actually given through the senses (e.g., the front side). The house is therefore not actually, but only intentionally, present in consciousness.

Every form of consciousness—not only perception, but also imagination, memory, thinking, judging, etc.—is thus characterized by its object reference or directedness, its intentionality. Just as being is linked to consciousness—things must be accessible to us in some form, i.e., experienceable—consciousness is also linked to being. It must have some kind of object reference to be comprehensible or even describable.

■ ■ Intentional Meaning-constitution

In contrast to psychic contents, the objects or things that become 'conscious' to us are not simply in consciousness "'as objects in a box' so that they can be found in it and snatched at in it". They are first constituted "as being what they are for us,

1

and as what they count as for us, in varying forms of objective intention" (Husserl, LI1, p. 275/Hua XIX/1, p. 169). The intentional givenness of the 'things' involves a certain performance of consciousness, which 'objectively interprets' or 'understands' a given sensation. Husserl calls this performance 'apprehension' or 'apperception'. Only in the context of an objective apprehension by consciousness can one speak of intentionality, i.e., of consciousness of a 'thing', since sensations or sensory data alone are not yet objects. A sensation can be strong or weak, painful or pleasant, but it does not yet have 'objective' characteristics, such as hardness, roughness, or color, which characterize, for example, a perceived piece of wood.

Moreover, the same sensory material can be apprehended completely differently by different subjects: one person might perceive what they think is a human, while another perceives it as a doll. Furthermore, different sensory data, in the unified course of perception and its changing perspectives, can belong to one and the same perceived object. The identity of a perceptual object beyond its temporal course and changes in its appearances cannot therefore be understood by a mere reference to sensory stimuli and a corresponding reaction. The meaning and unity that constitute a perception, according to Husserl, are the result of the intentional relation or institution of meaning, which Husserl later calls 'constitution' (cf. Wehrle 2009).

■■ **Perceptual Intentionality**

Although an object like a house is usually given to us in perception at a glance, such a constant and uniform perception, upon closer intentional analysis, turns out to be a kind of 'presentation', a gradual constitution, which is automatically 'performed' by consciousness, as Husserl puts it. Different perspectives must connect in a uniform way temporally and in content. Formerly 'empty' intentions, like the back of the house, which was merely anticipated, must be vividly fulfilled. The external perception of things (as opposed to their representation or imagination) is characterized by the fact that these things can never be completely given, i.e., in all their possible sides and aspects at the same time. Only one profile is given at any one moment. The fact that an object can be viewed from infinitely many perspectives, and can thereby undergo variations in appearance, leads Husserl to speak of 'adumbrations' (*Abschattungen*). To say that an object appears in adumbrations means that each perspective of it 'shadows' other possible perspectives. A transcendent object, be it a house or a melody, therefore presents itself in the course of perception only partially, but in every moment of perception as itself. This self-presence must necessarily be accompanied by a limitation of what appears from it, which is precisely what constitutes the transcendent character of the perceived thing. External perception is thus characterized by an "essential contradiction", as Husserl emphasizes; it is "a constant pretension to accomplish something that, by its very nature, it is not in a position to accomplish" (CW 11, p. 39/Hua XI, p. 3).

However, this is not to be understood as a deficiency of human perception, but an essential feature of any possible perception. Even God himself, if he existed, would not be able to see an object "in the entirety of its sensibly intuitive features" (Husserl CW 11, p. 40/Hua XI, p. 3), i.e., from all sides at once, at least not if we still want to call this 'seeing' or perception. Perceptual givenness is by its nature always perspectival and unfinished. It requires a subjective or bodily starting point as well as the potential to change one's attention or field of view (through the movement of the eyes or changes in physical position).

■ ■ Horizon-Intentionality

Perceptual intentionality is therefore not a static mental state, but a process in which a 'thing' gradually presents or gives itself. It is a process of constant acknowledgment (cf. CW 11, p. 49/Hua XI, p. 12), in which the experiencing subject is actively involved in gradually getting to know the object, by walking around it, changing perspectives, and retaining what has once been seen and known. Visual appearances and movements are so coordinated as to form a unity of the senses and the sensory object, e.g., the appearing house. Each current appearance of a side of the house stands in a horizon of further possible perceptions of the other sides, which have not yet been seen, but which can be, through a change of perspective. Perception therefore always functions within a *horizon*: It always anticipates more than is currently given, with an inner, deepening horizon (additional aspects of the side of the house already seen) and an outer, expanding horizon (spatial surroundings of the house, which have not yet been seen or have only been seen vaguely as background). Therefore, perception always refers to an embodied perceptual subject with kinesthetic (gr. kinere: 'move' and aisthesis: 'sense') possibilities, who can realize these horizons concretely. Husserl also speaks of this as horizon-intentionality.

■ ■ Paradox of Givenness

Here a seeming paradox is revealed: Although we are directly connected with things that are physically present and given, we can never fully grasp them; they always appear only partially. Husserl emphasizes both the objectivity and positivity of things as well as their subjective givenness. On the one hand, things present themselves in perception as themselves, i.e., they do not refer to something else in the way of a symbol, sign, or image. On the other hand, however, for things to present themselves in this way requires various synthetic processes in consciousness (temporal and content syntheses or performances of consciousness) and various bodily activities. So, we do not simply 'have' the object: Its being and appearance do not coincide directly. What we always directly 'have' is an apperception, i.e., a store of given sense data (which Husserl sometimes refers to with the Greek term 'hyle'), and an apperceptive apprehension of these data. The transcendent object is constituted through such an 'exhibiting' or 'presentative' appearance, in which an object gives itself in adumbrations, i.e., shows itself from different perspectives and from different sides (CW11, p. 55/Hua XI, p. 18).

Thus, we always have the external object "in the flesh (we see, grasp, seize it)", but it also seems infinitely distant: "What we do grasp of it, pretends to be its essence; and it is it too, but it remains so only in an incomplete approximation, an approximation that grasps something of it, but in doing so it also constantly grasps into an emptiness that cries out for fulfillment" (Husserl CW11, p. 59/Hua XI, p. 21).

1

1.3 Overview of Phenomenological Methods

» All scientific investigations up to that point were objectively directed; everywhere they had in advance, they presupposed, objectivity in naive experiencing and knowing. But never was the fundamental question taken up explicitly as to how the cognizing subjectivity in its pure conscious life brings about this achievement of meaning, this achievement of judgment and insight, "objectivity" [...]. For subjectivity is only in possession of what it accomplishes in itself. Already the simplest 'having an object over against oneself' in perception is consciousness and accomplishes meaning-giving and positing of reality in superabundant structures; it is only that reflection and reflective study are needed to know anything of this, and certainly anything that is scientifically useful. (Husserl, CW 14, p. 70/Hua VII, pp. 67–68)

The starting point and goal of phenomenology is thus to clarify how it is possible to identify the objective, general content of a thing—that is, the 'thing itself' in the essence, sense, or meaning that it has for us, but also for everyone else—despite, or precisely because of, its subjective givenness.

▪▪ Phenomenological Description

Starting anew philosophically means that we must not presuppose anything; we must start only from what presents itself to us in sense experience directly and "originarily (so to speak, in its 'personal' actuality)". We must initially simply accept it as "what it is presented as being, but also only within the limits in which it is presented there" (CW2, p. 44/Hua III/1, p. 51). This means that we must not simply presuppose the objective world in order to then measure and formalize it, as the natural sciences do: "Phenomenology involves describing, not analyzing and explaining"; this is its "first rule" (Merleau-Ponty 2012, p. lxxi).

Phenomenological description is thus supposed to teach us how to see 'properly' again, to open ourselves to things and the world before we impose our interests and established concepts on them. The phenomenologist tries to see the world anew and, in doing so, to clarify the habits, prejudices, and attitudes that always already constitutively co-determine our experience. This is what the motto of phenomenology 'to the things themselves' essentially means. Clarification does not mean that concepts, structures, or orders that always already co-determine our experience and thinking can simply be ignored or negated. Instead, these presuppositions should first become visible and thematizable in order to generate new attention to what shows itself to us and how it shows itself to us.

In a first step, we must bracket our presuppositions and our conceptual knowledge. (We bracket *in* and not *out*, since the assumptions are still visible, even though their validity has been suspended.) We do this in order to sharpen our attention and turn to the things as they actually appear to us (method: description and epoché, ▶ Chap. 2, ▶ Sect. 2.1).

■ ■ **Eidetic Determination**

Only afterwards can the general and the necessary (eidos/essence) within this appearance be identified with the help of an imagined 'eidetic variation' of the concretely perceived or imagined things (method: determination of essence as eidetic variation, ▶ Chap. 2, ▶ Sect. 2.2). To identify the essence is to determine it (in principle) in the same way that any other subject at any other time would determine it. If, for example, I now have the insight that 2 + 2 = 4 or that a pair of scissors is a device with which one can cut, this insight is not dependent on my concrete psychological experience, but can be recognized by any subject at any time. Phenomenology as eidetic determination of essence is therefore objective, i.e., in relation to its general validity. In this sense, all conceivable 'subject areas', such as physical nature, logical truths, or culture can be subjected to a determination of essence, which is why Husserl also speaks of eidetic ontology (doctrine of being). Such an ontology must always begin with the concrete experience of things and their description and proceed through an imaginative variation that strips away the particular, the accidental, and the arbitrary features to arrive at the invariant essence of the corresponding thing. The goal is to arrive at those core properties that can no longer be varied but must be given in all possible and actual (ontic) things of this kind (e.g., a table), if they are to count as things of this kind (table).

■ ■ **Epoché and Reduction**

However, if one wants to philosophically inquire back to the transcendental conditions of possibility of this appearance in consciousness itself, one must perform a transcendental-phenomenological epoché or reduction (▶ Chap. 2, ▶ Sect. 2.3).

In a first step, we bracket not only certain assumptions about the world or things, but also the immediate belief in the existence and pre-existence of the world itself. Such a comprehensive epoché thus suspends what Husserl calls our 'natural attitude' or 'general thesis'. With this, everything we experience is initially labeled with the index 'pure phenomenon'. However, this does not mean that the existence of the world is doubted or somehow eliminated. The world is merely deprived of its self-evidence; we can no longer simply assume it as given and objectively existing. Instead, we suspend our belief in the world in order to thematize it and then gradually demonstrate, clarify, and justify it. This allows us to find out why we are so sure of this world and how we achieve objectivity as a generally shared sense and as experienced transcendence.

1

> **Definition**
>
> 'Epoché' is an ancient Greek term from Pyrrhonian skepticism that means suspension of judgment. In Husserl, it denotes the methodical step of bracketing, which allows a reflective distancing from the object of investigation. The content of the judgment remains the same, only the validity of the judgment is initially suspended until the judgment, or its validity, has been checked. By equipping the judgment with the index of the bracket, it can become visible as a (pre-)judgment and thus become the subject of research. What changes is not what is bracketed, but our attitude towards it. The descriptive epoché brackets specific assumptions or beliefs about the object of investigation. The all-encompassing transcendental epoché brackets the most basic prejudice of all, the belief in the existence of the world, which implicitly accompanies every experience.

The transcendental-phenomenological epoché, also called the 'transcendental-phenomenological reduction', as a method of neutralizing our 'acceptance of being' (*Seinsglaube*), does not in any way affect the content of our experience of the world, but only modifies our attitude towards it. The clarification of this all-encompassing belief in the existence of the world and objectivity is dedicated to finding the conditions of the possibility of experiencing such a world (including all things, other subjects, and ourselves). Husserl—like Immanuel Kant—seeks these conditions in the experiencing subject. The neutralization thus opens the door to a transcendental enlightenment or inquiry, which Husserl describes as a process of 'reduction' or 'reducing'. Reduction in this sense does not refer to a mitigation or even a crossing out of the experienced, but rather to a condensing down to the transcendentally necessary and essential. This might be thought of as comparable to the lengthy culinary process of reducing a sauce, which thereby obtains a more intense flavor.

Thus, for example, the human psyche can be reduced to the transcendentally necessary and general structures and achievements of any conceivable subjectivity. Or the everyday, practical lifeworld, with its diverse practices and cultural meanings, can be reduced to its general—as well as its specifically historical—conditions. That is, is can be reduced to its subjective and, above all, intersubjective achievements and intentions.

The search for 'the things themselves' here takes a detour or goes all the way back to the conditions of their experience, to how meaningful and coherent things, and ultimately the world as a whole, can be given to us at all. It is about the question of how these things and the world receive meaning from us, how we intersubjectively and continuously constitute sense or meaning within experience. In doing so, we do not create the world. Phenomenology is not absolute idealism: it merely seeks to understand the sense that this world has for us before any interpretation or analysis. In this sense, phenomenology can be practiced as either a static or genetic analysis of constitution.

▪▪ Static Analysis

When performing a static analysis, we always start from an experienced or given object, such as the perception of a house, and then identify and describe those components that are constitutive for this perception. In this context, Husserl distinguishes between two directions of attention in the description:

- the *noetic direction* focuses on the subjective side of perception, i.e., the modes of consciousness (perceiving, imagining, taking-for-certain, evaluating, etc.) as well as the underlying sensory experiences (sensations),
- the *noematic direction* focuses on the given object in the *how* of its givenness.

In the case of the object as a noema of description or in the static intentional analysis, Husserl distinguishes between different layers:

- the *noematic core* (formal-ontological determinations: the house is a thing, not a fact or a cause; determinations of its properties: it is made of wood, has several doors, etc.),
- the *noematic characteristics* (how the object is given: as a remembered, desired, imagined, or perceived house) and
- the *objective unity* (the overall meaning 'house').

The objective unity, which combines all partial determinations, is at the beginning of every intention (we 'mean' to see a house, without already knowing the details), but in its determination as the intended whole or fully determined house, it remains merely an ideal target of possible verification in the further course of experience (Husserl Ms. BIII 12IV/84a).

The static phenomenological method thus deals with the *how* of the givenness of objects. Furthermore, it tries to determine general structures in relation to either the modes of appearance (noesis) or the object itself (noema). The former is a constitutive determination that asks what is constitutive for the appearance or the meaning of a particular object. The latter is an ontological determination that asks what this object in its essence is (▶ Chap. 2, ▶ Sect. 2.2).

▪▪ Genetic Analysis

Here, the necessity of a genetic analysis of constitution becomes apparent, as the given object is never given all at once in its entirety. The genetic analysis of constitution therefore asks about the temporal syntheses—the passive and active accomplishments of consciousness—that are necessary for the experience of a given object or a meaningful experience of the world in general. Here, three different stages of genesis can be distinguished:

1. The so-called *active genesis* that refers to an explicit act of thinking or judgment. Here, for example, various objects are thought together or linked within a judgement, so that a 'new' object or new insights are created.
2. The *receptive-bodily genesis* of perception, which combines both passive and active dimensions of experience. Thus, perception is not a thinking act and contains no explicit positioning or assertion; yet perception is not entirely passive, but 'actively' structured by the will, interests, feelings, preferences, and attention. It thus already contains implicitly evaluative elements, as was empha-

1

sized by Husserl early on (Hua XXXVIII; Hua XXXXIII/2) and made explicit in his late work (Husserl [1939]1973).

3. The *passive genesis* or primordial (first) constitution. This involves entirely passive processes in consciousness that integrate impressions temporally and content-wise into the stream of experience (Hua X; XI/CW IV; IX), without the involvement of an 'I', i.e., without the subject being 'aware' of it.

As is already clear here, genetic analysis goes beyond a static description of phenomena by seeking to clarify their origin or becoming. It describes constituting processes that underlie object perception and object intentionality in general. Therefore, genetic analysis is part of Husserl's transcendental-phenomenological investigation, which inquires into the necessary structures of experience. However, it does this not only formally, by identifying general 'necessary conditions', but also concretely, by trying to demonstrate elements that reside as (implicit or operative) moments of the overall experience, such as habits. It is no longer just about how a coherent object and world perception is possible, but also about the temporal genesis and development of subjectivity itself. For Husserl, the transcendental ego is not a mere formal synthesizing activity, which must always remain unknown. It is the concrete person or bodily subjectivity viewed transcendentally. In this sense, the transcendental ego or person must itself show a genesis, since subjectivity does not remain unchanged through its constitutional accomplishments. For Husserl, a bodily and temporal subject is behind the 'conditions of the possibility of experience' (cf. Kant [1781/1787] 1998).

In Husserl's genetic phenomenology, therefore, topics such as affection, motivation, habit, character, but also limit problems of phenomenology such as death, sleep, unconsciousness, etc. become subjects of investigation. At the same time, intersubjectivity becomes the center of transcendental phenomenology, since the coherence of our world-perception (objectivity, reality) and the meaning of objects cannot be constituted by a single subject. What and how the world is given to us also depends significantly on our ancestors, fellow human beings, and possible descendants. Therefore, a genetic phenomenology must be embedded in a generative phenomenology (cf. Steinbock 1995).

Genetic analysis does not necessarily have to be transcendental but can also be concrete. That is, it can aim at historical or psychological conditions. Here, the question is not what is necessary for experience as such, but what are the conditions of the development (individual, historical, biological, cultural) of a specific embodied and situated subject and its specific experiences (cf. Merleau-Ponty 2012).

> ### ❯ For further study
> #### Genetic stages of intentionality
> In his late phase, the genetic transcendental phenomenology, Husserl distinguishes between different stages of intentionality. Intentionality is no longer limited to the higher-level acts of consciousness such as thinking, imagining, judging, or perceiving but also includes lower-level, passive processes. To enable consciousness of something in the full sense, i.e., of a constant, identical object, various passive stages of constitution or passive intentionality must come first.

This preconscious layer of consciousness is first characterized by the formal regularity of time consciousness, which combines all sensory experiences into 'one consciousness'. In the passive synthesis of inner time consciousness, continuously incoming sensory data (impressions) are synthesized with forward-looking intentions (protentions) and past impressions (retentions). Husserl thereby differentiates between a 'longitudinal intentionality' and a 'transversal intentionality'. The former refers to the contents of temporal consciousness, for example, the incoming tones of an appearing melody, while the latter refers to the 'acts' or 'syntheses' of inner time consciousness as such. Transversal intentionality can therefore only appear through, or be abstracted from, longitudinal intentionality. Yet, for consciousness to be able to constitute a meaning—like a melody—as a unified whole, these transversal processes must be at work, as each succeeding impression transitions into a retention. In other words, each impression is held in consciousness, but in a modified form, as it continuously descends into the depths of consciousness (CW 4, p. 33/Hua X, p. 31). Here, there is an "intentional relation […] of phase of consciousness to phase of consciousness" (CW 4, p. 346/Hua X, p. 333). In other words, a passive temporal connection of experience is established in and by consciousness.

In addition to the formal temporal syntheses, the content-oriented syntheses also begin in passivity: Initial connections between impressions—as well as regular anticipations and corresponding fulfillments/negations—first emerge in passive syntheses of association by similarity and contrast (CW 4, p.407, p. 494–519/Hua XI p. 272, p. 398–416). At the level of passivity, there is no unstructured chaos of sense data, but rather a passive orientation towards the world, which is characterized by passive synthesizing on the one hand and passive-sensible units (pre-objective units) on the other (Hua XI, p. 76; cf. Merz et al. 2009).

In addition to passive intentionality, there is an operative functioning (*fungierende*) intentionality, in which the body aligns itself with the world or gives way to an affective tendency without a (conscious) ego or self having to be involved (Husserl (EJ) [1939] 1973, p. 78). This applies to all bodily actions that are not directly thematic as such, e.g., habitual actions. This concept is later explicitly developed by Maurice Merleau-Ponty and referred to as 'operative intentionality' (Merleau-Ponty 2012, p. lxxxii, 440–442). For Merleau-Ponty, the temporal connection of past, present, and future experiences is no longer established by consciousness, but by the acting body in an 'intentional arc' (Merleau-Ponty 2012, pp. 137, 160).

Husserl also discusses the so-called 'drive intentionality' (Nam-In Lee 1993; Yamaguchi 1982; Mensch 1998). Drive intentionality is a general openness or tendency towards the world, an as-yet indeterminate but immediate directionality that characterizes every consciousness or living being (cf. Wehrle 2015). Husserl uses the example of an infant, who has an original kinaesthesis, or instinct, to suckle, which is awakened by appropriate circumstances, but does not yet have a 'conscious' goal (Ms. C 16 IV, Bl. 36b; cf. Brudzińska 2013).

■ ■ **Self-clarification**

We ourselves are the most difficult to describe, as we are both the constituting, meaning-giving subject, i.e., the subject of experience and reflection, which we must always presuppose in all activities, as well as the constituted object, i.e., the

1

object of our own experience and reflection, which is always already given (i.e., constituted) with a certain meaning. The subject is thus the necessary starting point of any phenomenology, as any analysis of experience must begin from the first-person perspective of the one who is experiencing. Only in this way can certainty or evidence be ensured, as each person has original access only to their own experience. The inner life and experiences of other subjects are only indirectly accessible to us, through their bodily expression. Therefore, any methodologically rigorous phenomenology must begin with a 'self-clarification'. However, it must not stop there, because in such a self-clarification, the transcendence of other subjects and things phenomenologically reveals itself. They constantly elude our grasp precisely because we cannot perceive and determine them all at once, comprehensively, or originally; they remain forever embedded in an open horizon of further perceptions.

▪▪ Intersubjectivity

Comparison with the experiences of others is indispensable, especially to establish with certainty that what I experience is not an illusion and that there is an objective world. Not a single sense—not subjectivity, objectivity, world, or even self—can be constituted by a single concrete subject alone. These only have sense if there are also other experiencing and meaning-giving subjects who experience the same world, even if not always in the same way. Phenomenologists recognize that intersubjectivity must always precede the individual subject and its meaning-constituting acts: All contents that we find in our consciousness, such as world, nature, or culture, already refer to other subjects. Although every experience is necessarily subjective, what we come to know through experience is not: The content of the experience always points beyond the individual subject in its meaning to an intersubjectivity. Every subject is what it is, only as a child of its time or as heir to a tradition, and is thus genuinely historical (Hua XIV, p. 223).

To be able to get 'to the things themselves', phenomenological description, determination of essence, and transcendental enlightenment must thus take place in constant corrective exchange with others.

❯ For further study

Intersubjectivity and collective intentionality

Intentionality is always already intersubjective and socially shaped. This has long been, and still remains, one of the central themes of phenomenology. For example, the consciousness we have of ourselves as something (object, self) is determined by the gaze, i.e., the intentionality of others (Sartre 1943) as well as the social, cultural, and historical context (Beauvoir 1949; Fanon 1952). We can only speak of ourselves as a human, person, or subject when there are also other subjects with corresponding consciousness and intentionality (Husserl 1960 CM/Hua I), for whom we are objects. Furthermore, intentionality is not only embedded in social, cultural, and historical contexts, but also takes place with others, in an implicit or explicit way. Thus, we can speak of a common bodily operative intentionality and intercorporeality (cf. Merleau-Ponty [1960] 1964, pp. 242, 252; Waldenfels 2000, pp. 287ff.; Fuchs and De Jaegher 2009) as well as a 'we-intentionality' or 'collective intentionality' or a 'feeling-together' (Husserl, Hua XIII-XV; Walther 1923; Stein [1916] 1989; Scheler 1923 [2008]). These are topics that current phenomenology brings back to the center and relates to current academic debates, e.g., debates about social cognition or social ontology. Moreover, it engages in the analysis of political and social phenomena such as mass hysteria or populism that are prevalent in our times (Calcagno 2018; Moran and Szanto 2015; Zahavi 2001, 2018; Magri and Moran 2018; Zahavi and Salice 2017; Tranas and Caminada 2020; Thonhauser 2020; Szanto 2020; Zahavi 2025).

The motto 'To the things themselves' thus proves to be the unending task of phenomenology, its regulative ideal. Husserl describes his scientific program as a 'labor philosophy', to be continued from generation to generation, in which there are no final results. We start by approaching the 'things' with a prejudice-free description that then functions as a noematic guide. We then inquire further into how it is possible in the first place for us to have things and a world that appear to us in a unified and coherent way. Thus, we come from the experienced things to the correlatively necessary general structures and accomplishments of subjective consciousness or of intersubjective constitution. Only via this detour through the experiencing and meaning-constituting subject, and importantly, through the evidence of other experiencing and meaning-constituting subjects, do we philosophically return to 'the things themselves'. And only then are we able to ground and confirm the previously only assumed objectivity of things and the world.

▪▪ Modesty

All knowledge of things and the world is also a form of self-knowledge (cf. Husserl (CM) Hua I, pp.182ff.), as things and other subjects are always given to us only perspectivally and in subjective experience. This is not to say that things and the world should be reduced to our experience of them or are merely considered creations of subjectivity, or that we deny or ignore the status of a world independent of us. By insisting that consciousness and being, subject and object, modes of consciousness and contents of consciousness are always only to be had together, Husserl does not want to elevate the status of the subject or lead us to megalomania.

On the contrary, such a correlative a priori (i.e., a connection that determines the nature of this experience before any concrete experience) sets limits and calls for humility. Before we proclaim something that is only subjective or relative to be universal or objective, we must examine it thoroughly: What evidence do we have for this? Do further experiences and the experiences of other subjects agree with this? How can we bring our subjective assumptions, prejudices, habits, and interests, which co-determine this perception, into the light, discuss them or bracket them? Only through the detour of such strict self-knowledge, according to Husserl, do we come with small and modest steps, together with other phenomenologists, through a detailed description of what is given to us in experience, to 'the things themselves'.

1

Literature

In the text, the cited volumes of Husserl's Collected Works in German (Husserliana) are only indicated with the siglum Hua and the volume number. The individual volumes are always listed in
the bibliography. Where possible, a published English translation has been used. Where not possible, the texts have been translated automatically and subsequently edited by the author. The
English translations of Husserl are indicated either with the siglum CW, when they are published
within the series Collected Works or with the following abbreviations:

CES = The Crisis of European Sciences and Transcendental Phenomenology

CM = Cartesian Meditations

EJ = Experience and Judgment

LI1 = Logical Investigations, volume 1

LI2 = Logical Investigations, volume 2

PRS = Philosophy as Rigorous Science

Brudzińska, Jagna. 2013. Von Husserl zu Merleau-Ponty. Gedanken über die
Erfahrungsphänomenologie. In *Corporeity and Affectivity. Dedicated to Maurice Merleau-Ponty*,
eds. Karel Novotný, Pierre Rodrigo, Jenny Slatman, and Silvia Stoller, 15–34. Leiden: Brill.

Beauvoir, Simone de. (1949) 2011. *The Second Sex*. Trans. Constance Borde and Sheila Malovany-
Chevallier. New York: Vintage Press.

Calcagno, Antonio, ed. 2018. *Gerda Walther's Phenomenology of Sociality, Psychology, and Religion*.
Dordrecht: Springer.

Fanon, Frantz. (1952) 2008. *Black Skin, White Masks*. Trans. R. Philcox. New York: Grove Press.

Fuchs, Thomas, and Hanne De Jaegher. 2009. Enactive Intersubjectivity: Participatory Sense-
Making and Mutual Incorporation. *Phenomenology and the Cognitive Sciences* 8: 465–486.

Husserl, Edmund. (1900/1975) 2001. *Logical Investigations*, volume 1 (**LI1**). International Library of
Philosophy. Trans. J.N. Finlay. London: Routledge. German edition: Husserl, Edmund. 1975.
Logische Untersuchungen. Erster Band. Prolegomena zur reinen Logik. Husserliana: Edmund
Husserl—Gesammelte Werke XVIII (Hua XVIII), ed. E. Holenstein. The Hague: Martinus
Nijhoff.

Husserl, Edmund. (1900/1984) 2001. *Logical Investigations*, volume 2 (**LI2**). International Library of
Philosophy. Trans. J.N. Finlay. London: Routledge. German edition: Husserl, Edmund. 1984.
*Logische Untersuchungen. Zweiter Band: Untersuchungen zur Phänomenologie und Theorie der
Erkenntnis*. Husserliana: Edmund Husserl—Gesammelte Werke XIX (**Hua XIX**), ed. U. Panzer.
The Hague: Martinus Nijhoff.

Husserl, Edmund. (1910/1911) 2022. Philosophy as Rigorous Science (**PRS**). In *Phenomenology and
the Crisis of Philosophy*, trans. Q. Lauer, 71–147. New York: Harper & Row. German edition:
Husserl, Edmund. 1910/1911. Philosophie als strenge Wissenschaft. *Logos* 1: 289–341.

Husserl, Edmund. (1913/1976) 1982. *Ideas Pertaining to a Pure Phenomenology and to a
Phenomenological Philosophy. First Book: General Introduction to a Pure Phenomenology*. Trans.
F. Kersten. The Hague: Martinus Nijhoff. German edition: Husserl, Edmund. 1976. *Ideen zu
einer reinen Phänomenologie und phänomenologischen Philosophie. Erstes Buch*. Husserliana:
Edmund Husserl—Gesammelte Werke III/1 (**Hua III/1**), ed. K. Schuhmann. The Hague:
Martinus Nijhoff.

Husserl, Edmund. 1922. *Manuscripts* (Husserl Archives Leuven): *BIII 12IV/84a*.

Husserl, Edmund. (1931/1950) 1960. *Cartesian Meditations: An Introduction to Phenomenology*
(**CM**). Trans. D. Cairns. The Hague: Martinus Nijhoff. German edition: Husserl, Edmund. 1950.
Cartesianische Meditationen und Pariser Vorträge. Husserliana: Edmund Husserl—Gesammelte
Werke I (Hua I), ed. S. Strasser. The Hague: Martinus Nijhoff.

Husserl, Edmund. 1932. *Manuscripts* (Husserl Archive Leuven): *C 16 IV/36b*.

Husserl, Edmund. (1936/1976) 1970. *The Crisis of European Sciences and Transcendental
Phenomenology* (**CES**). Northwestern University Studies in Phenomenology and Existential
Philosophy. Trans. D. Carr. Evanston, IL: Northwestern University Press. German edition:
Husserl, Edmund. 1976. *Die Krisis der europäischen Wissenschaften und die transzendentale*

Phänomenologie: Eine Einleitung in die phänomenologische Philosophie. Husserliana: Edmund Husserl—Gesammelte Werke VI (**Hua VI**), ed. W. Biemel. Dordrecht: Springer.

Husserl, Edmund. (1939) 1973. *Experience and Judgement: Investigations in a Genealogy of Logic* (**EJ**). Northwestern University Studies in Phenomenology and Existential Philosophy. Trans. J.S. Churchill and K. Ameriks. Evanston, IL: Northwestern University Press. German edition: Husserl, Edmund. 1939. *Erfahrung und Urteil: Untersuchungen zur Genealogie der Logik,* ed. L. Landgrebe. Prague: Academia Verlagsbuchhandlung.

Husserl, Edmund. (1966) 2001. *Analyses Concerning Active and Passive Synthesis: Lectures on Transcendental Logic.* Collected Works 9 (**CW 9**). Trans. A. Steinbock. The Hague: Kluwer. German edition: Husserl, Edmund. 1966. *Analysen zur passiven Synthesis. Aus Vorlesungs- und Forschungsmanuskripten 1918–1926.* Husserliana: Edmund Husserl—Gesammelte Werke XI (**Hua XI**), ed. M. Fleischer. The Hague: Martinus Nijhoff.

Husserl, Edmund. (1969) 1991. *On the Phenomenology of the Consciousness of Internal Time (1893–1917).* Collected Works 4 (**CW 4**). Trans. J.B. Brough. Dordrecht: Kluwer. German edition: Husserl, Edmund. 1969. *Zur Phänomenologie des inneren Zeitbewusstseins (1893–1917).* Husserliana: Edmund Husserl—Gesammelte Werke X (**Hua X**), ed. R. Boehm. The Hague: Martinus Nijhoff.

Husserl, Edmund. 1973a. *Zur Phänomenologie der Intersubjektivität. Texte aus dem Nachlass. Erster Teil: 1905–1920.* Husserliana: Edmund Husserl—Gesammelte Werke XIII (**Hua XIII**). Ed. I. Kern. The Hague: Martinus Nijhoff.

Husserl, Edmund. 1973b. *Zur Phänomenologie der Intersubjektivität. Texte aus dem Nachlass. Zweiter Teil: 1921–1928.* Husserliana: Edmund Husserl—Gesammelte Werke XIV (**Hua XIV**). Ed. I. Kern. The Hague: Martinus Nijhoff.

Husserl, Edmund. 1973c. *Zur Phänomenologie der Intersubjektivität. Texte aus dem Nachlass. Dritter Teil: 1929–1935.* Husserliana: Edmund Husserl—Gesammelte Werke XV (**Hua XV**). Ed. I. Kern. The Hague: Martinus Nijhoff.

Husserl, Edmund. 1979. *Aufsätze und Rezensionen (1890–1910).* Husserliana: Edmund Husserl— Gesammelte Werke XXII (**Hua XXII**). Ed. B. Rang. The Hague: Martinus Nijhoff.

Husserl, Edmund. 1987. *Aufsätze und Vorträge (1911–1921).* Husserliana: Edmund Husserl— Gesammelte Werke XXV (**Hua XXV**). Eds. T. Nenon and H.R. Sepp. The Hague: Martinus Nijhoff.

Husserl, Edmund. 2004. *Wahrnehmung und Aufmerksamkeit. Texte aus dem Nachlass* (1893–1912). Husserliana: Edmund Husserl—Gesammelte Werke XXXVIII (**Hua XXXVIII**). Ed. T. Vongehr and R. Giuliani. Dordrecht: Springer.

Husserl, Edmund. 2021. *Studien zur Struktur des Bewusstseins (1896–1925).* Husserliana: Edmund Husserl—Gesammelte Werke XLIII/2 (**Hua XLIII/2**). Ed. U. Melle and T. Vongehr. Dordrecht: Springer.

Kant, Immanuel. (1781/1787) 1998. *Critique of Pure Reason.* The Cambridge Edition of the Works of Immanuel Kant. Trans. Paul Guyer and Allen W. Wood. Cambridge, UK: Cambridge University Press.

Lee, Nam-In. 1993. *Edmund Husserls Phänomenologie der Instinkte.* Phaenomenologica 128. The Hague: Kluwer.

Magrì, Elisa, and Dermot Moran, eds. 2018. *Empathy, Sociality, and Personhood: Essays on Edith Stein's Phenomenological Investigations.* Contributions to Phenomenology 94. Dordrecht: Springer.

Mensch, James. 1998. Instincts—A Husserlian Account. *Husserl Studies* 14: 219–237.

Merleau-Ponty, Maurice. (1945) 2012. *Phenomenology of Perception.* Trans. Donald M. Landes. New York: Routledge.

Merleau-Ponty, Maurice. (1960) 1964. *Signs.* Northwestern University Studies in Phenomenology and Existential Philosophy. Trans. Richard C. McCleary. Evanston, IL: Northwestern University Press.

Merz, Philippe, Andrea Staiti, and Frank Steffen. 2009. Intentionalität. In *Husserl-Lexikon,* ed. Hans-Helmuth Gander, 153–157. Darmstadt: WBG.

Moran, Dermot, and Thomas Szanto. 2015. Introduction: Empathy and Collective Intentionality— The Social Philosophy of Edith Stein. *Human Studies* 38(4): 445–461.

1

Sartre, Jean-Paul. (1943) 2018. *Being and Nothingness. An Essay in Phenomenological Ontology.* Trans. S. Richmond. London: Routledge.

Scheler, Max. (1923) 2008. *The Nature of Sympathy.* London: Transaction Publishers.

Stein, Edith. (1916) 1989. *On the Problem of Empathy.* The Collected Works of Edith Stein, volume 3. Trans. Waltraut Stein. Washington, D.C.: ICS Publications.

Staiti, Andrea, ed. 2015. *Commentary on Husserl's Ideas I.* Berlin: De Gruyter.

Steinbock, Anthony. 1995. *Home and Beyond: Generative Phenomenology after Husserl.* Northwestern University Studies in Phenomenology and Existential Philosophy. Evanston, IL: Northwestern University Press.

Ströker, Elisabeth. 1984. Intentionalität und Konstitution. Wandlungen des Intentionalitätskonzepts in der Philosophie Husserls. *Dialectica* 38(2,3): 191–208.

Szanto, Thomas. 2020. In Hate We Trust. The Collectivization and Habitualization of Hatred. *Phenomenology and the Cognitive Sciences* 19: 453–480.

Thonhauser, Gerhard. 2020. Zum Verhältnis von Phänomenologie und Massenpsychologie anhand von Max Schelers Unterscheidung von Gefühlsansteckung und Miteinanderfühlen. *Phänomenologische Forschungen* 2: 195–216.

Tranas, Linas, and Emmanuele Caminada. 2020. Gerda Walther and Hermann Schmalenbach. In *Routledge Handbook of Phenomenology of Emotion,* eds. H. Landweer and T. Szanto, 133–143. London: Routledge.

Waldenfels, Bernhard. 2000. *Das leibliche Selbst. Vorlesungen zur Phänomenologie.* Frankfurt a.M.: Suhrkamp.

Walther, Gerda. 1923. Zur Ontologie der sozialen Gemeinschaften. In *Jahrbuch für Philosophie und phänomenologische Forschung* 6: 1–158.

Wehrle, Maren. 2009. Konstitution. In *Husserl-Lexikon,* ed. Hans-Helmuth Gander, 172–174. Darmstadt: WBG.

Wehrle, Maren. 2015. 'Feeling as a Motor of Perception'? The Essential Role of Interest for Intentionality. *Husserl Studies* 31: 45–65.

Yamaguchi, Ichiro. 1982. *Passive Synthesis und Intersubjektivität bei Edmund Husserl.* Phaenomenologica 86. The Hague: Kluwer.

Zahavi, Dan. 2001. *Husserl and Transcendental Intersubjectivity: A Response to the Linguistic-Pragmatic Critique.* Series in Continental Thought 29. Trans. Elizabeth A. Behnke. Athens, OH: Ohio University Press..

Zahavi, Dan. 2008. Intentionalität und Bewusstsein. In *Edmund Husserl: Logische Untersuchungen.* Klassiker Auslegen 35, ed. Verena Meyer, 139–158. Berlin: Akademie Verlag.

Zahavi, Dan. 2018. Collective Intentionality and Plural Pre-reflective Self-Awareness. *Journal of Social Philosophy* 49(1): 61–75.

Zahavi, Dan, and Alessandro Salice. 2017. Phenomenology of the We: Stein, Walther, Gurwitsch. In *The Routledge Handbook of Philosophy of the Social Mind,* ed. J. Kiverstein, 515–527. London: Routledge.

Zahavi, Dan. 2025. Being We: Phenomenological Contributions to Social Ontology. Oxford: Oxford University Press.

Methods of Phenomenology

Contents

2

Every phenomenology begins with a description of concrete experience, whether in perception, imagination, or memory. This description can focus on either the content of the experience or the act of experiencing. Hence, two different directions of analysis can be methodologically distinguished.

▪▪ Two Methodical Directions

In describing an experience, one can inquire into the general or specific features of the object, or one can ask for the conditions of the possibility of having such an experience (or having object experience in general). In the former case, one applies the method of eidetics and seeks to determine the essence of the phenomenon in question. In the latter case, one applies the method of transcendental analysis and seeks to provide a transcendental justification or a genetic analysis of the constitution of the phenomenon. While eidetics is directed towards the given objects and aims to determine them according to their general and necessary essence, transcendental analysis is directed towards constituting acts and aims to clarify how and why we can experience objects in a constant and unified way. Transcendental phenomenological analysis thus takes a step back and investigates the conditions of the experience of things (objectivity) in the subject or consciousness.

The two methods are independent and can be applied separately from each other. For example, I can determine the general features of a thing, be it a house or the human psyche, without philosophically questioning the constitutive achievements (or better, processes) in (every) consciousness that make such an experience possible in the first place. While the former represents the starting point for a formal definition of a concept or for the determination of a regional ontology (i.e., the determination of general regions and genera of being), the latter is more likely to be assigned to a philosophy of knowledge or critique of knowledge (i.e., the question of what the conditions and limits of our knowledge of the world and being are) (cf. Schnell 2019, pp. 44–48).

2.1   Describing Without Prejudices

》 Phenomenology involves describing, and not explaining or analyzing. (Merleau-Ponty 2012, p. 4)

》 No conceivable theory can make us err with respect to the principle of all principles: that every originary presentive intuition is a legitimizing source of cognition, that everything originarily (so to speak, in its 'personal' actuality) offered to us in 'intuition' is to be accepted simply as what it is presented as being, but also only within the limits in which it is presented there. (Husserl, CW 2, p. 44/Hua III/1, p. 51)

What is phenomenological description? And why is description a philosophically relevant method? The following chapter attempts to answer these questions beginning from Husserl's theoretical perspective and with the help of examples.

According to the 'principle of all principles', the description should first begin with what is 'originally', that is, immediately, given to us instead of relying on existing theories, knowledge, or second-hand opinions. Only when I experience something firsthand, am I able to convince myself of its evidence (actuality, existence, completeness) and truth, and to recheck and update this evidence if necessary.

■ ■ Primacy of Experience

Speaking of experiences as given 'originally', should not be taken to imply that we somehow have insight into a pure, complete, or primal world that exists before any historical or cultural imprint. In fact, the terms 'original' or 'originary' do not refer to the *content* of experience at all. Rather, they refer to its *mode*. Everyone in the *first-person perspective* has a direct, 'in the flesh', or immediate experience of the world and of other subjects, even though that experience is only perspectival and thus partial. It is this mode of direct, first-person experience that we refer to as 'original' or 'originary'. No one has direct access to the experiences or mentally lived-through processes of other subjects. Even our own past experiences are accessed indirectly, although they were once lived through originally. Nevertheless, any further thinking or judging presupposes that something in experience has been given to us originally. This means that all other methods of philosophy, such as explanation, analysis, or formalization of something, must be founded in original experience. As Husserl and Merleau-Ponty emphasize in the above quotes, philosophy must start from the given, i.e., from experience. Every analysis, explanation, or formalization is first an explication or reduction of that which has been originally experienced.

■ ■ Lifeworld

All original experience takes place within a horizon of everyday, practical life. This horizon, which Husserl refers to as the 'lifeworld', is however, often forgotten or overlooked by science and philosophy (cf. Husserl, CES/Hua VI). We are so accustomed to the given world and to the everyday things and actions in it that that they no longer stand out as topics worthy of investigation in their own right. Therefore, we must first draw attention to our experience of the world and learn to see and describe it anew.

What is given to us now in the course of experience and in what way (clearly, vaguely, in the background)? What really falls into our field of view and what is merely anticipated based on previous perception? What is seen and experienced directly, and what is merely the result of a subsequent abstraction or expression of our knowledge about it? When we think we see a house or a cube, which 'intentions' are then fulfilled (the front of the house now visible), and which are merely empty or implied (the back of the house not actually seen now)? Why do we continuously see the same 'whole' house, even though we only have adumbrations of it, i.e., different temporally successive perspectives?

2

■■ Change of Attitude and Epoché

For the world and the things in it to shed their self-evidence and arouse our interest, a change of attention and attitude must first take place. For the existence, unity, and meaning of things to appear worthy of investigation, we must turn away from our everyday dealings with things towards a *description of their givenness* in our experience.

When describing an object, whether in perception, memory, or imagination, we try to 'bracket' our judgments and beliefs as well as our conceptual knowledge about the object for the time being. This is what Husserl calls, borrowing a term from Pyrrhonian skepticism, *epoché* (judgment abstention). This does not mean that this knowledge, these assumptions or judgments, can be made to disappear or that my consciousness becomes a *tabula rasa* in which the object appears to me for the very first time. The assumptions are merely 'bracketed', i.e., temporarily not considered. They remain 'out of play', as Husserl puts it, so that we can focus our attention on the manifest givenness of a thing and not on what we already (believe to) know or think about it.

It is not, therefore, the content that changes, but the way we attend to the content. The house that we previously saw while sitting at the laptop looking out the window, is the same; it does not lose its established meaning. Further, when we describe the house, we do not start with vague outlines or proto-objects, but with what we experience here and now. We do not describe individual sensory data, atoms, or outlines, but the house itself. We can also start our investigation with less material but more ideal objects, like the idea of love or the institution of science. We now take these familiar things along with their meaning as a guide for the description. The known object thus guides the description, but at the same time it is bracketed, i.e., it is given the status 'provisional' or 'under reservation': The validity of this known meaning must be proven in the course of the phenomenological description and may need to be adjusted or differentiated.

■■ From the *What* to the *How* of Givenness

As phenomenologists, we initially do not care *whether* the given thing really exists or not (this is actually also a knowledge claim or a pre-assumption), nor do we focus on *what* the thing is (conceptual categorization), or why it is (explanation), but first dedicate ourselves to the description of how this something, which appears to me now in experience, is given. We, for example, pay attention to the house, which now stands before us and describe it as a 'perceived house' in the *how* of its givenness, i.e., as a phenomenon that appears to me.

However, it is not the case that this phenomenon 'house' thereby appears in addition to the 'real house'. As already explained, every access to the world and things is always an experiencing one, and thus the intentional object or phenomenon of perception is exactly that which we experience from this world. The real house is the same as the perceived house; it is experienced 'in the flesh', literally standing before us, although never completely (i.e., never presenting all sides at once). However, it turns into a phenomenon for our description only through a change of attention or attitude, which renders the givenness of this object thematic and thus makes it describable as such. The aim of the phenomenological description is thereby to distinguish between different aspects, ways, qualities, or intensities in the appearance. In so describing, several things are achieved:

- **We discover differences:** for example, between those aspects of the house that fall into the field of view, like the front of the house, and those that do not, like the sides or back; or, for example, between the focus of perception and what appears merely as background.
- **We find connections:** for example, between actually and not actually seen sides, or between visual appearances and the corresponding movements of the perceiver.
- **We recognize general structures:** for example, every perception is directed at something, every object appears as embedded in a spatial horizon, every external perception presupposes potential movement of the perceiver.

Phenomenological description does not want to find arbitrary or one-time differences that constitute this or that factual experience (so my current perception of the house), but to find what is general and necessary to any experience of that kind—the features without which such an experience could not be described. Phenomenology attempts, through description, to identify structures and differences that apply not only to the perception of this house or that cube but to the perception of every possible and conceivable house or cube (regardless of who is perceiving them).

So doing phenomenology is always about a **reflective and descriptive seeing** (or imagining) with the aim of gaining a general insight—not for nothing is it called (in-) *sight*—into a given experience or experience in general. Phenomenology is thus not interested in how an individual experiences in particular; nor is it interested in merely internal processes, for example, how I feel right now, or how I feel while I do this or that, as would be the case in psychological approaches to introspection (see e.g., William James, Edward B. Titchener, Wilhelm Wundt). Although phenomenology describes not only things, but also the associated sensations and modes of consciousness, it does not understand itself as psychological self-observation, which seeks direct access to individual inner experience. Instead, it asks what makes up this or that experience—what is typical for a house perception, object perception, or perception in general—and emphasizes that this in turn implies subjective consciousness and its functions.

▪▪ From the Individual to the General

Phenomenology must therefore start with the *first-person perspective*, since it is only from there that we have access to the world and things, but it does not stop there. Rather, it aims to make general statements about this experience, i.e., statements that are valid not only for my experience here and now but for experience in general. A successful phenomenological description must therefore be intersubjectively verifiable: If my description is consistent, it will describe not only what I see but what anyone would see who assumed the same perspective. Of course, there might be individual and cultural differences in the perception of this house, due to differences in attention and interest as well as physical differences in the sensory organs, body size, etc. of the viewers. It might also be that where one per-

2

son sees a house, another sees a theater backdrop or a wall. However, regarding the *basic structures* of this experience (there are sides that are now actually seen and others not; something appears to me and not nothing, etc.) all possible descriptions must correspond.

So, the following applies: Not only do things always appear *to me* in a spatial horizon, but they appear that way to everyone. This is characteristic of every occurring or conceivable object perception, regardless of who is perceiving. It is not only *my* perception that is directed at something, but *every* perception, if it is to be called perception. Such general statements are reached, starting from the description, through a specific method that Husserl **calls eidetic variation** or **eidetic reduction**, in the sense of reducing to basic, general structures.

General statements about experience can therefore be *practically verified* or *theoretically secured, and transcendentally justified*: The aim is to:

— **Practically verify, through intersubjective comparison** with the descriptions of other phenomenologists or by comparison with special, deviating, or pathological experiences and cases as well as empirical research (▶ Chap. 3, ▶ Sect. 3.2).
— **Theoretically secure, through eidetic determination**, i.e., through the imaginative variation of the concrete experience, which is either affirmed by concordance and overlap of features or negated by exclusion of all non-essential moments, in order to identify and state the general (not otherwise thinkable) essence of the experienced things or ways of experiencing (▶ Sect. 2.2).
— **Transcendentally justify, through inquiring a questioning back** to the functions or stages of experience that *genetically* precede or *logically* underlie it, thereby making clear that these aspects are constitutively (logically or genetically) necessary to enable such an experience (▶ Sect. 2.3).

Ultimately, phenomenological description is not intended to highlight what is special, unique, or individual about a thing, person or experience—like the description of a work of art, a loved one, or a particularly extraordinary experience—but to capture the general or typical in the individual and singular.

Husserl's phenomenology in particular seeks to reduce the seen to the core or the essential, to identify the essence or *eidos*, starting with the determination and differentiation of certain types of experience or types of experienced things (e.g., dogs, houses, dice, etc.). At the highest level, it seeks to understanding the structures of experience and consciousness in general. The description of borderline cases like sleep, dreams, drug intoxication, pathologies, or death can help to determine the limits of experience and consciousness. What characterizes a certain pathology? What characterizes sleep? How do sleep, drug intoxication, and wakefulness differ? These, and similar questions, approach limiting cases in their typicality. By doing so, they illuminate not only the cases themselves but also the contours of so-called 'normal' experience.

2.1.1 Examples: Object Description

To illustrate what a phenomenological object description might look like, we now turn to Husserl's famous description of the dice.

> ▶ **Example: The dice: more than its visible front side**
>
> "Today we approach the discussion of an important phenomenological difference, which is manifested in well-known popular speeches. We say in a generally understandable way that we see the things around us, and at the same time we say that from them we actually only see the frontside [...]. We see a cube. For simplicity's sake, let's assume that the phenomenon remains unchanged, the cube does not move, and we also remain in the same position relative to it. Then the cube only presents a certain side to us, we see it as it "looks from this side". We then "actually" [often translated as 'genuinely', author] only see a piece of its surface, only the limiting squares with their colors and patterns. These are determinations of the cube that we ourselves "see" in a certain distinguished sense. We do not see the other determinations: the invisible surface parts, colors, the interior, etc. On the other hand, we do see the cube, and this perceived, seen object is more than the sum of those determinations [*Bestimmtheiten*], which were just said to be the only ones genuinely seen. The sense of the objective apprehension [*gegenständliche Auffassung*], the content of the cube, as it is meant in perception, certainly also includes the interior, the backside, etc. [...] The cube is more than its visible front side and what is "really" visible on the front side. Insofar as the cube, the whole cube, is meant in perception, it is the fully and completely seen, it falls entirely with all the determinations intended for it into perception. On the other hand, the examples again show that only a part of the determinations in a certain more poignant sense has a claim [...] to be considered as seen, as truly falling into perception. What is this difference, and how is it to be clarified phenomenologically?" (Husserl, Hua XXXVIII, pp. 26–27, automatic translation, edited) ◄

In the above example, Husserl describes only the phenomenon itself, i.e., how it appears to us. In doing so, *the question of the actual existence of the cube remains 'out of play'*. That is, he temporarily refrains from making a judgment or statement about it and focuses only on the perceptual experience. Instead of immediately judging whether this cube actually exists and why, an attempt is first made to describe how, i.e., through which aspects or elements, the cube appears to us as, and what in the appearance of this cube makes it appear as 'real' or existing.

▪▪ Actual and Potential Aspects of Perception

Using the description of the dice or cube, Husserl here makes clear the difference between what we 'actually' or 'genuinely' perceive, that is, what we ourselves see 'in a certain distinguished sense' (i.e., the now-present side, the surface of the cube) and what is 'meant' in perception, (i.e., the 'objective apprehension', 'cube', including the aspects not actually seen). The cube is more than its now-visible front side or what is 'genuinely' visible, and yet only some of its aspects fall into our current perception. The opinion or intention 'I see a cube' thus contains not only currently perceived aspects, but also aspects that have not yet been seen 'in a distinguished sense' (though they can potentially be seen in the further course of perception). Perception thus consists of the combination of actual or fulfilled and possible or emptily 'intended' aspects. Both belong to the sense 'cube'.

In a later text, Husserl elaborates on this and calls the actual 'consciousness' an **original consciousness**. In this context, he emphasizes that perception is always already a mixture of actual (i.e., original, genuine) and possible (or future) perceptions. Although every external perception is directed at the full object (house), it is only given in adumbrations. It thus consists of parts that are given originally and parts that are merely 'indicated' or co-present.

> ▶ **Example: The table (1): Originally given or indicated?**
>
> "That is a very curious situation peculiar to the very essence of the matter at hand. For proper to the very sense of every perception is perception's perceived object as its objective sense, that is, this thing, the table that is seen. But this thing is not merely the side genuinely seen in this moment; rather (according to the very sense of perception) the thing is precisely the full-thing that has still other sides [....]. Generally speaking, perception is original consciousness. We have, however, a curious schism in external perception: Original consciousness is only possible in the form of an actually and genuinely original conscious-having of sides and a co-conscious having of other sides that are precisely not originally there. I say co-conscious, since the non-visible sides are certainly also there somehow for consciousness, "co-meant" as co-present. But they do not appear as such, genuinely. [...] Noetically speaking, perception is a mixture of an actual exhibiting that presents in an intuitive manner what is originally exhibited, and of an empty indicating that refers to possible new perceptions. In a noematic regard, what is perceived is given in adumbrations in such a way that the particular givenness refers to something else that is not given, as what is not given belonging to the same object. We will have to understand the meaning of this." (Husserl, Hua XI, pp. 4–5/CW9, pp. 40–41) ◀

Such an indication or co-perceiving is by no means to be understood as an invention or imagination but genuinely belongs to the current act of perception. Only after such a perception or 'presentation' has taken place can one imagine, remember, or re-present the unified object as a whole. Indeed, it can be the case, that one explicitly represents, recalls, or imagines currently unseen sides of an object during a perception. However, this is not typical or usual for perception as such. Such explicit acts of re-presentation, Husserl argues, always imply, or refer to, an act of perception or presentation that has already occurred. What is specific to perception, in contrast to imagination or memory, is that there is an immediate match between the given and the indicated, which does not become thematic as such to the perceiver.

In a similar passage from a later text, Husserl focuses on the necessary correlation of modes of consciousness (appearing) and the object of consciousness (that which appears). Husserl further differentiates his description of object perception by introducing the concepts of inner and outer horizon on the side of the object, and that of 'horizon-intentionality' on the side of the subject. Every object appears in a horizon (of unnoticed, background, or not-yet-perceived aspects); every intentionality is thus also a horizon-intentionality ('*Horizontintentionalität*'), and fulfilled intentions (the perceived front of the house) are intertwined with (still) unfulfilled intentions, which point beyond the currently given. On the object side, we find 'indicative tendencies' or whole 'indicative systems', which in turn point to corresponding potential appearances and appearance systems.

▶ **Example: The table (2): Come closer and see me anew!**

"In other words, everything that genuinely appears is an appearing thing only by virtue of being intertwined and permeated with an intentional empty horizon, that is, by virtue of being surrounded by a halo of emptiness with respect to appearance. It is an emptiness that is not a nothingness, but an emptiness to be filled-out; it is a determinable indeterminacy. […] In spite of its emptiness, the sense of this halo of consciousness is a prefiguring that prescribes a rule for the transition to new actualizing appearances. Seeing the front side of the table, I am also conscious of the back side, along with everything else that is non-visible, through an empty pointing ahead, even though it be rather indeterminate. But no matter how indeterminate it may be, it is still a pointing ahead to a bodily shape, to a bodily coloring, etc. […] To our mind, the aspects are nothing for themselves; they are appearances-of only through the intentional horizons that are inseparable from them.

We thereby distinguish further between an *inner horizon* and an *outer horizon* of the respective aspect-appearance. […] Indeed, the call resounds as well with respect to the side that is already actually seen: "Draw closer, closer still; now fix your eyes on me, changing your place, changing the position of your eyes, etc. You will get to see even more of me that is new, ever new partial colorings, etc. You will get to see structures of the wood that were not visible just a moment ago, structures that were formerly only viewed indeterminately and generally", etc. Thus, even what is already seen is laden with an anticipatory intention. It—what is already seen—is constantly there as a framework prefiguring something new; it is an X to be determined more closely. There is a constant process of anticipation, of preunderstanding. In addition to this inner horizon there are then also outer horizons, prefigurings for what is still devoid of any intuitively given framework that would require only more differentiated ways of sketching it in."

(Husserl, Hua XI, pp. 6–7/CW9, pp. 42–42; emphasis M.W.; cf. also Hua IX, pp. 433ff.) ◀

In this description of the thing-appearance, it becomes clear to what extent the appearing object is coupled with the mode of appearance or the subjective appearance system. Although we cannot simply put something into the seen object that it does not itself show, a subjective activity must be added, a realization or determination of the still-indeterminate horizon, an anticipation of that which does not yet give itself. The table invites us (or at least Husserl) to look at it more closely, to see and determine it more clearly; with appropriate effort, concentration, and change of spatial position or eye movement, we get to see more and different aspects of it. Although we always anticipate, this anticipation is not arbitrary but follows certain regularities or a 'style'. It is pre-drawn or pre-guided by the form and content of what we have already seen of the object, and by the rules of object perception in general (intentionality, adumbrations, etc.). Perception does not,

2

therefore, involve a creative imagining or fantasizing of further sides of an object. When I perceive an object, such as a chair, I only anticipate within the realm of the possible and probable, e.g., more chair legs of the same shape and quality, similar to those I have already actually perceived.

■ ■ Object Perception and Movement

In other texts and contexts, Husserl makes clear that the realization of the inner and outer horizons is associated with the so-called *kinaesthetic possibilities of our physical body (Körper) and lived or living body (Leib)*. '*Leib*' is Husserl's term for the fact that our (human) body is not only extended like other bodies or material things (*Körper*), but is experienced also from within, that is lived. Moreover, from a phenomenological perspective, this lived, or better, living body is primary, since it refers to the body as subject of perception and action. It is the feeling, (freely) moving, and acting body (cf. Hua IV, pp. 143–162/CW 3, pp. 151–169).

Only free bodily movement makes it possible for us to see an object from different sides: The perceiver can walk around an object and assure herself that the corresponding house actually has a back side. At the same time she can experience the whole thing in all its sides (although never at the same time) by returning to the initial appearance at any time. Husserl argues, based on his description of thing-appearances in the lectures on *Thing and Space* from 1907 (Hua XVI/CW 7), that **three-dimensional spatiality** is related to the fact that we usually have two eyes and thus two integrated views of a thing. We can move these eyes and fix them on different aspects of a thing. Furthermore, we are able to move freely in space to view things from other perspectives. But even when standing still and viewing a stationary two-dimensional thing, such as a painting, the back-and-forth (stochastic) movement of the eyes makes possible our perception of the object in consciousness (Husserl, Hua XVI/CW7, section IV; cf. Mertens 2017). A perceiver who has only one eye from birth and is incapable of any movement (including of the eyes), would therefore not be able to experience the depth or three-dimensional spatiality of the object (cf. Husserl, Hua XVI, pp. 169–182, 227–229, 246–255/ CW7, pp. 143–153; Hua IV, p. 150/CW3, p. 157; Hua VI, pp. 120–123/CES, pp. 118–121; Mertens 2017, pp. 216–222).

One could say that, through movement in space or the exploration of one's environment, one gets to know objects and concretely realizes external horizons. Each visual appearance correlates with movements; if the movement changes, the appearances also change in a regular way. But embodiment (the feeling and self-moving body) is even more fundamentally a prerequisite for the perception of an object. Every experience of a thing, (i.e., sensory data that present features of the object or the environment), is simultaneously associated with movement or kinesthetic sensations. These are immediate subjective sensations or 'proprioceptions', that accompany our movements. If my perceiving activities and the perception of the given thing were not directly connected (through sensory feedback), how else could I experience the changing appearances as appearances of one and the same object? In sensory perception, self- and object-experience are thus necessarily combined, i.e., sensory information about things or the world is related to information about our own position and movement.

▪▪ Embodiment (*Leiblichkeit*) and Object Experience

Unified and coherent spatial object perception therefore goes hand in hand with:

- **an implicit bodily knowledge** or feedback, which links every experience back to me, i.e., my body and my bodily experience. A unity and continuity of different perceptions can only be guaranteed if these are felt as belonging to the same context of experience or consciousness;
- **an acquired practical knowledge** that, if I move and position myself in such and such a way, I will probably see this and that. The seen thereby motivates further kinesthetic movement sequences and thus further perceptions.

We constantly find this two-fold articulation: kinesthetic sensations on the one side, the motivating; and the sensations of features on the other, the motivated (Hua IV, p. 58/CW 3, p. 63). Thus, every perception includes possibilities for movement: "The processes of the kinesthetic sensations are free processes here, and this freedom in the consciousness of their unfolding is an essential part of the constitution of spatiality (Hua IV, p. 58/CW 3, p. 63; on the significance of embodiment in phenomenology, cf. Bernet 2009; Zahavi 1994; Heinämaa 2012; Taipale 2014; Alloa et al. 2019; Doyon and Wehrle 2020).

▪▪ From Individual Object to World

As becomes clear here, in everyday experience we do not deal primarily with separate or individual things. This is rather already a special form of perception, namely a focused perception or attention, in which we single out or highlight a special thing from a thing-like context (cf. Hua XXXVIII). And even here, the thing we are fixed on attentively necessarily points beyond itself to other things and the broader environment. But how do we get from the description of a particular thing to the experience of larger object complexes or even the world? How do we describe when what we perceive is not just a house but a residential settlement? Strictly speaking, only some objects and aspects that fall into our field of vision are perceived, but what happens to the surrounding houses that are part of the perception of a residential settlement?

> ▶ **Example: From the Perceived Thing to the World**
>
> "We see a room full of people, a forest with trees, a meadow, or a cornfield, and these cannot be grasped in one glance. What is at any time properly seen is not all that is there for our "seeing"; just as the back side of the Object is not properly seen and yet is co-apprehended and co-posited, so likewise is the unseen environment of the Object as well. The presented field of Objects is a field of Objects in a "world" [...]. The apprehension, and possibly the intending, reach beyond the proper perception. If the kinaesthetic circumstances change, then every phase ushers in a newly fulfilled visual field, and in it a new—even if partially identical—field of Objects is presented.
>
> In the successive elapsing of proper appearances, a sequential perception of a comprehensive Objectivity is carried out, and this is specifically such an Objectivity that it could never be perceived in a stationary perception (thus with kinaesthetic constancy). Each phase offers the proper perception of a restricted part of this Objectivity; but the apprehension reaches further. [...] *The world does not come to an end where the current*

2

kinetic perception ends. Phenomenologically, we obviously have to say that the fields of images which continually pass over into one another in the kinaesthetic sequence perpetually undergo such an apprehension that the continuous succession of appearances founds the unity of one appearance." (Husserl, Hua XVI, pp. 209–210/ CW 7, pp. 177–178, emphasis M.W.) ◄

▪▪ From Description to Philosophy

What becomes clear from the selected examples of phenomenological object description is that Husserl was not especially concerned with describing the given thing (cube, table) in its uniqueness. We learn little to nothing about what the cube or table looks like in detail—it could be any cube or table. In other texts, Husserl even speaks abstractly of things as 'objectivities' (*Objektitäten*), referring to their objecthood in general (see example "From the perceived thing to the world"). The experienced thing is only used here as an example to gain insight into the general nature of how physical things, objects, object complexes, or 'the world' appear to us.

Husserl thereby wants to point to the fact that already in describing how something concretely appears to us, a deeply philosophical question looms in the background. Namely, how something can appear to us (at all) as an object or objectivity, i.e., **how we experience objectivity in subjective experience** and why this is so self-evident to us. Upon closer inspection and description, this relationship becomes increasingly mysterious and complex; even an isolated perception of a thing requires several appearances linked temporally and in terms of content and thus implies what is not yet (or no longer) seen. The perceived thing in turn refers to other aspects of itself as well as to other things and the spatial environment. Perception in the full sense is therefore never directed only at one physical thing. It always picks out a section of a wider object field, which is itself a small section of the world.

▪▪ The Role of Consciousness

If one tries to phenomenologically describe a thing or the world, one almost automatically encounters the 'subjective' aspects of perception, i.e., the syntheses or 'achievements' of consciousness or the kinesthetic body, which guarantee the temporal and content unity of the perception. For an object to appear in a continuous and coherent manner, there must be a correlation of the subjective and objective parts of experience: the correlation of object appearance with eye position and eye movement; of movement with changing visual appearances; of the sensations of the thing with the sensations of the body (and its movement). This in turn shows that to be able to see a thing as a thing or to have the experience of an objective world, movement is needed (eye and body movement). Otherwise, we would only see a minimal section of the world and would not experience this as three-dimensional or as a mere section of a world beyond. Objectivity, as is clear from the above descriptions, is directly related to the possibilities of movement and the potentially constantly expanding horizon of perception of the experiencing subject.

And despite all these possibilities, we never fully grasp objects or the world. Some aspects always elude us; there is always more to discover and new ways to discover. The world does not end where our possibilities stop, as Husserl so beautifully puts it. Precisely this negative experience of withdrawal, gives the world its objective and transcendent character. Another moment that is indispensable for the experience of objectivity is what Husserl calls the 'unity of appearance'. Concretely, this means that the various sensations, appearances, and perspectives must somehow form a unity or a connection that makes entities or events appear as successive, simultaneous, or related in content. This unity, in turn, implies a relation to a consciousness or lived body. The experienced thing must appear as given to me and motivated by my actual and potential movements, even though we are not explicitly aware of this relation, or do not make it thematic in everyday experience.

2.1.2 Examples: Temporality and Experience

What stands out in all these descriptions of things is that something is never given suddenly or all at once; perception cannot be grasped statically but always refers to a temporal course (cf. Rinofner-Kreidl 2000; Rodemeyer 2006; Mensch 2010; Summa 2014). How temporality is experienced and constituted in consciousness is therefore a central theme in Husserl and other phenomenologists, such as Maurice Merleau-Ponty and Martin Heidegger. Here too, Husserl begins with the description of a temporal object, a melody, to determine from there the general essence of (inner) time consciousness (eidetic determination), or to inquire about the conditions for the unified appearance of temporal objects in general (transcendental justification), e.g., how the experiences are temporally and motivationally linked in the experience of a subject (genetic intentional analysis).

How does a temporal object appear to us? Why do we hear a melody and not disconnected tones or fragmented noises?

▶ **Example: The melody: first approach**

"Let us take the example of a melody or of a cohesive part of a melody. The matter seems very simple at first: we hear the melody, that is, we perceive it, for hearing is indeed perceiving. However, the first tone sounds, then comes the second tone, then the third, and so on. Must we not say: When the second tone sounds, I hear it, but no longer hear the first tone, etc.? In truth, then, I do not hear the melody but only the single present tone. That the elapsed part of the melody is something objective for me, I owe—or so one will be inclined to say—to memory; and that I do not presuppose, with the appearance of the currently intended tone, that this is all, I owe to anticipatory expectation. But we cannot be content with this explanation, for everything that we have said carries over to the individual tone. Each tone has a temporal extension itself. When it begins to sound, I hear it as now; but while it continues to sound it has an ever new now, and the now that immediately precedes it changes into a past. Therefore, at any given time I hear only the actually present phase of the tone, and the objectivity of the whole enduring tone is constituted in an act-continuum that is in part memory, in smallest punctual part perception, and in further part expectation. [...] Here, then, a deeper analysis must begin." (Husserl, Hua X, p. 23/CW 4, pp. 24–25) ◄

Husserl begins here, as he often does, with an everyday observation and takes this as his guide. The first intuition, however, does not seem to be sufficient; now we must add methodical distance and try to verify the above assumptions, and describe only what actually presents itself to us in the experience.

> ▶ **Example: The melody as inner time consciousness**
>
> "We now *exclude all transcendent apprehension* and *positing* and take the tone purely as a hyletic datum. It begins and ends; and after it has ended, its whole duration-unity, the unity of the whole process in which it begins and ends, 'recedes' into the ever more distant past. *In this sinking back, I still 'hold onto it'*, have it in a '*retention*'. And as long as the retention lasts, the tone has its own temporality; it is the same, its duration is the same. I can *direct my attention* to the *way in which it is given*. I am conscious of the tone and of the duration it fills in a continuity of 'modes', in a 'continual flow'. [...] 'Throughout' this whole flow of consciousness, one and the same tone is intended as enduring, as now enduring. 'Beforehand" (in the event that it was not expected), it is not intended. 'Afterwards', it is 'still' *intended* 'for a time' in '*retention' as having been*; it can be held fast and stand or remain fixed in our regard. The whole extent of the tone's duration or 'the' tone in its extension then stands before me as something dead, so to speak—something no longer being vitally generated, [...] but continuously modified and sinking back into 'emptiness'.
>
> What we have described here is the manner in which the object in immanent time 'appears' in a continual flow, the manner in which it is 'given'. To describe this manner does not mean to describe the appearing temporal duration itself, for it is the same tone with the duration belonging to it that, indeed, was not described but presupposed in the description. The same duration is present duration actually building itself up and then is past, 'elapsed' duration, duration that is still intended or that is produced in recollection 'as if' it were new. It is the same tone that now sounds of which it is said in the 'later' flow of consciousness that it has been, that its duration has elapsed. The points of the temporal duration recede for my consciousness in a manner analogous to that in which the points of an object stationary in space recede for my consciousness when I remove 'myself" from the object. The object keeps its place, just as the tone keeps its time. Each time-point is fixed, but it flies into the distance for consciousness. The distance from the generative now becomes greater and greater. The tone itself is the same, but the tone 'in the manner in which' it appears is continually different." (Husserl, Hua X, pp. 24–25/ CW 4, pp. 26–27, emphasis M.W.) ◄

In this description of the experience of a melody, it becomes particularly clear that the temporal object is the result of synthesizing processes of consciousness. The difference between the appearing table and the melody is that the former only gradually reveals itself or builds up over time. The melody, in contrast to a house objectively seen—and not related to the *how* of its appearance—is not simply there and cannot be experienced from different perspectives. The real duration of the sound-ing tone at first seems identical with its appearing duration, and yet their temporal-ity is different. The heard tone also has its temporal horizon; it is classified in the flow of consciousness, as a quasi-temporal structure, in which each incoming impression is retained in modified form as it sinks down into the depths of con-sciousness. In the case of visual object perception, it was the always-partial given-ness of the object that pointed beyond itself and motivated further intentions. Here it is consciousness itself that goes beyond the now-sounding tone.

The preceding tone (or tone datum) is retained in consciousness. That is, a retention of the tone is 'still somehow given' within consciousness and can thereby immediately connect with the now-sounding tone. Retention is not to be confused with the real echo of a tone; it is the *still-holding-on* of the faded tone in conscious-ness. Furthermore, a so-called **protention** takes place, i.e., there is an automatic anticipation of the following tone (or tone datum). The incoming tones are thus connected in consciousness with past tones and anticipations of tones still to come. This inner time consciousness allows us to experience sounding tones as uniformly successive and belonging together. The once-heard tones remain in consciousness, but in modified form. They lose, for example, intensity and clarity. They recede into the depths of consciousness, just like the visual appearance of a thing when I move away from it.

The **time object** is thus built up piece by piece. Only when the last note has faded can one refer back to the melody as a whole, as an immanent time object. From then on, I can remember this melody as a whole and specify the time at which I heard it. Only after the sequence of appearances is complete do we have a time object, but not while we are listening to the melody. The note as it appears to us, as Husserl so beautifully puts it, is experienced differently each time, as an impres-sion, retention, or anticipated protention, or afterwards as a remembered, i.e., 'newly created' (as it were) note. It becomes clear here that the 'object' of our per-ception, be it a house or a melody, is always the starting point or guide for any description when viewed statically: I do not merely experience parts of a house or isolated notes but a whole house or melody. In other words, I experience the object of perception as unified, complete, and continuous. At the same time, this unified object is also the goal of any description or the mystery that needs to be solved: How does such a stable and continuous object perception come about at all? What constitutive achievements of consciousness precede this temporal and content 'unity'? If one does not reduce the description to a certain 'static' section but pays attention to the changing modes of appearance—the connection between self-movement, temporality, and the appearance of the thing—it becomes clear that every object perception has a genetic dimension. The questioning of this genetic dimension belongs to transcendental phenomenology (▶ Sect. 2.3).

2.2 Determining the General

2

» This is a characteristic of the phenomenological method: That it gets its lawfulness [*Gesetzmäßigkeit*] neither from a supreme principle, nor through the inductive accumulation of individual examples, but by seeing and discerning [*erschauen*] the general essence [*Wesen*], the general lawfulness in the individual example. (Geiger [1925] 2009, p. 34, automatic translation, edited)

Already in his early lectures, such as *The Idea of Phenomenology* (*Die Idee der Phänomenologie*) from 1907, Husserl describes phenomenology as research into the analysis of essences. More concretely he believes that one can grasp the essence of a thing by a contemplative observation or essential seeing (*Wesensschau*) (Husserl, Hua II, p. 51/CW 8, p. 39; cf. Jansen 2017). The motto 'to the things themselves' initially aims at the essence of the corresponding things, i.e., what determines a thing or an object as such in its generality and necessity. Husserl is not only interested in how particular things are given in experience, but also in how and why generalities, that is, the characteristics of a thing or state-of-affairs in general, are given to us so self-evidently in experience.

Such an eidetic phenomenology, which focuses on the determination of the objective generality of perceived things or meanings, characterizes Husserl's philosophy until the so-called transcendental turn around 1913 (with the publication of *Ideas I*).

Definition

The 'essence' (*Wesen*) is what all objects of the same kind have in common (generality) as well as what is necessarily specific for this 'type of thing', i.e., what makes it this type of thing (specificity) and distinguishes it from other things.

The 'essence as eidos' is an idea in the Platonic sense, but without any metaphysical connotations: It does not exist as a separate object in a 'heaven of ideas'. Rather, it is the general that comes to us intuitively in and through the experience or imagination of something. Even though the essence does not have a separate existence next to the real, its determination is both necessary and a priori (before/independent of concrete experience), as it necessarily determines the scope and the limit of the object, whether that object is actually existing or merely conceivable.

■■ **Science of Essences vs. Science of Facts**
Although phenomenology begins with experience, and seeks to describe, determine, and clarify this experience, according to Husserl, it is not a science of facts, but a science of essences (eidetics). The essence to be determined is not the generality or generalization of empirical details (such as an inductive generalization of observed or measured properties of say, actually existing lions). Such empirical generality is always accidental, according to Husserl. That is, it happens to belong to a certain nature (due to environmental conditions or contingent natural laws),

but not a priori necessary. Only pure concepts, whose formation does not depend on the contingency of a factually given object (e.g., a lion) from which the general is then determined afterwards, are necessary in this sense. According to Husserl, the pure essence must determine the given individual thing not only afterwards, but also in advance, i.e., prior to, and independently of, any actual experience (Husserl 1973 (EJ), pp. 339–340/1939, p. 409). It is therefore about that without which a thing cannot be thought, i.e., about the realm of the necessary, not the actual.

▪▪ Eidetics in Science and Phenomenology
Eidetics is also practiced outside of phenomenology. Formal logic, for example, provides the general structures of valid argument forms. And geometry provides the general laws of spatial properties and relations. In the case of the latter, actually existing objects, such as a house, are taken merely as examples of general geometric shapes, such as triangles, straight lines, or right angles. Unlike geometrical objects, however, the things to which phenomenology refers (essence of perception, psyche, external things), do not lend themselves to exact determinations, so they cannot be used as axioms for a deduction or be proven without a doubt. Like biology, phenomenology is a descriptive science. Therefore, it only investigates 'vague' or morphological essences, as Husserl calls them. This refers to substantial essences that rely on the description of general forms or shapes, e.g., not unlikely to different forms of life as distinguished in biology. To describe experiences of consciousness in terms of their essences is therefore something completely different from conducting a logical or geometrical proof. In consciousness and the experienced world, nothing can be definitively fixed; everything is vague and in flux. And yet, Husserl deeply believed, it is also possible to recognize and identify necessary generalities by 'seeing' them with the help of relevant methods.

▪▪ Experience of the Typical and Determination of the Essence
In this context, one must distinguish between the intuitive grasping of generality within perception and the explicit act of determining and verifying such an intuited generality in the form of an essence. Husserl later understands the mere genetic experience of the general as the formation or constitution of a type in experience, e.g., when a child experiences something not only as a singular something, but automatically as a type, such as the type 'dog', based on previous experiences of similar things. Such a generality is formed by passive association, i.e., without conscious action in concrete experience, and is based on repeated individual experiences. Every similar thing is now immediately understood as this or that, i.e., endowed with a certain meaning. A typical experience or an experienced type is not yet an essence in the strict and pure sense, as these types can and must adapt to changing experiences and only vaguely encompass factual generalities (cf. Doyon 2024, pp. 140–149).

The pure essence, on the other hand, is supposed to determine the thing itself and not just our concept of it or our habit (what we are accustomed to seeing and therefore associate with it), but rather the essence that makes a certain thing what it is, independently of its determination and recognition. In determining the essence, it is necessary to

a. **make the merely (implicitly) experienced generality** explicit, and
b. **determine and verify the supposedly general** or invariant as such.

In determining the essence, we therefore want to find out what is common to every object of this kind (*generality*), what makes this object what it is (*necessity*), and at the same time what distinguishes it from other types of objects (*specificity*).

Even in determining the essence, there are gradual differences in generality and necessity. Thus, Husserl distinguishes between *material*, i.e., substantial, *essences* (like house, tree, color, sound, space, sensation, feeling, etc.) and *formal essences* (like object, quality, relationship, link, plurality, whole, part, size, etc.); (cf. Husserl, LI2, p. 19/Hua XIX/1, p. 256). Substantial essences, as the name suggests, are not merely formal; they are concretely content-determined and therefore less general than formal essences. Moreover, their generality can vary. It is possible to distinguish between levels with greater or lesser generality. For example, if we consider an individual dog, we first have the singular eidos 'dog', then genus and species concepts, such as 'mammal', 'animal', and 'living being'. Finally, at the highest level of generality, we reach the formal essence of 'object' or 'objecthood' The most general categories must always contain the other, more specific categories.

▪▪ Generalization and Formalization

Going from an individual dog to a thing in general seems to require a generalization. However, if one looks more closely, the formal essence of 'object in general' cannot be determined starting from a concrete perception (e.g., of a dog). It can only be determined by a formalization, never a factual generalization. 'Object in general' is not a content-related, but rather a formal-ontological, determination: For example, a triangle can be formalized first into a spatial figure and then into an object in general, or a seen 'red' can be formalized into a 'sensory quality'. A generalization, on the other hand, is a factual operation that goes from the specific or particular to the general. Material beings therefore always have a certain scope that needs to be delimited (e.g., what belongs to the genus 'mammals'? What falls under the category 'tree' or 'color'?). In this way, one can conduct a descriptive 'regional' ontology, which tries to determine the most general regions of being, such as nature, consciousness, or spirit (Husserl's as well as Hegel's term for the social and cultural world), and their subregions.

The more concrete or factual the description of the general becomes, the more difficult it is to determine the invariant in all things of that kind. Agreeing on the formal determination, for example, that it is part of the essence of color to be a sensory quality, is therefore easier than determining those characteristics that must be attributed to every conceivable dog or that make a dog (compared to other animals) a dog.

▪▪ Phenomenologically Perceiving Essence

According to Husserl, the general (e.g., 'house') of a perceived singular object or individual ('this house here') can not only be determined conceptually or terminologically in retrospect, i.e., in thinking, but can somehow be *seen,* that is, *intuited.* Husserl refers to this as an 'intuition of essence' or 'essential seeing' (*Wesensschau*).

This is not a direct sensory perception, as if one could catch a glimpse of a ghostly essence hovering on top of the everyday object. And yet Husserl insists that one can not only think, but *see* the ideal or categorical, not directly or all at once, but through repeated viewing of appropriate examples. He also calls this 'categorical intuition'. In this sense, one can mentally perceive general categories in a similar way as one sensually perceives concrete worldly things (Husserl, LI2, p. 282/Hua XIX/1, p. 674). Such an intuition of essence is not an immediate or simple act of perception, though it is always based on simple perceptions. For example, the higher-level category (eidos) 'color' can only be perceived on the basis of the simple perception of colored things. In this way, an intuition of essence always constitutes itself gradually.

If we look for the essence of 'red', for example, this generality can be seen from exemplary experiences of red objects. If we in turn look for the essence of 'perception', this can be intuited from exemplary experiences of perception (Jansen 2017, p. 145). Initially, we have the similarity of two or more things before our eyes, and almost automatically a "mental overlapping" takes place, "in which the common, e.g., the red, the figure etc., 'itself' emerges—that is, attains intuitive apprehension" (Husserl, EJ, p. 348/1939, p. 421).

This language of seeing should of course not be taken literally, as a sensuous seeing. As Husserl puts it: "One cannot see the universal red as one sees an individual, particular red" (Husserl, EJ, p. 348/1939, p. 421). However, there is an analogy here: A "common and general moment of as many examples as desired, seen one by one" is appropriated in an analogous manner "directly and as itself" (ibid.), just like an individual particular in sensuous perception. This, however, happens to be the result of a complicated intuitive process, in Husserl's words "the actively comparative overlapping of congruence" (ibid.).

> **For further study**
The pure essence as Eidos

In earlier texts, Husserl uses the term 'essence' (*Wesen*) to denote all possible forms of the ideal or general. For example, it might denote an idea in the Platonic sense (where a concrete object such as a table has a share in the idea 'table'), or in the sense of a species (where a concrete animal, such as an individual human being, falls under the species 'human') or as an ideal generality or meaning. The essence is therefore the general that can individualize itself in a multitude of particular objects, e.g., the essence 'human' or 'table' in countless actually existing and experienced humans or tables.

In later texts, such as the essay 'Philosophy as Rigorous Science' from 1910/1911 (PRS, 71–149/Hua XXV, pp. 29–41), Husserl speaks of the essence (*Wesen*) as 'eidos', which in a narrower sense refers to universals (e.g., 'human', 'red'), i.e., a kind of genus or general category with a determinate scope and predicates (everything that belongs to the category 'human' or 'red'). In the *Ideas I* (CW3/Hua III/1), Husserl then defines the eidos as a pure general in a certain sense, i.e., the general determination that we attribute to objects predicatively (terminologically) or prepredicatively (in categorical intuitions). 'Pure' here means purified of factual peculiarities, i.e., determined *formally*.

2

The pure essence or Eidos, therefore, does not include empirical essences. It must be so general that it is no longer bound to the empirical, i.e., to conditions and circumstances of this world (such as natural laws, the material environment, etc.). Thus, although one can speak in general terms of the 'human', the 'European', the 'Italian shoe' (Husserl's examples) or of zoological terms, such as 'lizard' or 'lion' etc., these empirical essences remain bound to a real context. They merely denote the scope of real lions or real possible lions. The pure essence, on the other hand, has no real scope of actual or possible individuals (e.g., future existing lions), but refers to a **scope of pure possibilities**, i.e., possibilities of pure imagination (cf. Sowa 2009, p. 70).

▪▪ Generality as Necessity

Although the seeing and determination of essences depends on the perception of concrete things, the concrete individual (a living being such as a human) must not be understood as the cause of the Eidos. The essence existed before and independently of any particular perception. To take another example, every color is subject to the essential laws of color in general (quality, intensity), and each individual (colored thing) is thus contained in the scope of the genus or species (color). This lawful generality or generality of essences (*Wesensallgemeinheit*) is thus at the same time an essential necessity, i.e., a prerequisite for belonging to this category (CW2, p. 14/Hua III/1, p. 19). This also applies to correct judgments about essences, such as that color cannot exist without extension. This applies not only generally, but also necessarily (if the essence has been correctly determined) to the essence of red.

The perceived things or individuals are therefore to be seen as arbitrary examples that individualize or exemplify the essence. To make this independence of the essence from the concrete perception clear, Husserl later emphasizes that the transition from the concrete thing or individual to the general or ideal can be realized just as well in free phantasy, i.e., in the imagination (LI2, p. 136/Hua XIX/1, p. 456). Genuine (i.e., free) eidetic variation is therefore primarily executable in the imagination; only there can the inspection of essence be protected from randomness (Husserl, EJ, p. 340/1939, p. 410).

> ▶ **Example: An essence is not an individual**
>
> "If, for example, we envisage to ourselves an individual house now painted yellow, we can just as well think that it could be painted blue or think that it could have a slate instead of a tile roof or, instead of this shape, another one. The house is an object which, in the realm of the possible, could have other determinations in place of, and incompatible with, whatever determinations happen to belong to it within the unity of a representation. This house, the same, is thinkable as *a* and as *non-a* but, naturally, if as *a,* then not *at the same time* as *non-a.* It cannot be both simultaneously; it cannot be actual while having *each* of them at the same time; but at any moment it can be *non-a* instead of *a.* It is, therefore, thought as an identical something in which opposite determinations can be exchanged.

[…] However, *what is seen as unity* in *the conflict is not an individual* but a concrete hybrid unity of individuals mutually nullifying and coexistentially exclusive: a unique consciousness with a unique content, whose correlate signifies concrete unity founded
    in conflict, in incompatibility […].

The *particular,* which is at the bottom of essential seeing, *is not* in *the proper sense* an *intuited individual as such.* The remarkable unity which is at the bottom here is, on the contrary, an 'individual' in the exchange of 'nonessential' constitutive moments."
    (Husserl, EJ, p. 344–345/1939, pp. 416–117) ◄

▪▪ Real and Ideal Possibilities

Why can an essence not be a generalization of actually existing things, such as lions, red roses, or humans? Because this would mean that it always remains bound to that which is current. Everything that really exists and happens, does so not without reason, motivation or rule, but the kind of necessity it possesses is real and not pure. Even natural laws, although generally valid, apply only to this temporally and materially existing world. Husserl thus strictly distinguishes between real and ideal possibilities, i.e., possibilities that apply to this world and these people, but not to objects and conscious subjectivity in general. Perception is always a concrete experience of individual objects (or living beings), such as the perception of this house. And individual objects, like this house, always appear as embedded in a spatial and temporal horizon. This means that the perception of the house necessarily comprises parts that are somehow 'pre-given' in a 'horizon-like way' as for example the back of the house that is not currently visible (cf. Husserl, Hua XXXIX, p. 65). Such a pre-givenness is prefigured in its content by what we have already actually experienced of this house (the front side). The changing perspectives and views of the house must therefore match, i.e., be concordant, if we want to speak of the perception as being of the same house (and not of different objects). This, in turn, is a fundamental law of the appearance of reality: For us, only what is experienced as concordant is experienced as real, i.e., what corresponds with what we or other subjects have already experienced.

▪▪ The Freedom of Imagination

Not so in the imagination. Here, starting from an imagined house, we can freely vary, and the variations do not have to match each other. We can imagine the house once yellow, once blue, once with this roof, once with that. This is important because it is not about the individuality of the object (i.e., the identification of a specific house), but about that which must apply to all houses as such. It is about finding that which remains the same in all possible (and infinitely extendable) variations, the invariant amidst the variations.

To now perceive and determine this invariant and to be able to check or judge it in future perceptions and ideas, according to Husserl, requires an active volitional effort and method that leads us from the concrete, individual, and contingent to the abstract, general, and necessary: the eidetic intuition or eidetic variation.

2

Definition

'Eidetic variation' is a method developed by Husserl to find the 'eidos', i.e., the essential or unchanging characteristics, of a given object. In 'eidetic variation' we take an experienced or imagined object as an example and then arbitrarily, imaginatively vary it, i.e., we generate open-ended free variants of this thing. What is revealed is the unity contained or maintained in the multitude of variants: That which remains the same in every possible variation. This invariant represents the necessary general form of the thing, without which such a thing (as a model of its kind) would not be thinkable, i.e., could not be vividly imagined as such (Husserl, EJ, p. 341/1939, p. 411).

The eidetic variation consists of three main steps:

1. the "**running through the multiplicity of variations**", as a productive activity of the imagination
2. the "**unitary linking in continuous coincidence**", as a passive process of association within the intuition of those variations that coincide in relation to one aspect (congruence), and
3. the "**identification of the congruent over against the differences**", as an active mental act of identification (Husserl EJ, pp. 346–347/1939, p. 419; Hua IX, p. 86).

2.2.1 Examples of Eidetic Variation

As we have seen, eidetically oriented phenomenology is not primarily interested in empirically existing things or individuals. Here, the call 'to the things themselves' is meant in an almost Platonic sense, as a call to identify the essence of things, i.e., what necessarily constitutes all things of this kind and determines them generally, i.e., according to their possibility (and not their actuality). One could therefore say that phenomenology practiced in this way is a **science of possibilities** and not of facts. Thus, the specific eidos of a thing, e.g., of a sound or color, must apply to every actual and possible existing sound or every actual and possible existing color. However, one can of course fail to grasp or determine an essence correctly, as the human capacity for variation (imagination) is limited and potentially biased. For example, due to new knowledge or facts, what was thought to be a necessary aspect of color could turn out to be merely contingent.

▶ **Example: From a tone to the tone in general**

"For example, if we take a sound as our point of departure, whether we actually hear it or whether we have it present as a sound 'in the imagination', then we obtain the *eidos* sound as that which, in the course of 'arbitrary' variants, is necessarily common to all these variants. Now: If we take as our point of departure another sound-phenomenon in order to vary it arbitrarily, in the new 'example' we do not apprehend *another eidos* sound; rather, in juxtaposing the old and the new, we see that it is *the same,* that the variants and the variations on both sides join together in a single variation, and that the variants here and there are, in like fashion, *arbitrary particularizations of the one eidos.*

And it is even evident that in progressing from one variation to a new one we can give this progress and this formation of new multiplicities of variation the character of an arbitrary process, and that […] the same *eidos* must appear 'again and again': the same general essence 'sound in general'." (Husserl, EJ, pp. 341–342/1939, p. 412) ◄

Phantasy, or the possibility of a free variation in the imagination, plays an important role here. Of course, generalities can also be determined on the empirical level. For example, I can compare a multitude of things existing and perceived here and now and determine what is common to them all. But even if I were to increase the quantity of particulars by means of digital technology (e.g., pictures of existing lions) to infinity, I would still end up with only an empirically limited scope. For this reason, if I want to determine the eidos or essence of something, it cannot be tied to the scope of actually existing things.

■ ■ Algorithmic Biases and Eidetic Variation

The problem with determining an eidos beginning from empirical generalizations can be illustrated in the current debate about so-called *implicit bias* (implicit 'prejudices') in algorithms. If you train a self-learning algorithm for face recognition with a non-representative empirical data selection, i.e., only with images of faces with white skin tones, it will not be able to recognize faces with other tones. This became known when the Facebook algorithm categorized vacation photos of users with darker-toned skin not as photos of people but as photos of monkeys. Similarly, when a software for detection of skin cancer was trained on people with light-toned skin, it could not identify cancer in people with darker-toned skin. These are examples not only of the prejudices of the particular programmers, the lack of diversity in the IT sector, or the limited selection of training data, but also of an automated, insufficient empirical generalization. If, however, the method of eidetic variation were applied here, one would not start with a selection of actually existing faces, but with an arbitrary face—or general details of a face—and then simulate potentially infinite variations of possible faces until stable congruences were discovered and then tested against reality. In this case, the starting example must be as arbitrary as possible and could also be an imagined face. It should not make a difference whether we start our variation with this or that face, or with this or that skin tone.

> ▶ **Example: The eidos is Not an Empirical Generalization**
> "[C]ertainly we obtain for this red here and that red there an identical and general element present in both, but precisely only as what is common to this and that red. We do not obtain pure red in general as *eidos*. To be sure, taking account of a third red or several, whenever they present themselves to us, we can recognize that the universal of the two is identically the same as the universal of the many. But in this way, we always obtain only commonalities and generalities relative to empirical extensions […]. However, as soon as we say that every arbitrary like moment, newly to be taken account of, *must* yield the same result, and if we repeat once more: the *eidos* red is *one* over against the

2

infinity of possible particulars which belong to this and any other red capable of being in coincidence with it, then we are already in need of an infinite variation in our sense as a foundation. This variation provides us with what belongs to the *eidos* as its inseparable correlate, the so-called *extension of the eidos,* of the 'purely conceptual essence'." (Husserl, EJ, pp. 349–350/1939, pp. 422–423) ◄

▪▪ Reduction to the Essential

To be able to formulate such a pure general or conceptual essence, it is necessary to ensure independence from empirical necessities and laws. For this, we must refrain from any assertion about reality or, in Husserl's words, from any 'positing of existence'. Husserl sometimes describes this in terms of an *eidetic reduction* (cf. LI2, p. 112/Hua XIX/1, p. 412), i.e., a reduction to the purely possible (in relation to a thing). However, this reduction needs to be strictly distinguished from the transcendental reduction. While the transcendental reduction reduces to the (formal, foundational) conditions for experience, i.e., what is constitutively necessary for this or that experience or experience in general, the eidetic reduction is supposed to direct the researcher's view to the ideal general of the thing to be determined. The thing to be determined can be the essence of sound or, in the context of transcendental phenomenology, the essence of consciousness. An eidetic reduction to the (e.g., factual or categorical) essence is not necessarily also transcendental in the Husserlian sense. The eidetic reduction can be called transcendental only when applied to determine the essence of consciousness or subjectivity, as these essential structures are also the conditions of the possibility of experience (► Sect. 2.3).

> ► **Example: The pure eidos, not bound to any reality**
>
> "First of all, it is necessary to point out that *even totally free variation is not enough* to actually give us the universal as pure. Even the universal acquired by variation must not yet be called *pure in* the true sense of the word, i.e., free from all positing of actuality.
>
> Although the relation to the contingent example, actually existing as a point of departure, is already excluded by the variation, a relation to actuality can still cling to the universal and in the following way: For a pure *eidos*, the factual actuality of the particular cases by means of which we progress in the variation is completely irrelevant. And this must be taken literally. The actualities must be treated as possibilities among other possibilities, in fact as arbitrary possibilities of the imagination. This treatment is achieved only when every connection to pregiven actuality is most carefully excluded. If we practice variation freely but cling secretly to the fact that, e.g., these must be arbitrary sounds *in the* world, heard or able to be heard by men on earth, then we certainly have an essential generality as an *eidos* but one *related to our world of fact* and bound to this universal. It is a secret bond in that, for understandable reasons, it is imperceptible to us […].
>
> Only if we become conscious of this bond, *putting it consciously out* of *play,* and so also free this broadest surrounding horizon of variants from all connection to experience and all experiential validity, do we achieve perfect purity. Then we find ourselves, so to speak, in a pure world of imagination, a *world of absolutely pure possibility.* […]

A pure *eidos*, an essential generality, is, e.g., the species red or the genus color, but only if it is apprehended as a pure generality, thus free from all presupposition of any factual existent whatsoever, any factual red or any teal colored actuality. Such is also the sense of the statements of geometry, e.g., when we designate the circle as a kind of conic section, that is, when we apprehend it in an eidetic intuition; we are then not speaking of an actual surface as an instance belonging to a real actuality of nature. Accordingly, *a purely eidetic judging 'in general,'* such as the geometrical, or that concerned with ideally possible colors, sounds, and the like is, in its generality, *bound to no presupposed actuality.*" (Husserl, EJ, pp. 350–351/1939, pp. 423–425) ◄

Let's now start with a variation based on an imagined arbitrary red color (step 1). In this case, the variation performed (as an achievement or creation of our imagination) shows both what matches or is congruent within these different variants, and what is different in each case (step 2). The second step involves a passive association or almost automatic recognition of congruence (overlapping coverage of the variants running through the imagination) and difference (non-overlapping coverage). For example, I imagine a red rose, a red chair, and a red cup; in this case, the form changes, but the color red is common to all. As Husserl makes clear, every experienced difference is closely linked to such congruence. I can only perceive given differences on the basis of a basic commonality. Every newly experienced difference or the 'conflict' between the variations thus leads back to a more foundational (i.e., more general) form of commonality, up to a basic generality, which encompasses all possible diversity as parts or possible formations of this Eidos.

► **Example: The eidos red: Congruence and difference**

"If, for example, we pass from a given red color to a series of any other red colors whatsoever—whether we actually see them or whether they are colors floating 'in the imagination'—we obtain the *eidos* 'red', which, as the necessarily common, is what is congruent in the alteration of the 'arbitrary' variants, while the different extensions in the coincidence, instead of being congruent, on the contrary come to prominence in conflict.

The *idea* of *the difference,* therefore, is only to be understood in *its involvement with the idea* of *the identically common element which is the eidos.* Difference is that which, in the overlapping of the multiplicities, is not to be brought into the unity of the congruence making its appearance thereby, that which, in consequence, does not make an *eidos* visible. […]

Consider, for example, an identical color; at one time it is the color of this extension and shape, at another time of that. In the overlapping, the one conflicts with the other, and they mutually supplant each other. But, on the other hand, it is clear that *things cannot enter into conflict which have nothing in common.* In our example, not only is an identical color already presupposed; it is even more important that, even if the one colored object were square, they still could not enter into conflict if both were not extended figures. Thus, every difference in the overlapping with others and in conflict with them points toward a new universal to be brought out." (Husserl, EJ, pp. 346/1939, pp. 417–418) ◄

2

In a final step (step 3), the general that one has intuited over and against differences must now be explicitly identified and formulated as such. Since every determination of essence can also be wrong or insufficient, for example, if possible variations were not considered, this must also be checked, i.e., confirmed or corrected. This can be done through eidetic variations of other subjects or examples from future experience or through empirical or scientific facts, which must then be used as pure examples (examples translated into pure possibilities).

Although the essence and possibility of things are, in terms of their status and validity, prior to the actual experience and existence of things, the determination and examination of these essences and possibilities remain bound to experience, even though one can temporarily free oneself from factuality via the imagination. However, this must not be understood as a disadvantage. Worldly experience can also provide us with new variants of things, and variants that were previously unimaginable for us. In Husserl, we read for example, that experience can function as a corrective. It alerts the phenomenologist as 'researcher of essences' to the fact that he may have made a mistake in his determination of an essence:

» If I have properly considered it as belonging to the essence of thing perception that things must be seen, and now the experience of a person born blind shows me that the sense of touch is sufficient for the constitution of spatial thingness, then I realize that I have not gone far enough in the free design of possible modifications of perception. (Husserl, Hua XXV, p. 248, automatic translation, edited)

For further study
Changing essences?
Especially when it comes to material (i.e., substantive) essences, such as world, nature, living beings, or individuals, which constantly change and develop, it becomes difficult to assume a 'timeless' (LI1, p. 249/Hua XIX/1, p. 129) or 'omnitemporal' (EJ, pp. 258–261/1939, pp. 309–314/) essence. Are these changes only variations or differences of a higher generality not yet seen and determined? Have we been unable to discern the essence of the 'human' because of variants we cannot imagine? Or has this essence changed in its nature (or is it constantly changing), i.e., not only in its real, but also in its ideal possibilities? Do we have to assume the changeability, i.e., **historicity of material essences**?

Merleau-Ponty would clearly say, 'Yes'. For him, sense (*Sinn*) is constantly temporally *instituted*: Sense (and thus every substantive determination) can only exist in relation to the past, i.e., in the resumption (reinstatement), which is then practically and even creatively continued (cf. Merleau-Ponty [1954] 2010; cf. Bedorf 2020). These processes of institution (which do not necessarily originate from a subject) not only actualize the respective sense or meaning but determine it anew each time and carry it forward into the future. Even here, sense and meaning can be fixed and generalities can be determined, but always only provisionally and temporarily. By determining the essence as historically determined, Merleau-Ponty tries to unite the general and necessary with the concrete and changeable. At the same time, however, he comes to define a new, more foundational generality that applies before any concrete experience, namely, that every sense, every individual, every experience, and thus every being qua being must be historical, i.e., temporal. Temporality is thus determined as the general essence of all things and individuals. With his treatment of institution as a comprehensive theory of historicity, Merleau-Ponty ties into Husserl's concept of constitution and historicity of the lifeworld (cf. Husserl, Hua IV/1970).

2.2.2 Criticism of Essentialism

Can the essences of all things, including living beings, be determined necessarily and generally, i.e., independently and in advance of concrete experience? Are these essences themselves timeless or omnitemporal as Husserl seems to assume? Are our determinations of essences possibly one-sided, faulty, or prejudiced, because we fail to grasp the truly general? Or must all material essences be understood as temporal and changeable (for example through evolution, development, or culture)? Are these the essences of things themselves that we grasp here, or just our historically and culturally relative concepts of them?

■■ 'Existence before essence'?

These are critical questions, which any eidetics, including Husserl's, must face. Are there omnitemporal essences or ideas that never change and that necessarily determine the world or our experience of the world in advance, e.g., like the categorical essence of logic? However, even in the field of propositional logic, there are cultural differences and different logics existing in parallel. The propositional logic of European languages is characterized by its subject-object structure, but this is not the case in all languages. Is the 'essence' of something then merely a subsequent determination or even political legitimation, which merely expresses our preferences, interests, or the norms and power relations of our time? Husserl's essentialism was heavily debated and criticized by his successors and by post-modern philosophers, including those in existentialist phenomenology, whose motto was 'existence before essence'. Feminist philosophy, critical theory, and gender and postcolonial studies also accuse the phenomenological eidetic descriptions of essentialism, which they criticize as naturalizing and thus justifying a gender-binary and Eurocentric universalism. Two things can be noted about this in the brief space allotted here.

First, it can be argued that such criticisms do not actually target what is at the center of Husserl's eidetics, namely the pure (only conceivable) essence. Here, the determinations are so formal-general that they do not affect concepts relevant to the above philosophies such as 'human' or even 'woman'. Even the determination of a factual or material essence (like color or sound in general) can only be applied to the genus category 'human' or even concretely to the identity determination 'woman' to a limited extent. Only structures of possible consciousness or subjectivity (for experience) or possible objects (of experience) as such can be determined phenomenologically in their generality.

Husserl is also not concerned with naturalization in eidetics, i.e., the assumption that a certain character is inherent in humans or in women by nature (such as weakness, care, or irrationality, which were long thought to characterize the 'nature'

2

of women) and that any deviations from this character should be evaluated negatively. Such a determination would have been exposed by Husserl as a category error. After all, existing women or humans are individuals and not essences. Their determination is therefore bound to real possibilities (natural laws, biological conditions, concrete circumstances, previous experiences, etc.) and not to necessary or ideal possibilities.

Secondly, it cannot be denied that we constantly make general statements about reality, and we experience generality and ideality, not just individuals or particulars. Philosophy, like any science, relies on those general insights. The ability to refer to something general, i.e., something that is valid for a whole area of things or facts, does not belong to logic or explicit concept formation alone; it is characteristic of sensuous experience. We do not arrive at the general only through formalization or abstraction, but experience things everyday as similar, belonging together, or of the same kind. Indeed, our concepts and orders of the world change, which is why they seem relative and arbitrary. And yet the concept must maintain its relation to the experienced thing if it still wants to be pertinent and express something meaningful.

▪▪ Concept and Essence

The concept and the essence of the thing must therefore be distinguished, even if they mutually influence each other. This is because new things (e.g., new technologies or problems) also create new concepts and because one cannot arbitrarily use a concept in any way one chooses. So, it is perhaps controversial, for example, whether a certain plant is to be called a tree or a bush. However, one could not imagine calling this green, growing thing a bottle. Its material or factual essence does not include 'thing you can drink from'. Furthermore, a concept can only be thought, not 'seen' or perceived, as is the case (according to Husserl) with essences.

Nevertheless, it is legitimate to ask whether and how such a general determination of essence is possible. A supposedly general determination may have been influenced by cultural and historical prejudices and possibly only generalizes subjective interests, historical discourses, or normative power structures. Here, the critical question must be asked to what extent the free variation in imagination is really 'free' and not shaped by certain ways of thinking or circumstances of a particular time (cf. Aldea 2016). However, this does not mean that one must altogether discredit the attempt to form such a general determination.

▪▪ The Dilemma of Free Variation

The motto 'To the things themselves' cannot therefore be reduced to conceptual analysis but remains dependent on the descriptive determination of essence. However, this must constantly be tested against empirical examples that do not coincide with the determined essence, just as in the practice of free variation. The difficulty here is that the result of the free variation must be general, but the process is always carried out by a specific, i.e., historically and culturally situated, subject. Therefore, the corresponding result must withstand any possible variation (carried out by past, present, and future subjects). And even if one never reaches the ultimate objective essence, then at least what can be revealed here are the limits of human practices of thinking and imagining.

2.3 Inquiring-back to the Conditions

▪▪ From Description to Transcendental Reduction

Let's take a closer look at the examples discussed in ▶ Section 2.1 (Describing without prejudice) focusing on the methodical attitude of the description. Husserl emphasizes in the first text, the lectures on perception and attention from 1907, that in the description of something such as a cube, the real existence of the thing does not matter, but only the appearance or how it is given to consciousness (*Wahrnehmungserlebnis*). The same idea can be found in the passage from Husserl's lectures on inner time consciousness from 1905; here too he takes the everyday perception of a melody as a starting point and then undertakes a 'deeper analysis'. In doing so, he switches off all transcendent conceptions and assumptions and describes the tone purely as a hyletic datum, i.e., a sensation or experience in the 'how' of its givenness.

In the description we thus limit ourselves to what appears. So, we *know* of course that a house has several sides, and we do not doubt its reality, but that does not mean that these sides or this reality also *immediately* appear to us. With the methodical bracketing of any pre-assumptions regarding the object to be described there is a change of attention, an opening or preparation for a new phenomenal perspective.

▪▪ Descriptive and Transcendental Epoché

In this context, one can distinguish between a *descriptive epoché*, i.e., the bracketing of certain preconceptions or judgments about the being or existence of the object to be described, and a *transcendental epoché*, i.e., the bracketing of preconceptions or judgments about the existence of the world. The descriptive epoché or bracketing does not yet have a transcendental meaning, i.e., the belief in the existence of the world, which characterizes every experience, is not completely set aside here. What is bracketed are only assumptions about the quality and existence of the object or fact to be described.

After his so-called transcendental turn in the *Ideas* of 1913 (*Ideas Pertaining to a Pure Phenomenology and Phenomenological Philosophy,* cf. CW2/Hua III/1; III/2), the epoché (bracketing) is determined as a preparation or **gateway to a transcendental investigation of experience**. While the pre-transcendental epoché also initially leaves out the question of the being or existence of the given object (thus not dedicating itself to the *whether* or *what* of the object, but initially focusing on the *how*), the epoché of the transcendental philosophy does something more. It brackets not only the existence of a certain phenomenon but also the entire *general thesis* or *natural attitude* (i.e., our implicit and ubiquitous belief that the world exists). This allows us to clarify how we come to assume an objectivity and transcendence at all and what role the achievements or processes of consciousness play in this.

2

With the transcendental reduction, we thus leave what Husserl calls the 'natural attitude' behind to thematize and understand what has always been self-evident and valid for us: the existence of an objective world.

» I find the 'actuality', the word already says it, as a factually existent actuality and also accept it as it presents itself to me as factually existing. No doubt about or rejection of data belonging to the natural world alters in any respect the general positing which characterizes the natural attitude. 'The' world is always there as an actuality; here and there it is at most "otherwise" than I supposed; this or that is, so to speak, to be struck out of it and given such titles as 'illusion' and 'hallucination', and the like; <it is to be struck out of 'the' world> which — according to the general positing —is always factually existent. (CW 2, p. 57/Hua III/1, p. 61)

▪▪ The Belief in the Being of the World

While the descriptive epoché suspends only local or subject-related assumptions or judgments, the transcendental epoché suspends the implicitly operating belief in the being of the world (and our being as empirically existing beings in it). Husserl also refers to this belief in the world as the '**general thesis**', although this phrasing is potentially misleading. He does not mean to assert that in all our experiences we make an additional, explicit judgment about the existence of the world. Such a consciousness of the world "in the mode of certainty of belief" is not a separately occurring act, where one posits or predicates the 'existence' of the world. Rather, every judgment and positing already presupposes such a passive "consciousness of the world in the certainty of belief". "It is this *universal ground of belief in a world*", says Husserl, "which all practice presupposes, not only the practice of life but also the theoretical practice of cognition" (Husserl 1973, p. 30/1939, p. 25). However, with the transcendental epoché, which brackets this general and passively operating belief in the world, neither the belief nor the world that is experienced in it disappears. The change of attitude that occurs here—turning from the existing world to its conditions of appearing—does not erase the self-evidence of this world, but rather thematizes it for the first time. The bracketing of the passive belief in the world thus functions like the marking of something that is now to be subjected to closer examination. This can be compared to a provisional assumption that is now to be subjected to a legal examination, i.e., whose validity must be clarified and proven in the further course of the investigation (cf. Lohmar 2002, p. 751). Therefore, we treat everything that we experience (the contents of our experience) from now on purely as a phenomenon, as how it appears to us, and hold back any assumptions, including the basic assumption of its existence.

▪▪ Conditions of the Possibility of Experience

After the all-encompassing transcendental epoché comes the methodological step that Husserl calls 'reduction'. Often both steps are taken together, without further distinguishing between the concepts of 'transcendental epoché' and 'transcendental reduction'. But the reduction, properly understood, refers to a questioning back to the ultimate conditions of givenness. It does not thereby mean that we doubt what we perceive or simply erase the contents of our experience (our beliefs, judgments, etc.), as is the case, for example, with René Descartes' methodical doubt. It is neither a doubting (skepticism) of the world, nor a denial of the world (idealism), nor a naive affirmation of the world (realism). It is a questioning-back to the conditions that allow the world to be given in the first place.

This form of reduction thereby aims at a thematic narrowing of focus: By bracketing the belief in the world, attention is now directed not only to how a certain object is given to us, but to how *anything* (objects, the world) can be given to us at all. We thus *reduce* to those *aspects that are necessary* for this (and not just to those that are incidental or accidental). These are then the conditions of the current experience (e.g., the perception of a house), but also of any possible experience of anything at all.

This transcendental questioning of the conditions of the possibility of experience is a **genuinely philosophical question** or task. Although it must start with a description of what is currently given to us, it goes beyond a mere description and asks how this particular experience (e.g., perception as a mode of experience) or any possible experience (as experience of something) is made possible. This is not to say that every phenomenological description, including, for example, those in applied phenomenology (e.g., in psychology or nursing studies), requires a transcendental epoché (cf. Zahavi 2021). Yet if we wish to approach ultimate questions about the givenness of an objective world, the transcendental epoché is essential.

■ ■ Why Transcendental?

Husserl (like Kant) seeks these conditions of experience in subjective consciousness, in cognition or experience. The transcendental reduction thus opens a view on the 'constitutive achievements' of our subjectivity. This is a reduction insofar as I am no longer interested in personal aspects of experience, such as my motivations and situation, or my appearance (empirical form). Instead, I now focus on those functions of experience that are necessary for any conceivable experience. These functions or achievements have the status 'transcendental', as they are not dependent on a particular experience, but are a priori necessary for experience to take place at all. These achievements are not individual, personal, or psychological; they are universal for every conceivable consciousness or subject.

> **Definition**
>
> Generally, 'transcendental' refers to knowledge that is independent of empirical principles. This distinguishes philosophical or metaphysical knowledge from merely empirical or historical, i.e., relative, knowledge. The 'trans' in 'transcendental' indicates that this type of knowledge transcends the boundaries of everyday empirical experience, just as the 'meta' in 'metaphysical' points beyond the realm of sensory experience. 'Transcendental knowledge' therefore refers to necessities and not to empirical, i.e., contingent or existing, facts; it is not dependent on the senses and in Kant's formulation 'a priori' (cf. Nenon 2005).

2

■ ■ I as Transcendental Subjectivity

The transcendental epoché directs our attention not only to the appearance of a phenomenon (i.e., to the content), but also to the *how* of knowledge (i.e., to the act of experience), whereby a kind of Copernican turn occurs: If everything experienced becomes a phenomenon, this naturally also applies to me as a psychophysical human being. After all, I also experience myself and therefore count as content or object of my own experience. But how can I be both **object and subject of my experience**, content and condition of the same? Here a kind of ego-splitting occurs, and a 'new' subject, or better, a new dimension of our subjectivity, comes to light. This is the transcendental consciousness, the transcendental subjectivity or the transcendental person (cf. Luft 2009, p. 152f.). However, it is not only the forms of intuition, such as time and space, or the categories of the understanding, such as quantity, quality, or modality that constitute transcendental subjectivity (cf. Kant). It is also the lived and physical body of the conscious subject along with its historicity, sociality, and culture. These are no less necessary for having a coherent experience of a stable, meaningful, and objective world. They allow the experiencing subject to experience itself and the world, and to acquire meaning as well as lasting abilities and knowledge.

❯ For further study

Kant and Husserl: From the transcendental I to the transcendental Person

Kant's critical philosophy is called 'transcendental', because it identifies the necessary conditions for the experience of empirical objects. Kant thus opposes a common conception of his time, in which transcendental knowledge refers to knowledge of the transcendent (i.e., the supernatural or divine). A transcendental investigation is indeed the search for the non-empirical conditions of experience. However, Kant no longer seeks these principles in the supernatural, but derives them from finite, sensory appearances in experience. The end goal is to arrive at necessary and invariant, i.e., a priori, conditions for that experience. He initially proceeds *analytically*, by dissecting our experience and identifying those elements that are necessary for such an experience, such as the forms of intuition, i.e., time and space; and then *deductively*, by deriving the necessity of the forms argumentatively: Since a sensory perception without time (temporal unity) and space (spatial arrangement) is not conceivable, these categories must be necessary, i.e., the conditions for every possible perception (cf. Nenon 2005, p. 292).

Husserl joins Kant's project in intention and goal and partly comes to similar results. However, there are decisive differences. First, Husserl does not use the term 'transcendent' to refer to the supernatural, but rather to everything that is not immanent to consciousness, i.e., all sensually appearing things or the world. The transcendental question is therefore directed at what conditions must be fulfilled in the subject/consciousness for a transcendent world to appear (cf. Nenon 2008). Another crucial difference is that Husserl does not arrive at the transcendental conditions through logical analysis or deduction but through a *descriptive transcendental philosophy*: The sought-after conditions must be *intuitively given* for each subject, i.e., they must be experienceable and describable. Therefore, Husserlian transcendental philosophy always begins with the description of one's own experience and presupposes an individual, personal subject to whom something appears here and now.

The singularity and facticity of the transcendental ego is relevant for Husserl, as he borrows the meaning of the term 'transcendental' not only from Kant but also from Descartes. Husserl traces it back to the *Cartesian insight* that the characteristic mode of being of consciousness differs essentially from that of worldly or thingly beings. For example, it is possible to imagine a consciousness without a world, but not a world without a consciousness to which it is given. For this reason, consciousness is the transcendental condition of all transcendence, of the world. While we cannot derive this condition from individual experiences, it manifests itself constantly in and through our experience. We implicitly experience ourselves as this condition and can at any time explicitly reflect on ourselves as the subject, i.e., the starting point and condition of our experience. This makes the *transcendental ego* something that, according to Kant, it could never be: a necessarily *singular being* (cf. Heinämaa et al. 2014, p. 8). This also means that the realm of transcendentality is nothing other than that of the concrete, worldly person; the difference between empirical and transcendental is not the difference between two people but between two *different aspects within the conscious life of an individual*. This insight becomes clear when we turn to the topic of embodiment or the living body (*Leiblichkeit*) (▶ Sect. 2.3.2.1; cf. Heinämaa et al. 2014., p. 9; Wehrle 2022).

In summary, Husserl's transcendental philosophy represents a *radicalization*, *rearticulation,* and *expansion* of the Kantian concept of the transcendental (cf. Heinämaa et al. 2014, p. 8). It is a radicalization and *rearticulation* insofar as the 'transcendental' in Husserl must be part of concrete subjective experience and not something to be deduced. It is an *expansion* insofar as Husserl extends the area of transcendental investigation to include the temporal development of the ego, its embodiment, and intersubjective relationships. Instead of focusing only on the inner life of the subject, the realm of the transcendental also includes its lifeworld as well as culture and sociality. This transforms the purely formal transcendental ego in Kant (as a formal starting point) into a transcendental person who is embodied, situated, passive, active, and above all intersubjectively sense-constituting.

■■ Genetic Constitutional Analysis

This turn from the appearing object to the conditions of its appearance in the subject was already evident in the description of temporal objects such as a melody. Here, the necessity of a genetic intentional analysis that deals with the conditions of the emergence or the 'constitution' of an object perception becomes apparent. This analysis is transcendental insofar as it questions back to general genetic conditions that are necessary for any possible experience. For example, it asks how consciousness itself is temporally constituted (Hua XXXIII; cf. Bernet 2010; Held 1966); it examines how judgement is founded in sensual experience (Husserl EJ [1939] 1973); or it demonstrates that every activity (thinking) points back to a passivity (affection, reception). In such a *genetic constitutional analysis*, which focuses on underlying developments, processes, and associated motivations in the subject, it becomes clear that every perception of an object is already the result of temporal constituting processes and of passive syntheses operating within the experiencing

2

consciousness. Every *static intentional analysis*, which thematically has either noet-ically a mode of appearance (perception, judgement, representation) as its subject, or noematically an intentional object, such as a house, therefore points back to the passive achievements of founding processes *in consciousness*, which first enable such a unified object experience.

▪▪ Transcendental Phenomenology and Eidetics

The transcendental in Husserl thus refers to the insight that the conditions that allow the world and things to uniformly appear to me as such are to be found in the (passive and active) achievements of subjectivity itself. In considering oneself as a transcendental subject, everyone can understand themselves not only as a thing in the world, but as a perceiving and sense-instituting or constituting subject. In a second step, the general and necessary structures of every possible subject, i.e., of pure consciousness (cleansed of all concreteness), are determined. The first step is the transcendental turn or reflection on the subjective conditions; the second, the general determination of these conditions through an eidetic variation of my concrete subjectivity. To get to the transcendental principles, therefore, requires eidetic determination. However, it turns out that every eidetic variation of one's consciousness is always already transcendental.

2.3.1   The Three Ways to Transcendental Reduction

In Husserl's transcendental phenomenology, strictly speaking, the naively assumed 'world' is no longer described but the transcendental person or the transcendental subjective life. In this, both the ego as the pole of all activities of consciousness and the ego as the substrate of habitualities acquired through experience, as well as all current and possible contents of experience (and thus the world as appearance or phenomenon) are included. Three influences from the history of philosophy are central to this insight: First, the methodical doubt of René Descartes' *Meditations on First Philosophy* (1641), second, the descriptive psychology of inner experience of Husserl's teacher Franz Brentano, and third, the so-called 'Copernican turn' from ontological investigation to the transcendental interpretation of the world as a world of possible experience in Immanuel Kant's *Critique of Pure Reason* (1781). Accordingly, there is also talk of 'three ways' to transcendental reduction or transcendental subjectivity, the 'Cartesian', the 'psychological', and the 'ontological' way (cf. Bernet et al. 1993, pp. 65–75).

2.3.1.1   The Cartesian Way

As the name suggests, Husserl follows a Cartesian model in the eponymous *Cartesian Meditations* (Husserl, CM/Hua I), first published in 1931 in a French translation by Emmanuel Levinas. Descartes sought to reach an indubitable first foundation that could ground all sciences. He went about this by strategically negating any beliefs for which he could find even the slightest doubt. He started by negating belief in the world, since it is given to us by our sometimes-deceptive senses, which can therefore easily be doubted. He went on to negate belief in our own body, about which we can also be mistaken—for example, when we dream of strolling through Paris while we are actually sleeping in our beds. He even went so far as to doubt universal mathematical and logical truths, which can also be doubted if we imagine that an evil demon who deceives us in everything has implanted those beliefs in us. What remains then, when all objects, material as well as ideal, are thrown into doubt? Here Descartes encounters the 'I' or ego, which must always be presupposed in all this doubting: Descartes cannot think that he is being deceived and at the same time think that he does not exist. And so it is for any being that thinks. That I should not exist while I am thinking this, is, so to speak, unthinkable. What remains as indubitable, therefore, is the thinking 'I', or ego cogito. The insight that I, while I think (doubt etc.), also must exist, is necessarily true whenever I think or pronounce it.

▪▪ The Apodictic Evidence of the 'I think'

This idea of the apodictic (necessary, in the sense of not being able to be otherwise) certainty of the *ego cogito* ('I think') is also taken by Husserl as the starting point of his considerations. Although we can be deceived about the *content of every experience*, for which there is always only partial evidence (never, for example, have all sides and aspects of an object been present at the same time), the *actual act of experiencing* is apodictically evident, i.e., when, and as long as, I experience, I necessarily exist (this is not doubtful). However, this certainty is only limited to the moment of the execution of the current experience and not equally valid for past acts or my past I. Husserl spends much effort and energy on clarifying how far this apodicticity extends, and advocates for an apodictic critique, in which we must continually clarify how certain our experiences are. Nevertheless, he emphasizes that every subject has an original, i.e., direct access to its own experiencing and the contents experienced therein. Therefore, every phenomenological philosophy or critique of knowledge must begin with one's own experience, as this is more evident than the mediated experience of our fellow subjects. Only within our own experience can we convince ourselves of the truth or falsity of something, bring something 'into view' or to evidence. The contents of the experience, although never fully given, thus have a share in the apodictic evidence of the 'I think' or 'I experience'. Just as with Descartes, every philosophical and scientific investigation must therefore begin with subjective experience or knowledge in order to test and assure further evidence, such as that of experienced objects and the world as a whole, from this indubitable foundation.

▪▪ Descartes' Mistake

Despite sharing a common starting point in the subject and a common emphasis on the practice of meditation as a shift in attention away from the world and towards one's own experience, Husserl clearly distinguishes himself from Descartes' understanding of the *ego cogito*. For Husserl, this unquestionable foundation can no longer be the empirical ego of the meditator (such as Descartes), as this ego would then still be part of the same world that Descartes had negated through doubt. This led to a separation between mind and body in Descartes: two worldly substances, a thinking one (*res cogitans*) and a material one (*res extensa*), with only

2

the former remaining after methodical doubt. According to Husserl, this was Descartes' mistake: He assumed that the *ego cogito* is still a "little tag-end" of the world (CM, p. 24/Hua I, p. 63), i.e., it has the same status as worldly objects. As Husserl further expresses it: Descartes opened the door to a transcendental perspective but did not go through it.

> ### For further study
>
> #### In defense of Descartes: The integral Cogito
>
> In defense of René Descartes, it should be noted that in other writings, such as in the letters to Elisabeth (1643–1649) or *The Passions of the Soul* (*Les Passions de l'âme* 1649), he pays attention to feelings and embodiment and emphasizes the interaction of mind and body. Paul Ricœur, a famous representative of hermeneutic philosophy and phenomenology, refers to this and speaks of an 'integral cogito' (Ricœur [1950] 1966), which includes corporeality, affectivity, and will in addition to the reflective *cogito* or the *res cogitans*. More recently, the French phenomenologist Jean-Luc Marion has presented a reinterpretation of Descartes, which also advocates for an integrative understanding of the *ego cogito* in Descartes (cf. Marion [2013] 2018). However, Husserl's criticism of the formulation and argumentative positioning of the *ego cogito* in the *Meditations* is still justified as it does not address Descartes' supposed dualism but rather the transcendental status of embodiment that Descartes had missed.

▪▪ Transcendental experience

The 'knowing ego', according to Husserl, does not stand for an ontologically independent substance, as it does in Descartes. Rather, it stands for a transcendental change of perspective, from which we can now view ourselves and the world as part of our experience from a distance. What we can thereby see and examine is our transcendental experience. In this, we now encounter everything as actual or possible content of our experience. Above all, we encounter ourselves as the object and subject of our experience, recognizing the latter as the constitutive condition of any experience at all. Descartes' methodical doubt can therefore—properly understood—serve as a model for us to reach transcendental subjectivity in one fell swoop, i.e., the possibility of recognizing ourselves, not as an already-constituted meaning (as this person or content of our experience), but also as the condition of experience. It thus allows us to see ourselves as sense-constituting. In this regard, it is we who constitute (together with other transcendental subjects) the sense of the world, mathematical truths, as well as the sense of ourselves and other people as embodied, feeling, thinking, and thus also transcendental subjects.

▪▪ *Ego-cogito*-cogitatum

The ego cogito as transcendental subjectivity is therefore not a formal starting point of thinking or experiencing, but includes all current, past and future contents of experience and thus the entire appearing world. Since consciousness is always consciousness of something, we are dealing with the structure *ego-cogito-cogitatum*. Since the appearing as a phenomenon is part of transcendental subjectivity, there is no separation between body and mind, but only a distinction between the empirical human (as content of experience) and the transcendental subject (as subject of cognition and constitution). The latter is not a second subject, but a specific (i.e., transcendental) perspective on the same subject. Since neither the human subject nor the world disappear but rather become thematic as experienced phenomena in the 'how' of their givenness, the epoché and reduction are not about any kind of doubt. Neither the world nor the human subject are negated or doubted. Instead, the belief that they are 'objectively existing' is suspended in order to investigate what is meant by 'objective', and which aspects and steps are constitutive for the sense of 'human', 'nature', or 'world', respectively.

▪▪ The Epistemological Primacy of the Subject

With the Cartesian way, Husserl wanted to emphasize the epistemological primacy of the cognizing subject or consciousness. In this respect, the world (its appearance) depends on the cognizing subject, but not vice versa. This idea, however, is sometimes misconstrued as advocating for a *solus ipse*, a single subject, which can exist independently of the world and other subjects. But this suggests an artificial separation between subject and world as well as subject and other subjects, which Husserl certainly did not intend. The subject, for Husserl, has no ontological primacy, but only an epistemological one. Of course, every concrete empirical subject is always already situated in the world and part of an intersubjective community. However, since the world after the reduction is only examined as a correlate of possible consciousness i.e., as an appearing phenomenon, it remains as such principally bound to the possibility of consciousness.

The Cartesian approach is sometimes also seen as beset by the difficulty of having to bridge an unbridgeable gulf between the thinking 'I' and the external world. However, the question of how I get from my inner experiences to something outside of me, i.e., to the world and other subjects, is also misguided from Husserl's point of view. It assumes that subject and world are separated by an abyss. After the transcendental epoché and reduction, however, it turns out that the appearance of both the world and other subjects are part of transcendental subjectivity. If one wants to distinguish between experience of self, world, and others, this distinction *must be immanent* (cf. Husserl, CM, 5th Meditation; CW8, p. 27/Hua II, p. 35), i.e., it must be shown that other subjects, material objects, and I myself are each given in a different way. The **meaning of transcendence and objectivity must manifest in subjectivity**, if it is to manifest at all. Nevertheless, in later texts, Husserl preferred the other two ways that lead to the transcendental reduction—the psychological and the ontological—to the Cartesian way, because they do not lend themselves so easily to misunderstandings about a *solus ipse* or a world negated by doubt.

2.3.1.2 The Psychological Way

With the path from the description of the human psyche to the conditions of experience in general, Husserl wants to point out both the close connections between transcendental phenomenology and psychology in terms of content, and their differences in method and epistemological status. When Husserl speaks of psychology in this context, he is not so much thinking of the empirical psychology of his

2

time, but of a descriptive psychology, as was envisaged by his teacher Franz
Brentano. Such a psychology is supposed to investigate the unique essence of the
psyche (over and against other natural objects). Instead of causally explaining the
psyche with the means of natural science and thus equating it with other material
objects, attention should be paid to how the psyche differs from other objects and
which method is appropriate for its investigation. One fundamental characteristic
of the psychic, over and against the material, is its intentionality, i.e., that it relates
to the world: through imagining, thinking, perceiving, but also feeling, valuing,
and judging. Just like transcendental phenomenology, such a phenomenological
psychology turns to the subject and its experience. It tries to perceive and determine the essence of this inner experience. However, the subject of psychology is the
empirical human being, while in transcendental phenomenology it is transcendental subjectivity in general. For psychology, the psyche is still always an *object in the
world* (constituted) and not a *subject for the world* (constituting). In Husserl's sense,
the psyche is thus a dependent layer of being (CW 8, pp. 562–66/cf. Hua VIII,
Beilage XIX, p. 427), which refers to an experiencing and sense-constituting
instance. The **psyche is an object of investigation** (part of being/the world), but not
the condition of the possibility of the experience of being in general.

▪▪ Phenomenology as Psychology and Philosophy

Even though the status of the investigated subjectivity (as psyche or transcendental
subject) differs in phenomenological psychology and transcendental phenomenology, this does not apply to the contents of these investigations. In terms of their
content, i.e., the general structures of consciousness, psyche and transcendental
subjectivity are identical. Both are characterized by their intentionality, temporality, processes of association, and motivational relations (not causal relations). The
transcendental level does not refer to an additional subject that somehow hovers
above the empirical human being. Psyche and transcendental subjectivity are not
two coexisting, different realms of being. Rather, the transcendental is a reflective
view of oneself as an empirical human being or psyche. It is the same psyche, only
considered according to its necessary properties for an *experience in general*. What
differs, therefore, is the status and not the content of the investigation. While one is
about the general determination of the psyche of empirical humans, the other is
about the pure description of a consciousness in general and its transcendental
necessity for any form of experience. Thus, a strictly descriptive-eidetic psychology
can pave the way for a transcendental consideration but is not yet transcendental
itself.

As Husserl emphasized later, his own earlier phenomenology (as well as a purely
theoretical psychology) can be understood as a phenomenological (because eidetically descriptive) psychology. However, such a phenomenological determination
can only be considered 'philosophy' when one includes the question about the conditions of the possibility of experience in the subject. In Husserl's transcendental
philosophy, the determination of essence is therefore used to determine the general
(or as Husserl calls it: the 'pure', consciousness), i.e., the general and necessary
structures of every concrete and conceivable consciousness. However, such a determination is then necessarily transcendental, as this minimal determination of those

attributes that every conceivable consciousness must have, simultaneously represents the conditions for experience in general. The question here is about the necessity of various processes in the subject for the perception of a tone, a melody, a house, etc. In this sense, certain structures such as intentionality or temporal synthesis are thus necessary for the appearance of a particular tone—as I hear it now—to be heard by a particular empirical subject—the author of this introduction. And these conditions then apply independently and before any concrete experience, i.e., a priori.

▪▪ Factual (Objective) and Constitutive Necessity

Transcendental structures therefore possess a different form of necessity than that possessed by the eidetic a priori. For example, if we judge that every (general) material object must necessarily also be extended, this determination is factually (objectively) general and necessary. However, if we judge that every consciousness must be intentionally constituted, this determination is at the same time *constitutively necessary*. The latter determination is a **transcendental necessity**, not just a factual one. While in a factual eidetic a priori the essence denotes that without which an object of this kind cannot be recognized as such, the constitutive a priori denotes those conditions that are necessary to meaningfully speak of the experience of an extended thing (or the world as a whole). The intentional constitution and the constitutive achievements of consciousness are therefore not only independent of a particular experience, but necessary for any experience of objectivity at all.

Although eidetic description and transcendental phenomenology represent independent methodological directions, for Husserl in his late philosophy, they are inseparably linked. Here, the eidetic method is embedded in a transcendental justification and analysis that seek to determine the general and pure essence of consciousness or transcendental subjectivity. Both the description (as a noematic guideline) and the determination of generality and the pure possibility of a thing now serve as a gateway to transcendental questions (how is experience of meaningful objects possible at all?). In this context, the determination of essence is mainly applied to the transcendental subject itself to determine the necessary general structures of consciousness without which (a) concrete consciousness would not be conceivable (essence of consciousness), and (b) experience or knowledge would not be possible (transcendental condition). In the case of consciousness or subjectivity, the **determination of essence is thus always also transcendental**, i.e., the general essence of the transcendental subject (including its body, its history, and intersubjectivity) is nothing other than the condition of the possibility of experience in general.

2.3.1.3 The Lifeworldly (or Ontological) Way

Instead of critically examining the validity of knowledge of the world, or limiting ourselves to the subject, we can just as well begin our transcendental investigation with a positive description of this very world. It is a world that is always already there for us before we begin to practice science or philosophy. It is a world into which we are born and to which we refer in all practical and theoretical matters. It is a world in which we live, which we know, in which we *find our way*: the *lifeworld* (cf. Carr 1970; Held 2003; Moran 2012; Luft 2011). The lifeworld and the 'natural attitude' founded therein thus form the starting point and also the motivation for any theoretical reflection or investigation, whether in the sciences or in philosophy. The lifeworld is therefore pre-theoretical or pre-reflective. It is always already in effect, along with its cultural and social institutions, meanings, traditions, and practices. Even while we practice science or philosophy, we always remain situated in this horizon. Here too, one can genetically trace back to the subjective (or better, intersubjective) origin or constitution of this practical, meaningful, and self-evident world.

» *Briefly reminding ourselves* of our earlier discussions, let us recall the fact we have emphasized, namely, that science is a human spiritual accomplishment which pre-supposes as its point of departure, both historically and for each new student, the intuitive surrounding world of life, pregiven as existing for all in common. Furthermore, it is an accomplishment which, in being practiced and carried for-ward, continues to presuppose this surrounding world as it is given in its particular-ity to the scientist. For example, for the physicist it is the world in which he sees his measuring instruments, hears timebeats, estimates visible magnitudes, etc.—the world in which, furthermore, he knows himself to be included with all his activity and all his theoretical ideas. (CES, p. 121/Hua VI, p. 123)

Here Husserl criticizes the natural sciences for having completely forgotten their connection to the lifeworld. They establish an image of reality that reduces it to formulas and numbers, without making it clear that these formulas are not the origin of reality, but the result of a certain practice or method of abstraction or formalization. This practice presupposes the pre-theoretical reality or world, which can then be calculated and formalized. For example, abstract geometry originated in the practical need to measure distances and determine the spatial relationships between things in order to handle them better or facilitate intersubjective coopera-tion. Martin Heidegger formulates a similar criticism somewhat earlier when he emphasizes that we initially stand in a practical relation to the world; things are first 'ready-to-hand' or available to us, before we look at them from a distance, think about them, or analyze them, i.e., they become 'present-at-hand' for us (Heidegger [1927] 1962; cf. Dreyfus 1990; Cerbone 2021).

▪▪ Constitution and Constitutional Analysis
In contrast to Heidegger, Husserl wants to describe the lifeworld and being (and us humans as part of this being) not merely ontologically, but also to clarify and ground them epistemologically and genetically. Although Heidegger's approach is not epistemological, it can still be understood as transcendental (in a different sense than Kant and Husserl) when he, for example, in *Being and Time* (1927) describes the 'transcendentals' of Dasein (cf. Crowell and Malpas 2007). In Husserl's understanding of a transcendental constitutional analysis, however, one cannot simply assume an objective world or an objective being but must first ask *how* we can know or recognize them at all. Heidegger would reply that such recog-nition is secondary and only possible because we are always already in-the-world.

In other words, we ourselves are part of that being, which we not only question, but to which our care is dedicated. However, Husserl wants to distance himself from a mere ontology or anthropology (which he also counts Heidegger's approach as), as well as from the naive objectivism of the natural sciences. According to Husserl, such an objectivism moves "upon the ground of the world which is pregiven, taken for granted through experience" and seeks "the 'objective truth' of this world" or the world as such. Transcendentalism, however, means that "the ontic meaning [*Seinssinn*] of the pregiven life-world" is a "subjective construct" (CES, p. 68–69/Hua VI, p. 70):

» [A]chievement of experiencing, prescientific life. In this life the meaning and the ontic validity [*Seinsgeltung*] of the world are built up—of that particular world, that is, which is actually valid for the individual experiencer. As for the "objectively true" world, the world of science, it is a structure at a higher level, built on prescientific experiencing and thinking, or rather on its accomplishments of validity [*Geltungsleistungen*]. (CES, p. 69/Hua VI, p. 70)

What we encounter in the lifeworld, cultural objects, language, meanings, institutions, etc. are the result of a subjective—or better, intersubjective—constitution. Here, constitution can refer to an explicit constitution of meaning or practice of a subject or several subjects, as well as to a passive constitution, such as in the passive synthesis of temporality or association. The phenomena we encounter in our lifeworld, therefore always already refer to an **intersubjective meaning or previous constitution**, whether passive or active, voluntary or involuntary, practical or theoretical. To clarify this intersubjective constitution and meaning as well as its genesis, we must go back to the subject, i.e., ourselves and our experience. Only in subjective experience can we experience other subjects and intersubjectivity as such at all.

Although the constitution is always already intersubjective, just as the content of all our experiences, the analysis or clarification of this constitution initially takes place **in one's own reflection**. Only here can we bring experienced things to evidence through further experiences; only our experiences are directly accessible to us and verifiable by us. Therefore, we cannot start with the world or the other subjects but must first check how they are given to us and whether we find here hints and evidence for their existence (their being) and their specific nature (their suchness). Therefore, despite his emphasis on the importance of the lifeworld, Husserl also insists on the significance of a transcendental reduction. A reduction that, after bracketing belief in the world, now questions itself. We find that the world, along with all objects (and ourselves as an object of our experience) and their validity, is part of our experience. And we find that subjective consciousness contributes to the fact that we experience something like a unified and objective world at all, continuously, and quite self-evidently:

» Only a radical inquiry back into subjectivity—and specifically the subjectivity which *ultimately* brings about all world-validity, with its content and in all its prescientific and scientific modes, and into the 'what' and the 'how' of the rational accomplishments—can make objective truth comprehensible and arrive at the ultimate ontic

2

meaning of the world. Thus it is not the being of the world as unquestioned, taken for granted, which is primary in itself; and one has not merely to ask what belongs to it objectively; rather, what is primary in itself is subjectivity, understood as that which naively pregives the being of the world and then rationalizes or (what is the same thing) objectifies it. (Husserl, CES, p. 69/Hua VI, p. 70)

❯ For further study
Constitution and transcendental intersubjectivity

The concept of constitution refers to a **process of sense-making** or appropriation of sense. In so-called constitutional analysis, elements or steps are identified, which are constitutive for the sense of a thing, action, process, etc. To speak of constitution by one or more subjects is therefore not the same as claiming that the world or things are merely a subjective or social construct. Constitution rather refers to passive and active, individual and intersubjective, processes of association, or sense-making. It also refers to the understanding and appropriation of existing (perceptual) sense, including established linguistic meanings. As this shows, Husserl uses the term in an ambivalent way. It can refer to the intersubjective constitution of cultural meanings and cultural objects, where this sense, along with the associated material objects and practices, first arises through joint actions. At the same time, the term can also refer to the first appropriation or understanding of sense or meaning 'constituted' by other subjects (or meaningful objects and practices). As an example of a foundation or constitution, Husserl mentions the first-time recognition of scissors as scissors: As soon as we have linked the perceived thing with this practical purpose, we immediately see it as scissors, which allows us to cut something with it.

In this case, constitution denotes the *appropriation or grasping of a cultural or purposeful (practical) sense*, which already existed, and does not denote the act of inventing the sense 'scissors'. Constitution is therefore not necessarily a creative act that generates a new sense or meaning but can also refer to automatic processes of association and temporal synthesis in consciousness. Constitution therefore denotes everything that brings organization, context or sense in consciousness and experience, i.e., a normal (concordant and optimal) object and world experience, from passive to active syntheses, from perception through practical action to thinking and judging to we-intentionality. This whole range of passive and active institutions or 'achievements' of embodied subjects Husserl refers to as constitution. For the constitution of the world as an open horizon of possible perception and action, other constituting subjects are necessary. The sense of the world is inherently not only subjective, but objective, i.e., for all factual and possible subjects, it is experienceable and valid. Almost every sense that we find in our lifeworld points to other subjects. This is particularly clear in the case of cultural objects, institutions, and of course in language. The condition of the possibility of (concordant and meaningful) experience is therefore no longer only in the constituting transcendental subject (as with Kant), but points to a transcendental intersubjectivity.

2.3.2 Examples: Self-experience and Other-experience

2.3.2.1 Self-experience

As we have seen, when we speak about transcendental subjectivity this refers not to the human being as the subject of scientific investigation, but to the knowing subject, without which there would be no knowledge, evidence, or objects of investigation. In this transcendental turn, a kind of I-split occurs. Through this change of view or attention, a different kind of self-experience opens up, in which we can literally look over ourselves and thereby experience and thematize ourselves in a double way: **as object and as subject of experience**.

A beautiful illustration of this possibility, which already requires a transcendental perspective or distancing, is Husserl's example of the *double sensation*: When we touch our own hand, we feel in a double way. We feel touched and touching. Our body thus makes double 'sense' to us or is, in Husserl's words, 'doubly constituted'.

> ▶ **Example: Double sensation**
>
> "Touching my left hand, I have touch-appearances, that is to say, I do not just sense, but I perceive and have appearances of a soft, smooth hand, with such a form. The indicational sensations of movement and the representational sensations of touch, which are Objectified as features of the thing, 'left hand', belong in fact to my right hand. But when I touch the left hand I also find in it, too, series of touch-sensations, which are '*localized*' in it, though these are not constitutive of properties (such as roughness or smoothness of the hand, of this physical thing). If I speak of the *physical thing*, 'left hand', then I am abstracting from these sensations (a ball of lead has nothing like them and likewise for every 'merely' physical thing, every thing that is not my Body). If I do include them, then it is not that the physical thing is now richer, but instead *it becomes Body, it senses*." (Husserl, CW 3, p. 152/Hua IV, p. 145) ◀

In the 'natural attitude' I first touch my left hand and am interested in it as an object, i.e., in feeling its shape and its properties. Along with these representing sensations (so called because they re-present properties like roughness, smoothness, etc. of the hand) I also have localized 'sensations' in the right hand, but I am initially not aware of these. While sensations thus refer to the representing properties (content of the touch sensation) of the felt hand, Husserl with the term *sensings* (*Empfindnisse*), wants to emphasize the proprioceptive sensations in the feeling hand: In self-perception we are thus both subject and object of sensation. Only after a change of attention do I experience or realize that this physical thing also feels, so it is not only a body (i.e., externally visible and tangible, like any other material thing), but also a body that feels, i.e., (internally) senses.

Our own body, or *Leibkörper*, as Husserl puts it, in bringing together *Leib*, the living/lived body, and *Körper*, the physical body, can therefore not only be experienced by us as an object (with properties), but also in its subjectivity (as a subject of sensations).

2

> **For further study**
> **Merleau-Ponty and the body as subject**
> Maurice Merleau-Ponty emphasizes in his *Phenomenology of Perception* (1945), in which he presents a situated phenomenology of bodily perception and lifeworld, that the body is not only a constituted object of a somehow shaped transcendental consciousness, but itself the subject of perception, which in its movements and inter-actions with the world and others constitutes or institutes practical sense. After all, bodiliness and corporeality, as Husserl also acknowledges, also belong to the tran-scendental conditions of the possibility of experience (Wehrle 2022). Isn't the know-ing subject, which recognizes its own sensing subjectivity, then necessarily bodily? Don't we have to consider consciousness, bodiliness, and the factual situation in the world as co-original? Although in Husserl's genetic phenomenology many descrip-tions and other pieces of evidence can be found that point in this direction, he also ambiguously speaks of the 'body' as a form of self-objectification of the transcen-dental subject, as if the latter were primary and could be thought of without a body. It was Merleau-Ponty who put bodiliness at the center of a description of subjectiv-ity and world: a bodily subject, which is both passively situated in the world, and actively relates to this world and its factual situation. Intentionality, temporality, and sense-making are thus existentially reinterpreted and described as a dialogue between body and world. Merleau-Ponty thus turns phenomenology from the head (consciousness) to the feet (the body) (cf. Carman 1999; Waldenfels 2000; Morris 2008; Heinämaa 2012; Doyon and Wehrle 2020).

▪▪ Recognizing Oneself as Transcendental

Every empirical 'I' also has the ability to recognize itself as transcendental, namely, as that which is necessary for experience (of the world): formally (that there is expe-rience), but also in terms of content (constitution of sense, e.g., the sense of sci-ence). This **insight into the constitutive dimension** must be performed by every empirical subject itself, just like the clarification of the sense found in our con-sciousness and life. Phenomenology is in this transcendental sense always a form of self-inquiry or self-investigation (*Selbstbesinnung*).

> **For further study**
> **Sartre and the problem of self-experience**
> How can it be possible to experience oneself as a subject at all? Whenever I reflect on myself, I immediately make myself an object, since any thematization or reflec-tion needs a 'something' to which it is related. After all, consciousness is always consciousness of something. Jean-Paul Sartre raises this objection to Husserl. For Sartre, self-experience is necessarily an object experience, a 'thetic' consciousness, as he calls it. As the subject of my experiences or actions, I am a non-thetic con-sciousness: I am with the things or the world, but not thematic or conscious as such (as operating subject). As Sartre tries to show in his ontological investigation *Being and Nothingness* (1943), it follows that we, in our function as subjects, cannot be determined qua content and therefore in the true sense are NOTHING. If we are SOMETHING (i.e., part of being), we are this something always as being seen,

thematized, i.e., as content-determined object. This being, the content, is however primarily determined by other subjects, whose gaze objectifies us and thereby simultaneously assigns a specific meaning and a specific significance to us. This is illustrated by Sartre in his famous analysis of the gaze in which a person peeps through a keyhole out of jealousy or curiosity. If this person is initially completely absorbed in the act of peeping and fully with the couple being spied on, this suddenly changes when he hears steps behind them. At once, he becomes aware of themselves as an object among others in the world, visible to other subjects in a way that remains inaccessible to him. What this person is at that moment is determined by how, and as what, the other sees him: In this case, as a person peeping through a keyhole without permission, or in short, as a voyeur.

Sartre comes to the radical conclusion in his phenomenological ontology: Either I am a subject, i.e., nothing, but have the world for myself, or I have myself (as an object), but only at the price that I lose my self-evident and carefree acting in the world (at least temporarily). Either I am a consciousness (*pour-soi*) and the world is 'for-me' in subject mode, or I am, but then primarily as an object for others (*pour-autrui*). One is either subject or object, either I objectify, or I am objectified.

Husserl would admit that every explicit self-thematization necessarily leads to a shift or renewed split within the I (*Ich-Spaltung*), and this in potentially infinite repetition. For example, I can now have my coffee cup as a topic, then perceive myself as perceiving this cup, then reflect on myself perceiving this cup, then reflect on the reflection on me perceiving this cup, and so on. Again and again a new reflecting I (as subject) and an I that is reflected upon (object) appears. According to Husserl, however, this infinite regress can be neglected. What is important is only that one can transcendently reflect on oneself at all times and has the opportunity to catch oneself in one's reflection, operation, and thinking.

■■ The Negative Determination of Ownness

If after the transcendental reduction all current and possible contents of experience are part of transcendental subjectivity, how can I then still distinguish between myself and my experience and other subjects and their experience? After all, everything counts as content of my experience, thus as immanent to this experience. Husserl confronts this problem, for example, in the famous and often criticized fifth 'Cartesian Meditation' (CM/Hua I). First, he tries with an additional thematic reduction to the so-called *sphere of ownness*. For this, he needs to provisionally bracket all contents of experience that already refer to other subjects. This seems to be an almost absurdly hopeless endeavor, in which we realize that any sense we find in our experience, memory, perception, etc. already somehow directly or indirectly refers to others (e.g., 'cultural objects', the meaning 'human', but also the determination of 'subjectivity' against an 'objectivity' itself). Husserl also emphasizes that such a reduction to 'ownness' only gives us a negative definition of the peculiar ownness, as that which is left when we have abstracted from everything that refers to other subjects. However, such a definition remains dependent on all that it wants to delimit itself against (the alien) and thus already presupposes it. After such a thematic separation of the intentional contents of our experience, into own and alien, only the experience of ourselves remains, including that of our lived and

2

physical body (*Leibkörper*) as well as a pre-objective quasi-spatial environment (in which this body is located and able to move). This however appears as an artificial abstraction that cannot function as a positive definition of the sphere of peculiar ownness.

▪▪ A Positive Determination of Self-experience

What Husserl wanted to achieve with this additional thematic reduction is a provisional differentiation of the intentional contents of transcendental consciousness into those that have me as their content and those that have another subject as their content. How am I to recognize the other subject as another subject if, after the transcendental reduction, everything initially only appears as a phenomenon or content of my experience? After his unsatisfactory first attempt to delineate a sphere of ownness, Husserl now tries a more positive definition of self-experience, which he finds not in the **contents of experience (Noema)**, but in the **way we experience (Noesis)**. Each subject experiences things and also itself firsthand; it has an 'original' access to its appearances. The contents of experience of another subject can never be given to me originally; I can only infer what another experiences, thinks, and feels, based on his bodily expression, behavior, or communication. This is the real difference between self and other, experience and empathy: My self and my experiences are originally, i.e., directly, given to me, while the other and their experiences are only indirectly given, through their bodily and linguistic expressions. Even if other bodies appear to me directly as humans with feelings, intentions and consciousness, I never have direct access to their 'inner life', as it is lived and experienced. If I had, it would be my consciousness and my experiences, and not those of another autonomous subject that transcends my transcendental subjectivity. In this positive determination, the peculiarity of self-experience is therefore not so much something that differs in content from the alien or precedes it temporally but is characterized by its type of direct accessibility: What characterizes everyone's peculiar ownness is that it can be accessed originally, it is an **original sphere**. This was already clear in the example of double sensation: In my experience I have both representative sensations of the properties of things and proprioceptive *sensings*. Every experience of the outer world and things (including myself as a body) is therefore accompanied by an implicit, but direct, self-reference. At the same time, I am aware of this subjectivity as I can at all times attend or reflect on it. On top of automatic sensory feedback, and the self-reference implicit in every worldly (thing-oriented) experience, there is for conscious (human) subjects always the possibility of making this subjectivity explicit. One could express this with Helmuth Plessner, a phenomenological anthropologist, like this: Humans not only have experiences, they also experience their experiences (cf. Plessner [1928] 2019).

> ▶ **Example: Original and alien/other consciousness**
>
> "Experience is original consciousness:, and in fact we generally say, in the case of experiencing a man; the other is himself there before us 'in person'. On the other hand, this being there in person does not keeps us from admitting forthwith that, properly speaking, neither the other Ego himself, nor his subjective processes or his appearances themselves, nor anything else belonging to his own essence, becomes given in our experience

originally. If it were, if what belongs to the other's own essence were directly accessible, it would be merely a moment of my own essence, and ultimately he himself and I myself would be the same. The situation would be similar as regards his animate organism, if the latter were nothing else but the 'body' that is a unity constituted purely in my actual and possible experiences, a unity belonging as a product of *my* 'sensuousness' exclusively in my primordial sphere. A *certain mediacy of intentionality* must be present here, going out from the substratum, 'primordial world', (which in any case is the incessantly underlying basis) and making present to consciousness a 'there too', which nevertheless is not itself there and can never become an 'itself-there'. We have here, accordingly, a kind of *making 'co-present'*, a kind of *'appresentation'*." (Husserl, CM, pp. 108–109/ Hua I, p. 139) ◄

▪▪ Primordial Transcendence

In this second positive distinction between original self-consciousness and mediated or appresented alien consciousness, Husserl now makes a clear content-based distinction between the experience of ourselves and of the other. Self-experience is primordial, that is, phenomenologically prior to the experience of others. This does not mean that the self is ontologically primary and the other secondary. Rather, it means that, in the **order of constitution**, the self comes first. That is, when we consider what is constitutive for understanding the meaning of 'other subject', original self-consciousness is foundational.

Self-experience must serve as a model or starting point: Only because we experience ourselves both as subject (from within) and as object (from without), can we directly transfer this to the perception of the other. Here, the body or embodiment plays a crucial role (cf. Heinämaa 2012): We never see others merely as physical bodies, but always also as lived bodies (felt from within), because we experience ourselves in this way. For us to experience the other as transcendent (i.e., existing outside our consciousness), we already need the experience of transcendence, namely, our own temporal and bodily transcendence. Already in our discussion of the perception of things, it became clear that a coherent and continuous perception requires both forms of transcendence. Insofar as this perception consists of the synthesis of different adumbrations of the thing and different perspectives, the current experience is always already temporally transcended, that is, refers to future adumbrations and perspectives of the same object. Our extended body with its kinesthetic abilities thereby also represents a 'primordial transcendence' insofar as it presupposes an environment, even if this environment cannot yet have the full meaning of a transcendent world or objectivity (thus primordial transcendence). Husserl's controversial argument is that for the constitution of the sense 'other' or 'alien', one's own experience is indispensable and, in a way, also primary, since it is always already presupposed.

❯ For further study

Against a primacy of the own/self

Jean-Paul Sartre, Emmanuel Levinas, and the German phenomenologist Bernhard Waldenfels have, each in their own way, argued against a primacy of owness or self-experience, claiming instead that the other, the alien, is always primary. In their view, every experience and all knowledge is a reaction to the world and other subjects. What we do and what we are therefore must be understood as an indirect or direct response, i.e., human existence means responsiveness and not pure intentionality. In defense of Husserl, it could be argued here that he very much emphasizes that on the noematic level, the meaning of 'mine' and 'yours', 'I' and 'other' necessarily constitutes itself reciprocally. Thus, the word 'subject' or 'mine' makes no sense without an experience of the other. If there were only me, why would I need to point out that something is 'mine'? These concepts are necessarily *relative* to each other. And yet he emphasizes the special role of self-experience: For the constitution of the sense of other subjects, for example, my lived and physical body must always be present as the instituting original. If I did not constantly experience myself in this way or if I had no body at all, I could not immediately recognize the other as a subject with a lived (sensing and moving) body, and hence as another consciousness.

These three phenomenologists (and many others after them) rightly emphasize that both my existence and my meaning are secondary to an already-existing, intersubjective world. However, we can perhaps reconcile these differences by noting that both sides, self and other, are equally important. Every subject is already situated, unwillingly thrown into a world that existed long before it. And every subject is completely determined by others, owing their existence and their name to others (cf. Waldenfels 1997, 1998a, 1998b, 1999). But as soon as this subject tries to recognize itself philosophically and to understand this meaning, self-experience is the necessary point of departure. Self-experience or first-person experience is paramount in both a good and bad sense. It is paramount in a good sense insofar as it enables and motivates empathy. It is paramount in a bad sense insofar as our experience often begins from prejudices, habits, or *implicit bias*. We always start from ourselves, our habits, and the environment familiar to us, from what is normal for us, what we are used to. Everything we experience is experienced and judged against this background, the 'home-world' (cf. Held 1991; Steinbock 1995; Renker 2009), as Husserl calls it, without this becoming thematic for us. Here it becomes clear that it makes phenomenological sense to critically reflect on this desired or undesired primacy of the experiencing subject and what is own or familiar to it.

2.3.2.2 Experience of the Other

Let's now look at the description of the experience of the other. The guiding question here is: How is it possible that the other appears in my experience as another subject—with the sense 'transcendent', 'existing outside of me', 'with the same mental and physical abilities'—and not merely as a product of my imagination? Husserl tries to answer this question by conducting a thought experiment in which he traces, step by step, how the sense 'another transcendent subject with consciousness' is constituted. This leads directly to another question: How does the experience of another subject differ from ordinary object perception? Both, after all, refer to external things. However, those things do not both reduce to the immanence of intentional content. So, why can the experience of a thing be reduced to a representation when that of another bodily subject cannot?

■■ Perception of Another Inner Life

Normally, I perceive other subjects directly as people, as fellow human beings, just like you and me. However, in the analysis of their constitution, all these already-constituted meanings are initially bracketed. So, what do I actually see as soon as a subject enters my field of perception? I see an extended body or a bodily expression, behavior, and movement. Just as I cannot see the back of a neighbor's house when I am standing in front of it, so I cannot see the inner life of the other directly. However, unlike the house, which I can walk around to fill my empty intentions, I can never directly fill my empty intentions of the other as other. I cannot immediately experience what makes the other a subject of experience: his body felt and lived from within, his psyche, his thoughts, and ultimately his transcendental dimension. All this I can only anticipate based on what I already know from my own experience.

How does this work in detail? First, another human being appears as a body in our field of perception. We can recognize this as the body of another because we had previously separated the self-experience from the (possible) experience of the other by reducing it to 'ownness'. What belongs to me in terms of content includes my own self with my lived and physical body (*Leibkörper*) and a pre-objective environment or world. Husserl calls this the **'primordial sphere'**. Here we already have a kind of pre-objective environment, but neither my lived and physical body nor its spatial environment have an objective meaning (as a human or world) at this moment. This must first be established in the proof that we experience other subjects as others and can verify their evidence. So, these are primary transcendences that are necessary and take precedence in the analysis of the constitution of the other.

We automatically perceive the body that now appears as similar to, and belonging together with, ours. Just as we perceive several people or birds in one place without further thinking as a 'group'. According to Husserl, this immediate **co-perception due to similarity** is achieved by a passive synthesis in consciousness. He refers to the co-perceived objects, in reference to mathematical processes, as a **'pairing'**. This is followed by various processes of 'sense transfer' (*Übertragung des Sinns*) from my lived and physical body to that of the other.

> ▶ **Example: My Experience of the Other**
>
> "Let us assume that another man enters our perceptual sphere. Primordially reduced, that signifies: In the perceptual sphere pertaining to my primordial Nature, a body is presented, which, as primordial, is of course only a determining part of myself: an 'immanent transcendency'. Since, in this Nature and this world, my **lived body** [*Leib*] is the only body that is or can be constituted originally as a 'lived' body (an operating organ), the body over there, which is nevertheless apprehended as a lived body, must have derived this sense by an *apperceptive transfer from my lived body*, and done so in a manner that excludes an actually direct, and hence primordial, showing of the predicates belonging to a 'lived' body specifically, a showing of them in perception proper. It is clear from the very beginning that only a similarity connecting, within my primordial sphere, that body over there with my body can serve as the motivational basis for the *'analogizing' apprehension* of that body as another lived body [...]."

2

If we attempt to indicate the peculiar nature of that analogizing apprehension whereby a body within my primordial sphere, being similar to my own lived and physical body [*Leib-Körper*], becomes *apprehended as likewise a lived body* [*Leib*], we encounter: first, the circumstance that here the *primally institutive original is always livingly present*, and the primal instituting itself is therefore always going on in a livingly effective manner; secondly, the peculiarity we already know to be necessary, namely, that what is *appresented* by virtue of the aforesaid analogizing can never attain actual presence, never become an object of perception proper. Closely connected with the first peculiarity is the circumstance that *ego* and *alter ego* are always and necessarily given *in an original 'pairing'* […]." (Husserl, CM, pp. 110–111, p. 112, translation revised MW/ Hua I, p. 140, p. 141–143) ◄

▪▪ Sense transfer

What Husserl refers to as a 'sense transfer' begins passively (not as a thought act or judgment) with my experience and gradually becomes 'more active', until it reaches a full *empathizing* (cf. Zahavi 2023). After an immediate pairing, which perceives the body in connection with mine, there follows a kind of appresentation or apperception, which is based on a receptive presentation and is motivated by it, i.e., by the visible body, its bodily expression and its way of moving. From there, step by step, first passively, then actively, further anticipations take place. Central to this is my lived and physical body, i.e., my experience as subjective and objective body. This makes it clear that the other is also a lived and physical body like me but can never take my spatial position. My body is always the 'absolute here', the other 'there', and vice versa. At the same time, I can now actively put myself in her position and anticipate what I would see and feel if I were standing there, where she is now. The other is thus perceived as 'if I were there'. Husserl borrows a concept from the psychologist Theodor Lipps to refer to this final phase as 'empathizing' (*Einfühlung*).

This analysis makes clear that sense transfer needs my self-experience as a starting point but can never be reduced to this self-experience. The sense of the Other is thus traced epistemologically to a kind of 'modification' of the self, but at the same time, its actual constitution takes place reciprocally, and can only be understood as a result of an intersubjective institution of sense. Therefore, the other cannot simply be a mirror or a duplicate of myself; he is necessarily his own subject with his own bodily 'here', his own perspective, and his own constitutive abilities.

> ▶ **Example: The Other is not a duplicate of myself**
>
> "As reflexively related to itself, my physical lived body [*körperlicher Leib*] has the central 'Here' as its mode of givenness; every other body, and accordingly the 'other's' body, has the mode 'There'. This orientation, 'There', can be freely changed by virtue of my kinesthesias. Thus, in my primordial sphere, the *one spatial 'Nature'* is constituted throughout the change in orientations, and constituted moreover with an intentional relatedness to my **perceiving and moving lived body**. Now the fact that my **physical and lived body** [*körperlicher Leib*] can be (and is) apprehended as *a natural body existing and movable in space like any other* is manifestly connected with the possibility expressed in the words:

By free modification of my kinesthesias, particularly those of locomotion, I can change my position in such a manner that I convert any There into a Here that is to say, I could bodily occupy any spatial locus […].

After all, I do not apperceive the other ego simply as a duplicate of myself and accordingly as having my original sphere or one completely like mine. I do not apperceive him as having, more particularly, the spatial modes of appearance that are mine from here; rather, as we find on closer examination, I apperceive him as having spatial modes of appearance like those I should have if I should go over there and be where he is. Furthermore, the Other is appresentatively apperceived as the 'Ego' of a primordial world, and of a monad, wherein his lived body is originally constituted and experienced in the mode of the absolute Here, precisely as the functional center for his governing. In this appresentation, therefore, the body in the mode *There*, which presents itself in *my* monadic sphere and is apperceived as another's lived body (the animate organism of the alter ego) that body indicates 'the same' body in the mode *Here*, as the body experienced by the other ego in *his* monadic sphere. Moreover, it indicates the 'same' body concretely, with all the constitutive intentionality pertaining to this mode of givenness in the other's experience." (Husserl, CM, pp. 116–117, translation revised MW/Hua I, p. 145f.) ◄

We therefore perceive the Other in our experience as another subject with its own experience, and this directly and immediately (i.e., without having to think explicitly about it). However, what is each time co-perceived or anticipated (that this body is indeed 'animated', i.e., sensuous, feeling and moving, being), is never given with absolute certainty, since the consciousness or feelings of the other can never actually appear. The appearing body must thus continuously prove itself in further experience through its expressions and behavior as 'animated' or 'human'. In this process, our intention could also be disappointed: If the supposed human suddenly stops, steams, blinks, and beeps, it may actually turn out to be a humanoid robot with technical problems.

► **Example: The Other as original inaccessibility**

"The experienced lived body [*Leib*] of another continues to prove itself as actually a lived body [*Leib*], solely in its changing but incessantly *harmonious behavior* (as having a physical side that indicates something psychic appresentatively) must present itself fulfillingly in original experience, and do so throughout the continuous change in behavior from phase to phase. The lived body [*Leib*] becomes experienced as a pseudo-lived body [*Schein-Leib*], precisely if there is something discordant about its behavior. The character of the existent 'other' has its basis in this kind of verifiable accessibility of what is not originally accessible. Whatever can become presented, and evidently verified, originally is something *I* am; or else it belongs to me as peculiarly my own. Whatever, by virtue thereof, is experienced in that founded manner which characterizes a primordially unfulfillable experience an experience that does not give something itself *originally* but that consistently verifies something indicated is 'other'. It is therefore conceivable only as an analogue of something included in my peculiar ownness. Because of its sense constitution it occurs necessarily as an '*intentional modification*' of that Ego of mine which is the first to be Objectivated, or as an intentional modification of my primordial 'world': the Other as phenomenologically a 'modification' of myself (which, for its part, gets this

2

character of being 'my' self by virtue of the contrastive pairing that necessarily takes place). It is clear that, with the other Ego, there is appresented, in an analogizing modification, everything that belongs to his concretion: first, *his* primordial world, and then his fully concrete ego. In other words, *another monad* becomes constituted appresentatively in mine." (Husserl, CM, pp. 114–115, translation revised MW/Hua I, p. 144) ◄

▪▪ The Experienced Transcendence of the Other

On the one hand, the other subject is directly accessible through his bodily expression, i.e., we always experience others directly as subjects like us, but on the other hand, he is never originally accessible: We cannot crawl into the heads or bodies of others and feel their feelings or think their thoughts. We can only perceive this indirectly or anticipate it. In everyday life, this (for the most part) works fine; we can rely on our intuition. However, this everyday evidence is corrigible; it is valid only until further notice. Something perceived as a human might turn out to be a mannequin upon closer inspection.

This uncertainty—that the other subject in its very presence also simultaneously withdraws—marks the difference between self-experience and experience of others in a positive sense. The essence of the other subject constantly eludes us; we can neither hold it, control it, nor fully recognize it, and this constitutes its transcendence. If the Other were originally experienceable, she would merely be one of my experiences, an immanent representation. The fact that we cannot originally experience the Other means that she cannot be reduced to my experience. She always transcends it, always exists independently and outside of it.

▪▪ Experience of the Alien and Objectivity

Conversely, the Other has the same status and the same general abilities as me, which means that I am also an object of the experience of others. I am also constituted in my sense by others. As Husserl shows step by step in his description, this Other, who initially appears as a mere perceived body in my field of perception, necessarily also has a sensing and moving body and thus a primordial spatiality and environment. A body that is for me always *there*, is, for the Other always *here*. The other also has a psyche, a consciousness and finally a transcendental dimension. The other sees the same things I see, but from a different perspective. She stands on the same ground as I do, but in her *here*. To experience the other evidently as an existing bodily subject is thus constitutively necessary for securing objectivity. As soon as we can demonstrate the transcendence of the other in our experience, it follows, that the world and the things that I experience, exist not only for me but also for others, i.e., they are not only subjective, but objectively valid.

2.4 Phenomenological Method after Husserl

Historically, phenomenologists have engaged Husserl's methods in a variety of ways. Some have subjected them to criticism, while others have developed them further or adapted them to new ends. One could even say that phenomenology is characterized by a constant critical reflection on its method. Many have sought a more or less explicit eidetic determination of general structures of experience or a determination of general structures of different regions of being (regional ontology). Still others have devoted themselves to a transcendental phenomenological critique of knowledge and experience and sought to investigate the genetic development, that is, the passive and active achievements of consciousness in general or of the situated bodily subject. However, what all phenomenologists can agree on is that **description of experience lies at the core of phenomenology**.

■ ■ Critique of Husserl's Eidetics

As already mentioned, Husserl's eidetics have often been met with criticism. In analytic philosophy, for example, it was doubted that 'essences' can be intuited or that general structures can be experienced directly. How could such a thing be verified, and what role does language play here? In critical theory or feminist philosophy, Husserl's determination of essence was seen as a regression to a Platonic world of ideas or as an example of an essentialism that plays into a political strategy of naturalizing human differences (e.g., gender, origin, abilities). Through such a universalization, differences or deviations from the supposed (ideal) essence of man could then be used to legitimize unequal treatment, marginalization, exclusion, or violence (cf. Oksala 2022). These objections are particularly justified with reference to the unspeakable atrocities committed during the time of National Socialism. Who determines what is universal and ideal? And how are the supposedly purely descriptive determinations of the general linked with value judgments? In the face of such questions, Husserl can appear a little naïve. While it might be theoretically possible to neutrally determine general structures, in actual practice, prejudices, ideologies, interests, and power relations always play a role. For most thinkers after the Second World War, it is simply no longer possible to refer to the 'essence' of things.

Yet the problem of how we can have access to the general, despite—and within—our subjective experience, remains. Husserl has made clear that we, in our experiencing, thinking, and communicating with others, must always already assume more general structures and invariants. Therefore, the method of eidetics still seems unavoidable. However, the essence is no longer the goal so much as the provisional starting point. Now the goal is to find out whether and how general structures can be recognized, or how we come to (implicit or explicit) assumptions of the general.

■ ■ New Approaches

Phenomenologists after Husserl are therefore no less concerned with ways to determine the general within the plurality of human experiences. Examples of this include Merleau-Ponty's existential phenomenology (cf. *Phenomenology of Perception*, 1945), Heidegger's early and late thinking of being (cf. *Being and Time*, 1927; *On the Essence of Truth*, 1930; *The End of Philosophy and the Task of Thinking*, 1964) Sartre's phenomenological ontology (cf. *Being and Nothingness*, 1943) and Simone de Beauvoir's description of the situation of women or the elderly (cf. *The Second Sex*, 1949; *The Coming of Age*, 1970). Although there is no explicit implementation of eidetic variation in any of these projects, the determination of general modes of experience or ways of being remains at the forefront of all of them. For example, Merleau-Ponty examines the difference between normal and pathological ways of being-in-the-world, while de Beauvoir examines the different material, socio-cultural, and thus experiential situations of women and men, respectively. Furthermore, all of these projects distinguish between different regions of being. Heidegger distinguishes between being 'ready-to-hand' (*Zuhanden*) and 'present-at-hand' (*Vorhanden*). The later Merleau-Ponty makes an ontological distinction between the visible and the invisible (Merleau-Ponty [1954–1955] 2010). Sartre distinguishes between being 'for-itself' (*pour-soi*) and being 'in-itself' (*en-soi*). And Beauvoir traces the artificial allocation of genders to the regions of transcendence on the one hand (men) and immanence on the other (women). These projects also contain numerous reflections on the relationship between the factual and the essential. For example, Heidegger distinguishes between the ontic and the ontological and describes the essence of technology. So too, the later Merleau-Ponty studies how sense becomes instituted, while Sartre famously characterized existentialism with the battle cry 'existence before essence'. In all of these philosophies, the essential or the general is no longer seen as strictly a priori, but more and more as connected with—or dependent on—the factual, and thus also the historical and changeable. Nevertheless, all these approaches are characterized by the determination of a general, from which the particular, the other, or the concrete as such, first becomes visible and graspable.

▪▪ New Methodological Procedures

In phenomenology after Husserl, we also find special methodological procedures, not unlike eidetic variation, that aim at a determination of the general (or particular). Merleau-Ponty, for example, uses empirical case studies of pathologies to trace 'normal' experience. Heidegger goes back to the original use and meaning of concepts in ancient philosophy (like *techné* or *poiesis*) or draws on his rural, Black-Forest environment (through common terms like '*Gestell*') to determine the essence of causality and technology or to describe our relationship to being in new terms. These are methods of variation that reveal the similarities or differences between things, perceptions, or ways of experiencing and determine the underlying common principle. Through the detour of history, pathology, or the everyday (which is often not self-evident for philosophers) an epistemological distance or alienation is created, which allows for different ways of thinking.

❯ For further study

Early realistic phenomenology: The Munich and Göttingen Circles

The so-called 'early' or 'realistic phenomenology' of the Munich and Göttingen Circles (from about 1890 to the time of the First World War) follows Husserl's object-oriented, eidetic descriptive approach and develops it independently. These circles trace back to the "Academic Association for Psychology" founded in Munich in 1895 by Theodor Lipps and the "Philosophical Society Göttingen" founded in 1907 by Theodor Conrad (cf. Salice 2015). Other members include Hedwig Conrad-Martius, Johannes Daubert, Herbert Leyendecker, Paul F. Linke, Alexander Pfänder, Adolf Reinach, Max Scheler, Dietrich von Hildebrand, Hermann Ritzel,

Gerda Walther, Wilhelm Schapp, and Edith Stein. The works of these early phenomenologists deal with a wide variety of topics, such as questions on the foundations of logic, mathematics and mathematical physics, the experience of religious and mystical phenomena, emotion and will, perception, aesthetics, ethics, collective intentionality, and ontology. What they have in common is a general commitment to the faithful description of concrete objects and states of affairs.

From the outset, these thinkers are critical of Husserl's assumptions that take us beyond the concrete givenness of things or types of intentionality. For example, they are skeptical of the idea that intentionality can be generally characterized as a structure of intention (intended object) and fulfillment (what is currently directly given of this object). Husserl's transcendental turn, which includes questions of epistemology, is therefore rejected. Such a turn to the (transcendental) subject or ego appears to these early phenomenologists as a relapse into psychologism or transcendental constructivism and thus as a betrayal of the phenomenological slogan: to the things themselves.

Instead of speculating about subjective conditions of experience, the Munich and Göttingen phenomenologists primarily devote themselves to the description of specific things (cf. e.g., Schapp [1910] 2013; cf. also De Santis and Nuccilli 2025), facts (cf. Lipps 1927) or intentionalities, such as legal considerations (Reinach [1913] 2007), acts of will and emotion, empathy, 'We-experiences', or forms of community (cf. Pfänder 1900; Scheler 1923; Stein 1916; von Hildebrand 1930; Walther 1923). Working in this vein, Edith Stein and Gerda Walther made important contributions to debates in social ontology and joint action (cf. Zahavi 2025b; Luft and Hagengruber 2018; Andrews and Calcagno 2022; Calcagno 2018). Another female philosopher in this tradition, Hedwig Conrad-Martius (1923), made significant contributions to phenomenological ontology in general. Conrad-Martius develops an ontology, which is supposed to investigate how being is founded in itself, and distinguishes three phenomenological attitudes: a narrower phenomenological or epistemological attitude in the sense of Husserl (cf. transcendental epoché), a broader phenomenological attitude, in which the activation or deactivation of the natural attitude plays no role (cf. descriptive epoché), and a real ontological attitude, in which the world is presupposed as factual, whether it exists or not (cf. Avé-Lallemant 1975, p. 34; cf. Hart 2020; Miron 2021).

Recent years have seen a revival of interest in early phenomenology: New research has shed light on its connection to Husserl's phenomenology and on its independent relevance to a range of philosophical problems. Only now—after more than a century of neglect—is the richness of these investigations becoming apparent (Moran and Parker 2015, pp. 12–13; cf. Salice 2015; De Santis 2021). Of special interest are the many female philosophers who belonged to early phenomenology. The presence of so many female voices in a philosophical movement was extremely rare, since women at this time were not allowed to become professors (though they were allowed to study at German universities) (Moran and Parker 2015, p. 13).

■ ■ **Transcendental Phenomenology after Husserl**
Husserl's transcendental orientation was also met with skepticism by his immediate successors in phenomenology who saw it not as a relapse into Platonism but as an

2

uncritical continuation of German Idealism. On this reading, the reduction is understood as a denial or elimination of the world, and the transcendental subject is (mis)understood as an omnipotent, creative, and completely transparent subject. This negative reception is undoubtedly due in part to Husserl's situation as a Jewish professor in 1930s Germany and in part to the fact that most of his manuscripts were at that time still unpublished (cf. Vongehr 2017). Especially in the English-speaking world, the reception of phenomenology has therefore been shaped mainly by Heidegger and Merleau-Ponty. Husserl is often mistakenly seen as representing an intellectualism and representationalism that needs to be overcome (cf. Dreyfus 1982). Only recently have central concepts of the transcendental-genetic approach, such as passivity, passive synthesis, temporality, affection, emotions, embodiment, normality, intersubjectivity, and lifeworld been gaining traction in the general philosophical discourse.

Particularly in contemporary political phenomenology, a transcendental approach has begun to play a role again as a critique of knowledge. Here eidetics and transcendental reduction are understood as methodological forms of an immanent critique, i.e., a critique of our experience that allows us to recognize our own assumptions, think differently, and thus gain more openness and understanding for the perspectives of others (cf. Aldea 2016; Aldea et al. 2021).

Contemporary transcendental phenomenology (referring to Eugen Fink, Martin Heidegger, Emmanuel Levinas, Marc Richir) also plays a vital role in recent debates on metaphysics, for example as counterpart of the so-called 'speculative realism' (cf. Quentin Meillassoux), and is well represented in recently founded research institutes like the *Institute for Transcendental Philosophy and Phenomenology* (ITP, University of Wuppertal, Germany).

However, initially, phenomenology after Husserl criticized his transcendental turn as being too Cartesian or too Kantian. Here it was argued that phenomenology should no longer create distance from the concrete, the everyday, or situated existence. There is no disinterested observer. Rather it is the very facticity, situatedness, engagement, and worldliness of the observer that provide the motivation and the motor for the description in which the world is to be captured, so to speak, *in actu*. Thus, for example, it is neither possible nor desirable to simply bracket all prejudices and worldly interests in order to get to the things themselves. After all, isn't every experience, including the phenomenological one, guided by certain interests in knowledge? And what actually motivates us to perform such an epoché or reduction?

Although Husserl's transcendental methods were often criticized or even rejected by subsequent phenomenologists, we see a variety of transcendental considerations come into play in their work. Almost all phenomenological approaches, for example, reflect on the conditions of the possibility of experience and investigate how we can recognize and describe the world without implicitly presupposing its status and meaning. For example, Sartre defines non-thetic (i.e., operative and non-thematic to the subject) consciousness as a prerequisite for the experience of a world. Merleau-Ponty understands his phenomenology of perception as a transcendental investigation in which the very passivity and situatedness of every factual subjectivity are themselves seen as prerequisites for knowledge and freedom.

As he emphasizes in his preface to *Phenomenology of Perception*, the central insight of Heidegger's being-in-the-world only appears on the basis of the transcendental reduction (Merleau-Ponty 2012, p. lxxviii). Heidegger himself, who decidedly rejects the transcendental philosophy of Kant and Husserl as too rationalistic, nevertheless aims in his description of *Dasein* at the conditions of the possibility of the experience of the meaning of being (cf. Gethmann 1993; Crowell 2002; Luft 2005). Instead of adopting an epistemologically critical account, however, he advocates an openness towards being (cf. Heidegger [1955] 1966).

In all these ways, phenomenologists after Husserl can be understood as continuing his transcendental project even while critiquing it or attempting to replace it with something more adequate. The problem of the beginning of phenomenology and the aim for an adequate description of the world therefore accompanies phenomenologists up to the present day.

> ### ❯ For further study
> #### Heidegger: *Gelassenheit* instead of epoché
> Heidegger's work—both early and late—can be understood as a critical engagement with Husserl's transcendental method, in which he seeks an alternative starting point for phenomenology (cf. Hadjioannou 2018). According to Heidegger, the epoché or transcendental method does not penetrate to the things themselves. It merely places things into a rationally ordered form. Instead of bracketing, one should take the stance of *Gelassenheit* (letting-be, releasement) towards being or things. In his essay 'The Question Concerning Technology' (1953) and in the 'Meßkircher Speech' (1955), he explicitly speaks of *Gelassenheit*, which allows a free relationship to being. 'To the things themselves' thus means in Heidegger to be open to how being reveals itself to us. That is, one should try to let being appear from itself, to open oneself to it, through a practice of questioning. Reflective inquiry or bracketing as a theoretical attitude is therefore not the gateway to phenomenology. Instead of trying to clarify or secure something, we should open ourselves to the world or the deeper meaning of words and things. However, such a 'releasement' can also be interpreted as a form of distancing oneself from what is self-evident. It is achieved by questioning common theories and going back to original concepts and meanings, to move from what is considered correct in our time (the 'correct') to the actual essence of being (the 'true').
>
> Already in *Being and Time* (1927), Heidegger speaks in this vein of a *formal indication*, which does not categorize the phenomena, but merely indicates them, i.e., refers to phenomena in a non-objectifying way. Here, Heidegger tries to find a kind of description that does not define or freeze things but captures them in their dynamic liveliness. What Heidegger gives us in *Being and Time* is thus not so much a depiction of facts as a descriptive indication of "a way of approaching what 'to be' means" (Dahlstrom 1994, p. 782; Heidegger 1985, pp. 60–61).
>
> Heidegger also uses methods designed to prepare the way for an 'event of revelation', with the aim of prejudice-free description. However, one risk of this approach is that it eludes intersubjective criticism and verification. Even if we refrain from engaging with Heidegger's antisemitic biographical background, his philosophy comes with an inherent danger: it seems to assume that some enlightened few are

2

able to achieve a genuine access to being. However, in recent decades, research has increasingly tried to crack this hermetic character of Heidegger's philosophy and open up new interpretations, topics, and interdisciplinary discourses.

▪▪ The Self-evidentness of the World

Phenomenology after Husserl shifts its focus away from knowledge of the world, towards existing *in the world* (e.g., Heidegger, Merleau-Ponty, Sartre, Beauvoir, Fanon). Existential phenomenology starts with concrete, that is, worldly and historically situated, experience. If there is to be objectivity and transcendence, it must also be experiential before all measurement and formalization: "The world is there prior to every analysis that I could give of it" as Merleau-Ponty emphasizes (2012, p. lxxiii). And this confirms our first intuition: In everyday experience, we do not doubt in the least that things and the world exist independently of us and are equally accessible to everyone. To philosophically illuminate this self-evidence of the world is also a basic motivation of existential phenomenology.

▪▪ Committed Description

Phenomenologists after Husserl argue that it is not reflective distance, but precisely being affected by, and practically engaged in, the world, that are prerequisites for an adequate description of experience. One representative of such an approach of direct description is Maurice Merleau-Ponty, who sees it as the task of phenomenology to study the sense of the world in its *nascent state*, that is, in its becoming (Merleau-Ponty 2012, p. lxxxv). However, subsequent reflection also plays a role here. After all, one cannot immerse oneself in a particular experience and simultaneously describe that experience philosophically. In contrast to the ideal of the detached observer, which characterizes Husserl's early descriptions, here the relationship between observer and lived experience is emphasized: there is a constant alternation between experience and reflection, without the two ever existing in strict separation. Because of this, reflection must always be aware that it already presupposes a pre-reflective world, meaning, and subject. Therefore, the experience being thematized is always preceded by a still 'silent experience', and the Cartesian 'spoken' cogito is preceded by a tacit cogito (see box for further study "Merleau-Ponty and the Problem of Reflection").

▪▪ Hermeneutic Phenomenology

As we can see, the perspectives and focal points, as well as the methods of phenomenology, are constantly shifting. While the Munich and Göttingen phenomenologists advocated for a realistic phenomenology, which focused on the concrete description of things and opposed a transcendental-subjective orientation, others advocated for an existential or hermeneutically oriented phenomenology. In hermeneutics after Heidegger, e.g., with Hans-Georg Gadamer and Paul Ricœur, an approach to understanding develops that is less interested in immediate experience and its description than in (linguistic or symbolic) expression and its interpretation (cf. Tengelyi 2007). The term 'expression' can refer to textual traditions as well as symbols, myths, or works of art. Hermeneutics is therefore concerned with a form of understanding that accesses meaning indirectly, i.e., through interpretation. Expressions in this sense always contain a surfeit of meaning; they are never limited to the intentions of the author or artist expressing themselves. The aim of interpretation is thus not only to interpret what was meant, for example by a text or artwork, but rather to look for and reveal the hidden sense behind an obvious meaning (cf. Gadamer [1960] 2010).

As the founder of phenomenological hermeneutics, Martin Heidegger was critical of the reflective distancing of the phenomenological description from the outset. His hermeneutic phenomenology assumes that we can only deal with being because we ourselves belong to being (as Dasein) (Heidegger 1927). The human being as being-in-the-world can therefore not go behind his implicitly given horizon of understanding. We can only try to understand this horizon and to demonstrate its individual moments. This form of understanding is necessarily circular, as the individual only makes sense in relation to the whole, and the whole in relation to the individual. Thus, we ask about our being because it concerns us and we already have a notion of its meaning, but we do not yet understand this meaning in detail. The hermeneutic philosophy of Paul Ricœur and Hans-Georg Gadamer subsequently dealt with the temporality and horizonality of understanding as well as the temporality and narrativity of subjective identity.

In each of these post-Husserlian approaches, the goal of phenomenology shifts. From Husserl's strict, scientific demand for ultimate justification, it shifts towards visualization of the ambiguity, situatedness, finiteness, and vulnerability of human existence on the one hand, and towards the interpretation or even revelation of the 'hidden meaning' of human expression in its historical diversity on the other hand. However, all these approaches still refer to their phenomenological roots, take description as their starting point, and share *the ethos of Husserl's 'self-responsibility'*, which states that one can only accept what one can demonstrate as evident in experience, reflection, and comparison with others.

❯ **For further study**

Merleau-Ponty and the problem of reflection

Whenever I refer to myself in reflection and thought, this presupposes an already existing and implicitly operating subject. With reference to Descartes, Merleau-Ponty therefore emphasizes that every spoken cogito is preceded by a tacit cogito. The situatedness and the passive determinations of the subject (biological dispositions, cultural and social influences, habits, etc.) make it impossible to capture all these aspects and make them explicit. A complete bracketing of all assumptions—the aim of the epoché—is thus impossible. Nonetheless, Merleau-Ponty's existential phenomenology is a transcendental project insofar as it inquires into the conditions of the possibility of experience and locates these in the temporality, and thus the situatedness, of subjectivity itself. This means that for him the most important insight that the transcendental reduction can offer is the impossibility of its complete execution (Merleau-Ponty 2012, p. lxxvii). We cannot detach ourselves from all lifeworldly ties and motivations and simply neutralize them or thematize them as disinterested spectators. Nor can we separate the determination of the necessary constitutive conditions from our factual circumstances. Merleau-Ponty therefore emphasizes the intertwining of facticity and eidetics as well as of facticity and transcendental

2

questioning. Here he agrees with Heidegger; the essence of subjectivity is its being-in-and-to-the-world. And it is this that motivates and enables all epistemological clarification.

■■ Phenomenology is a Practice Rather Than a School

It is striking that phenomenology after Husserl, despite various demarcations, transformations, and changes of direction, continues to affirm the term 'phenomenology'. As Husserl and many others after him pointed out, this is because phenomenology refers more to a movement, a practice, or a style of philosophizing which is determined by its method or by constant reflection on its method, than to a clearly defined research program or a philosophical school. With Merleau-Ponty we can still affirm that, even today, phenomenology is in a nascent state. This is both a problem and a promise (cf. Merleau-Ponty 2012, p. lxxi; Spiegelberg 1994).

Common to all phenomenologists is the question and the task of a philosophical determination of the experience of the world, the self, and other subjects (or living beings). Here, the focus might be on consciousness, the subject, the body, existence, being, intersubjectivity, perception, or language. However, in all these cases, sensual and meaningful experience—that is, the relation or interrelation of subject and world—plays a central role. The call 'To the things themselves' is thus followed by all phenomenologists, but in various ways.

This presupposes that phenomenologists do not rely on predefined scientific definitions or prefabricated norms and opinions but instead try to bracket these assumptions in order to clarify their meaning. This is intended to address the limits and contexts of knowledge and perception, in order to enable new and different perspectives on the world, things, ourselves, and others.

■■ Science and the Mathematization of the Lifeworld

Phenomenology always addresses the world as a totality of experience, as a practical horizon of experience, or as a lifeworld. Within such an all-encompassing experiential horizon, the natural sciences represent merely a special perspective: If one defines water as H_2O, this does not mean that the previous appearing reality is thereby reduced, replaced, or eliminated. The scientific definition only adds a layer of knowledge, that is, the determination of water in relation to its chemical composition. However, such a determination always presupposes the previous givenness, i.e., the everyday experience of water. Even afterwards, water remains something that is visible and tangible in its own way—not like an ordinary physical object, but like something in which one can swim and which one can drink. Science thus undertakes an idealization, formalization, abstraction, or mathematization of the lifeworld, which enables new perspectives and applications. But it remains founded on our lifeworld and always refers back to it (cf. Husserl CES/Hua VI; Heidegger 1927; Merleau-Ponty 2012). In no version of phenomenology is there an assumption of two worlds, one apparent and one real. From a phenomenological point of view, there is only *one* world, the one we experience (cf. Zahavi 2025a, p. 18). Truth, error, evidence, illusion, or reality must therefore be identified or proven within experience as such. Only the experience that my perspective is incomplete, that I have deceived myself, or that my experience does not coincide with others, leads me to the insight that reality must be more, or different, than what I had previously experienced. The difference between appearance and reality, right or wrong, normal or abnormal (cf. Doyon 2024; Wehrle 2024) itself originates from within experience or is a judgment about this experience.

▪▪ Current Phenomenology and its 'Things'

Phenomenological analyses and concepts such as intersubjectivity, intentionality, embodiment, temporality, passivity, affectivity and lifeworld have been taken up, further developed, adapted, differentiated, critically modified, and transformed since the time of Husserl. Further genuinely phenomenological, or phenomenologically interpreted, concepts have been added, such as the situation, freedom (Merleau-Ponty, Sartre, Beauvoir), body-schema, flesh (Merleau-Ponty) or the 'historical-racial schema' (Fanon 1952). In addition to classical text- and author-based studies, current phenomenological research is increasingly dedicated to the 'things'. Recent studies include descriptions and analyses of feelings and emotions, we-intentionality, joint action, practice and sociality, facticity and truth, imagination, normativity and normality of experience, disability, aging, and illness.

In recent years, classical phenomenology has been accompanied by applied phenomenologies that place the 'things' in political and historical context, apply them interdisciplinarily (in conjunction with nursing science, sports science, psychiatry, neuroscience, etc.), expand phenomenological descriptions, and critically look at hasty essential determinations or general statements (e.g., Feminist Phenomenology, Political Phenomenology, Critical Phenomenology). What unites all these different approaches despite their criticism of the classical phenomenology of consciousness (and its subject-centeredness) and makes them genuinely phenomenological approaches, is the conviction that a philosophical and critical description and analysis of subjective experience is indispensable if we want to understand or even change ourselves in relation to our world and our living environments. (For more on these different approaches, see also ► Chap. 3).

▪▪ Description—A Relentless Phenomenological Work

The meticulous and differentiated work of description remains at the core of phenomenology despite some profound changes in its questions and orientation over the years. Phenomenologists from Husserl's day down to the present have taken on this task in various ways and tried to describe the experienced meaning of the world, of themselves and others in a way that is prejudice-free, differentiated, open, and critical. In the end, the attempt to do justice to experience is what unites old and new, classical and critical, philosophical and non-philosophical (psychological, sociological, medical, neuroscientific) phenomenology.

Literature

In the text, the cited volumes of Husserl's Collected Works in German (Husserliana) are only indicated with the siglum Hua and the volume number. The individual volumes are always listed in
the bibliography. Where possible, a published English translation has been used. Where not possible, the texts have been translated automatically and subsequently edited by the author. The
English translations of Husserl are indicated either with the siglum CW, when they are published
within the series Collected Works or with the following abbreviations:

CES = The Crisis of European Sciences and Transcendental Phenomenology

CM = Cartesian Meditations

EJ = Experience and Judgment

LI1 = Logical Investigations, volume 1

LI2 = Logical Investigations, volume 2

PRS = Philosophy as Rigorous Science

Aldea, Andreea Smaranda. 2016. Phenomenology as Critique. Teleological-Historical Reflection and
Husserl's Transcendental Eidetics. *Husserl Studies* 32(1): 21–46.

Aldea, Andreea Smaranda, Sara Heinämaa, and David Carr, eds. 2021. *Why Method Matters: From
Phenomenology to Critique*. London: Routledge.

Alloa, Emmanuel, Thomas Bedorf, Christian Grüny, and Tobias Nikolaus Klass. 2019. *Leiblichkeit.
Geschichte und Aktualität eines Konzepts*, 2nd edition. Tübingen: Mohr Siebeck.

Andrews, Michael F., and Antonio Calcagno, eds. 2022. *Ethics and Metaphysics in the Philosophy of
Edith Stein. Applications and Implications*. Dordrecht: Springer.

Avé-Lallemant, Eberhard. 1975. Die Antithese Freiburg-München in der Geschichte der
Phänomenologie. In *The Munich Phenomenology*. Phaenomenologica 65, eds. Helmut Kuhn,
Eberhard Ave-Lallemant, and Reinhold Gladiator, 19–38. The Hague: Martinus Nijhoff.

Beauvoir, Simone de. (1949) 2011. *The Second Sex*. Trans. Constance Borde and Sheila Malovany-
Chevallier. New York: Vintage Press.

Beauvoir, Simone de. (1970) 1972. *The Coming of Age*. Trans. Patrick O'Brian. New York: Putnam.

Bedorf, T. 2020. Instituting Institutions. An Exploration of the Political Phenomenology of Stiftung.
In *Political Phenomenology. Experience, Ontology, Episteme*, ed. T. Bedorf T and S. Herrmann,
pp. 239–256. New York/London: Routledge.

Bernet, Rudolf. 2009. Leiblichkeit bei Husserl und Heidegger. In *Heidegger und Husserl. Neue
Perspektiven*, eds. Günter Figal and Hans-Helmuth Gander, 43–72. Frankfurt a.M.: Klostermann.

Bernet, Rudolf. 2010. Husserl's new phenomenology of time consciousness in the Bernau Manuscripts.
In *On Time—New Contributions to the Husserlian Phenomenology of Time*, eds. Dieter Lohmar
and Ichiro Yamaguchi, 1–19. Dordrecht: Springer.

Bernet, Rudolf, Iso Kern, and Eduard Marbach. 1993. *An Introduction to Husserlian Phenomenology*.
Northwestern University Studies in Phenomenology and Existential Philosophy. Evanston, IL:
Northwestern University Press.

Calcagno, Antonio, ed. 2018. *Gerda Walther's Phenomenology of Sociality, Psychology, and Religion*.
Dordrecht: Springer.

Carman, Taylor. 1999. The Body in Husserl and Merleau-Ponty. Philosophical Topics 27 (2):205–226.

Carr, D. 1970. Husserl's Problematic Concept of the Life-world. *American Philosophical Quarterly*
7(4):331–339.

Cerbone, David R. 2021. Availableness (*Zuhandenheit*). In *The Cambridge Heidegger Lexicon*, ed.
Mark A. Wrathall, 78–81. Cambridge, UK: Cambridge University Press.

Conrad-Martius, Hedwig. 1923. Realontologie. In *Jahrbuch für Philosophie und phänomenologische
Forschung* 6: 159–333.

Crowell, Steven. 2002. Does the Husserl/Heidegger Feud Rest on a Mistake? An Essay on
Psychological and Transcendental Phenomenology. *Husserl Studies* 18(2): 123–40.

Crowell, Steven, and Jeff Malpas, eds. 2007. *Transcendental Heidegger*. Stanford: Stanford University
Press.

Dahlstrom, Daniel O. 1994. Heidegger's Method: Philosophical Concepts as Formal Indications. *The
Review of Metaphysics* 47(4): 775–795.

De Santis, Daniele. 2021. Theodor Conrad, Zum Gedächtnis Edmund Husserls (Ein unveröffentlichter Aufsatz aus der Bayrischen Staatsbibliothek). *Husserl Studies* 38(1): 55–66.

De Santis, Daniele, and Daniele Nuccilli, eds. 2025. *The Philosophy of Wilhelm Schapp: From Phenomenology to Jurisprudence and the Hermeneutics of Stories.* London: Bloomsbury.

Descartes, René. (1641) 1990. *Meditations on First Philosophy / Meditationes de prima philosophia. A Bilingual Edition.* Trans. George Heffernan. Notre Dame: University of Notre Dame Press.

Descartes, René. (1643–1649) 2007. *The Correspondence between Princess Elisabeth of Bohemia and René Descartes.* Trans. Lisa Shapiro. Chicago: The University of Chicago Press.

Descartes, René. (1649) 1989. *The Passions of the Soul.* Trans. Stephen H. Voss. Indianapolis: Hackett.

Doyon, Maxime. 2024. *Phenomenology and the Norms of Perception.* Oxford: Oxford University Press.

Doyon, Maxime, and Maren Wehrle. 2020. Body. In *The Routledge Handbook of Phenomenology and Phenomenological Philosophy*, eds. Daniele De Santis, Burt C. Hopkins, and Claudio Majolino, 123–137. London: Routledge.

Dreyfus, Hubert L., ed. 1982. *Husserl, Intentionality, and Cognitive Science.* Cambridge, MA: The MIT Press.

Dreyfus, Hubert L. 1990. *Being-in-the-World: A Commentary on Heidegger's* Being and Time, Division I. Cambridge, MA: The MIT Press.

Fanon, Frantz. (1952) 2008. *Black Skin, White Masks.* Trans. R. Philcox. New York: Grove Books.

Gadamer, Hans-Georg. (1960) 1989. *Truth and Method*, 2nd revised edition. Trans. Joel Weinsheimer and Donald G. Marshall. New York: Crossroad.

Geiger, Moritz. (1925) 2009. Phänomenologische Ästhetik. In *Anthologie der realistischen Phänomenologie*, eds. Josef Seifert and Cheikh Mbacké Gueye, 391–398. Frankfurt a.M.: Ontos Verlag.

Gethmann, Carl Friedrich. 1993. *Dasein: Erkennen und Handeln. Heidegger im phänomenologischen Kontext.* Berlin: De Gruyter.

Hadjioannou, Christos. 2018. Heidegger's Critique of Technoscience as a Critique of Husserl's Reductive Method. In *Heidegger on Technology*, eds. Aaron J. Wendland, Christopher Merwin, and Christos Hadjioannou, 57–74. London: Routledge.

Hart, James G. 2020. *Hedwig Conrad-Martius' Ontological Phenomenology.* Ed. Rodney K.B. Parker. Dordrecht: Springer.

Heidegger, Martin. (1927) 1962. *Being and Time.* Trans. J. Macquarrie and E. Robinson. Oxford: Basil Blackwell.

Heidegger, Martin. (1930) 1993. On the Essence of Truth. Trans. J. Sallis. In *Martin Heidegger: Basic Writings*, revised and expanded edition, ed. D.F. Krell, 115–38. London: Routledge.

Heidegger, Martin. (1953) 1993. The Question Concerning Technology. Trans. W. Lovitt with revisions by D.F. Krell. In *Martin Heidegger: Basic Writings*, revised and expanded edition, ed. D.F. Krell, 311–41. London: Routledge.

Heidegger, Martin. (1955) 1966. Memorial Address. In *Discourse on Thinking: A Translation of* Gelassenheit, trans. and ed. J.M. Anderson and E.H. Freund, 43–57. New York: Harper and Row Publishers.

Heidegger, Martin. (1964) 1993. The End of Philosophy and the Task of Thinking. Trans. J. Stambaugh. In *Martin Heidegger: Basic Writings*, revised and expanded edition, ed. D.F. Krell, 373–92. London: Routledge.

Heidegger, Martin. 1985. Phänomenologische Interpretationen zu Aristoteles, Einführung in die phänomenologische Forschung, ed. Walter Bröcker and K. Bröckwer-Oltmanns, Early Freiburg lectures of the winter semester 1921/22. In Heidegger Gesamtausgabe, Bd. 61. Frankfurt am Main: Vittorio Klostermann.

Heinämaa, S. 2012. The Body. In The Routledge Companion to Phenomenology, ed. S. Luft and S. Overgaard, pp. 222–232. New York/London: Routledge.

Heinämaa, Sara, Mirja Hartimo, and Timo Miettinen. 2014. Introduction: Methodological, Historical, and Conceptual Starting Points. In *Phenomenology and the Transcendental*, Routledge Research in Phenomenology, eds. Sara Heinämaa, Mirja Hartimo, and Timo Miettinen, 1–20. New York: Routledge.

Held, Klaus. 1966. Lebendige Gegenwart: Die Frage nach der Seinsweise des Transzendentalen Ich bei Edmund Husserl, Entwickelt am Leitfaden der Zeitproblematik. Dordrecht: Martinus Nijhoff (Springer).

Held, K. 1991. Heimwelt, Fremdwelt, die eine Welt. Phänomenologische Forschungen 24/25:305–337.

Held, Klaus. 2003. Husserl's Phenomenology of the Life-World. In *The New Husserl: A Critical Reader*, ed. Donn Welton, 32–65. Bloomington, IN: Indiana University Press.

Hildebrand, Dietrich von. 1930. *Metaphysik der Gemeinschaft: Untersuchungen über Wesen und Wert der Gemeinschaft*. Augsburg: Haas & Grabherr.

Husserl, Edmund. (1900a) 2001. *Logical Investigations*, volume 1 (**LI1**). International Library of Philosophy. Trans. J.N. Finlay. London: Routledge. German edition: Husserl, Edmund. 1975. *Logische Untersuchungen. Erster Band. Prolegomena zur reinen Logik*. Husserliana: Edmund Husserl—Gesammelte Werke XVIII (**Hua XVIII**), ed. E. Holenstein. The Hague: Martinus Nijhoff.

Husserl, Edmund. (1900b) 2001. *Logical Investigations*, volume 2 (**LI2**). International Library of Philosophy. Trans. J.N. Finlay. London: Routledge. German edition: Husserl, Edmund. 1984. *Logische Untersuchungen. Zweiter Band: Untersuchungen zur Phänomenologie und Theorie der Erkenntnis*. Husserliana: Edmund Husserl—Gesammelte Werke XIX (**Hua XIX**), ed. U. Panzer. The Hague: Martinus Nijhoff.

Husserl, Edmund. (1910/1911) 2022. Philosophy as Rigorous Science (**PRS**). In *Phenomenology and the Crisis of Philosophy*, trans. Q. Lauer, 71–147. New York: Harper & Row. German edition: Husserl, Edmund. 1910/1911. Philosophie als strenge Wissenschaft. *Logos* 1: 289–341.

Husserl, Edmund. (1913/1976) 1982. *Ideas Pertaining to a Pure Phenomenology and to a Phenomenological Philosophy. First Book: General Introduction to a Pure Phenomenology*. Trans. F. Kersten. The Hague: Martinus Nijhoff. German edition: Husserl, Edmund. 1976. *Ideen zu einer reinen Phänomenologie und phänomenologischen Philosophie. Erstes Buch*. Husserliana: Edmund Husserl—Gesammelte Werke III/1 (**Hua III/1**), ed. K. Schuhmann. The Hague: Martinus Nijhoff.

Husserl, Edmund. (1931/1950) 1960. *Cartesian Meditations: An Introduction to Phenomenology* (**CM**). Trans. D. Cairns. The Hague: Martinus Nijhoff. German edition: Husserl, Edmund. 1950. *Cartesianische Meditationen und Pariser Vorträge*. Husserliana: Edmund Husserl—Gesammelte Werke I (**Hua I**), ed. S. Strasser. The Hague: Martinus Nijhoff.

Husserl, Edmund. (1936/1976) 1970. *The Crisis of European Sciences and Transcendental Phenomenology* (**CES**). Northwestern University Studies in Phenomenology and Existential Philosophy. Trans. D. Carr. Evanston, IL: Northwestern University Press. German edition: Husserl, Edmund. 1976. *Die Krisis der europäischen Wissenschaften und die transzendentale Phänomenologie: Eine Einleitung in die phänomenologische Philosophie*. Husserliana: Edmund Husserl—Gesammelte Werke VI (**Hua VI**), ed. W. Biemel. Dordrecht: Springer.

Husserl, Edmund. (1939) 1973. *Experience and Judgement: Investigations in a Genealogy of Logic* (**EJ**). Northwestern University Studies in Phenomenology and Existential Philosophy. Trans. J.S. Churchill and K. Ameriks. Evanston, IL: Northwestern University Press. German edition: Husserl, Edmund. 1939. *Erfahrung und Urteil: Untersuchungen zur Genealogie der Logik*, ed. L. Landgrebe. Prague: Academia Verlagsbuchhandlung.

Husserl, Edmund. (1950) 1999. *The Idea of Phenomenology*. Collected Works 8. Trans. W.P. Alston and G. Nakhnikian. Doredrecht: Kluwer. German edition: Husserl, Edmund. 1950. *Die Idee der Phänomenologie: Fünf Vorlesungen*. Husserliana: Edmund Husserl—Gesammelte Werke II (**Hua II**), ed. W. Biemel. The Hague: Martinus Nijhoff.

Husserl, Edmund. (1952) 1989. *Ideas Pertaining to a Pure Phenomenology and to a Phenomenological Philosophy. Second Book: Studies into the Phenomenology of Constitution*. Collected Works 3. Trans. R. Rojcewicz and A. Schuwer. Dordrecht: Kluwer. German edition: Husserl, Edmund. *Ideen zu einer reinen Phänomenologie und phänomenologischen Philosophie. Zweites Buch: Phänomenologische Untersuchungen zur Konstitution*. Husserliana: Edmund Husserl—Gesammelte Werke IV (**Hua IV**), ed. M. Biemel. The Hague: Martinus Nijhoff.

Husserl, Edmund. 1959. *Erste Philosophie (1923/24): Zweiter Teil Theorie der Phänomenologischen Reduktion*. Husserliana: Edmund Husserl—Gesammelte Werke VIII (**Hua VIII**). Ed. R. Boehm. Hague: Martinus Nijhoff.

Husserl, Edmund. (1966) 2001. *Analyses Concerning Active and Passive Synthesis: Lectures on Transcendental Logic*. Collected Works 9. Trans. A. Steinbock. The Hague: Kluwer. German edition: Husserl, Edmund. 1966. *Analysen zur passiven Synthesis. Aus Vorlesungs- und Forschungsmanuskripten 1918–1926*. Husserliana: Edmund Husserl—Gesammelte Werke XI (**Hua XI**), ed. M. Fleischer. The Hague: Martinus Nijhoff.

Husserl, Edmund. 1968. *Phänomenologische Psychologie. Vorlesungen Sommersemester 1925*. Husserliana: Edmund Husserl—Gesammelte Werke IX (**Hua IX**). Ed. W. Biemel. The Hague: Martinus Nijhoff.

Husserl, Edmund. (1969) 1991. *On the Phenomenology of the Consciousness of Internal Time (1893–1917)*. Collected Works 4. Trans. J.B. Brough. Dordrecht: Kluwer. German edition: Husserl, Edmund. 1969. *Zur Phänomenologie des inneren Zeitbewusstseins (1893–1917)*. Husserliana: Edmund Husserl—Gesammelte Werke X (**Hua X**), ed. R. Boehm. The Hague: Martinus Nijhoff.

Husserl, Edmund. (1973) 1997. *Thing and Space. Lectures of 1907*. Collected Works 7. Trans. R. Rojcewicz. Dordrecht: Kluwer. German edition: Husserl, Edmund. 1973. *Ding und Raum. Vorlesungen 1907*. Husserliana: Edmund Husserl—Gesammelte Werke XVI (**Hua XVI**), ed. U. Claesges. The Hague: Martinus Nijhoff.

Husserl, Edmund. 1987. *Aufsätze und Vorträge (1911–1921)*. Husserliana: Edmund Husserl—Gesammelte Werke XXV (**Hua XXV**). Ed. T. Nenon and H.R. Sepp. The Hague: Martinus Nijhoff.

Husserl, Edmund. 2001. *Die Bernauer Manuskripte über das Zeitbewusstsein* (1917/18). Husserliana: Edmund Husserl—Gesammelte Werke XXXIII (**Hua XXXIII**). Ed. R. Bernet and D. Lohmar. Dordrecht: Kluwer.

Husserl, Edmund. 2004. *Wahrnehmung und Aufmerksamkeit. Texte aus dem Nachlass* (1893–1912). Husserliana: Edmund Husserl—Gesammelte Werke XXXVIII (**Hua XXXVIII**). Ed. T. Vongehr and R. Giuliani. Dordrecht: Springer.

Husserl, Edmund. 2008. *Die Lebenswelt. Auslegungen der vorgegebenen Welt und ihrer Konstitution. Texte aus dem Nachlass (1916–1937)*. Husserliana: Edmund Husserl—Gesammelte Werke XXXIX (**Hua XXXIX**). Ed. R. Sowa. Dordrecht: Springer.

Jansen, Julia. 2017. Eidetik. In *Husserl Handbuch. Leben—Werk—Wirkung*, eds. S. Luft and M. Wehrle, 142–149. Stuttgart: J.B. Metzler (Springer Nature).

Kant, Immanuel. (1781/1787) 1998. *Critique of Pure Reason*. The Cambridge Edition of the Works of Immanuel Kant. Trans. Paul Guyer and Allen W. Wood. Cambridge, UK: Cambridge University Press.

Lipps, Hans. 1927. *Das Ding und seine Eigenschaften*. In *Hans Lipps Werke in fünf Bänden*, volume 1. Frankfurt a.M.: Vittorio Klostermann.

Lohmar, Dieter. 2002. Die Idee der Reduktion. Husserls Reduktionen und ihr gemeinsamer methodischer Sinn. In *Die erscheinende Welt. Festschrift für Klaus Held*, eds. H. Hüni and P. Trawny, 751–771. Berlin: Duncker & Humblot.

Luft, Sebastian. 2005. Husserl's Concept of the 'Transcendental Person': Another Look at the Husserl–Heidegger Relationship. *International Journal of Philosophical Studies* 13(2): 141–177.

Luft, Sebastian. 2009. Husserl's Theory of the Phenomenological Reduction: Between Lifeworld and Cartesianism. *Research in Phenomenology* 35(1): 198–234.

Luft, Sebastian. 2011. *Subjectivity and Lifeworld in Transcendental Phenomenology*. Evanston, IL: Northwestern University Press.

Luft, Sebastian, and Ruth Hagengruber, eds. 2018. *Women Phenomenologists on Social Ontology: We-Experiences, Communal Life, and Joint Action*. Dordrecht: Springer

Marion, Jean-Luc. (2013) 2018. *On Descartes' Passive Thought: The Myth of Cartesian Dualism*. Trans. C.M. Gschwandtner. Chicago: The University of Chicago Press.

Mensch, James. 2010. *Husserl's Account of our Consciousness of Time*. Milwaukee, WI: Marquette University Press.

Merleau-Ponty, Maurice. (1945) 2012. *Phenomenology of Perception*. Trans. Donald M. Landes. New York: Routledge.

Merleau-Ponty, Maurice. (2003) 2010. *Institution and Passivity: Course Notes from the Collège de France (1954–1955)*. Trans. L. Lawlor and H. Massey. New York: Routledge.

2

Mertens, Karl. 2017. Phänomenologie des Raumes und der Bewegung. In *Husserl Handbuch. Leben— Werk—Wirkung*, eds. S. Luft and M. Wehrle, 216–222. Stuttgart: J.B. Metzler (Springer Nature).

Moran, D. 2012. From the Natural Attitude to the Life-World. In Husserl's Ideen, ed. L. Embree and T. Nenon Dordrecht, pp. 105–124. Dordrecht: Springer.

Moran, Dermot, and Rodney K.B. Parker. 2015. Editor's Introduction. In *Resurrecting the Phenomenological Movement. Studia Phaenomenologica XV: Early Phenomenology*, 11–24.

Morris, David. 2008. Body. In *Merleau-Ponty: Key Concepts*, ed. Ros Diprose and Jack Reynolds, 111–20, London, UK: Acumen Publishing.

Miron, Ronny. 2021. *Hedwig Conrad-Martius: The Phenomenological Gateway to Reality*. Dordrecht: Springer.

Nenon, Thomas. 2008. Some Differences between Kant's and Husserl's Conceptions of Transcendental Philosophy. *Continental Philosophy Review* 4: 427–439.

Nenon, Thomas. 2005. Kants und Husserls unterschiedliche Bestimmungen der Transzendentalphilosophie. *Jahrbuch für Recht und Ethik/Annual Review of Law and Ethics* 13: 287–298.

Oksala, Johanna. 2022. The Method of Critical Phenomenology: Simone de Beauvoir as a Phenomenologist. *European Journal of Philosophy* 31(1): 137–150.

Pfänder, Alexander. 1900. *Eine Phänomenologie des Wollens. Eine psychologische Analyse*. Leipzig: Johann Ambrosius Barth.

Plessner, Helmuth. (1928) 2019. *Levels of Organic Life and the Human. An Introduction to Philosophical Anthropology*. Trans. M. Hyatt. New York: Fordham University Press.

Reinach, Adolf. (1913) 2007. *Zur Phänomenologie des Rechts. Die apriorischen Grundlagen des bürgerlichen Rechts*. Saarbrücken: VDM Verlag Dr. Müller.

Renker, J. 2009. Heimwelt/Fremdwelt. In Husserl-Lexikon, ed. H.-H. Gander, 131–133. Darmstadt: WBG.

Ricœur, Paul. (1950) 1966. *Freedom and Nature: The Voluntary and the Involuntary*. Northwestern University Studies in Phenomenology and Existential Philosophy. Trans. Erazim Kohák. Evanston, IL: Northwestern University Press.

Rodemeyer, Lanei M. 2006. *Intersubjective Temporality: It's about Time*. Phaenomenologica 176. Dordrecht: Springer.

Rinofner-Kreidl, Sonja. 2000. *Edmund Husserl. Zeitlichkeit und Intentionalität*. Freiburg: Verlag Karl Alber.

Salice, Alessandro. 2015. The Phenomenology of the Munich and Göttingen Circles. *Stanford Encyclopedia of Philosophy*, ed. Edward N. Zalta. https://plato.stanford.edu/archives/win2020/entries/phenomenology-mg/

Sartre, Jean-Paul. (1943) 2018. *Being and Nothingness. An Essay in Phenomenological Ontology*. Trans. S. Richmond. London: Routledge.

Schapp, Wilhelm. (1910) 2013. *Beiträge zu einer Phänomenologie der Wahrnehmung*, 5th edition. Frankfurt a.M.: Vittorio Klostermann.

Scheler, Max. (1923) 1954. *The Nature of Sympathy*. Trans. P. Heath. London: Routledge & Kegan Paul.

Schnell, Alexander. 2019. *Was ist Phänomenologie?* Frankfurt a.M.: Vittorio Klostermann.

Sowa, Rochus. 2009. Eidos. In *Husserl-Lexikon*, ed. Hans-Helmuth Gander, 69–75. Darmstadt: WBG.

Spiegelberg, Herbert. (1960) 1994. *The Phenomenological Movement. A Historical Introduction*, 3rd revised and enlarged edition. Dordrecht: Kluwer Academic Publishers.

Stein, Edith. (1916) 1989. *On the Problem of Empathy*. The Collected Works of Edith Stein, volume 3. Trans. Waltraut Stein. Washington, D.C.: ICS Publications.

Steinbock, Anthony. 1995. *Home and Beyond: Generative Phenomenology after Husserl*. Northwestern University Studies in Phenomenology and Existential Philosophy. Evanston, IL: Northwestern University Press.

Summa, Michela. 2014. *Spatio-Temporal Intertwining. Husserl's Transcendental Aesthetic*. Phaenomenologica 213. Dordrecht: Springer.

Taipale, Joona. 2014. *Phenomenology and Embodiment: Husserl and the Constitution of Subjectivity*. Evanston, IL: Northwestern University Press.

Tengelyi, László. 2007. *Erfahrung und Ausdruck. Phänomenologie im Umbruch bei Husserl und seinen Nachfolgern.* Phaenomenologica 180. Dordrecht: Springer.

Vongehr, Thomas, 2017. Die Geschichte der Rettung von Husserls Nachlass. In *Husserl Handbuch. Leben—Werk—Wirkung*, eds. S. Luft and M. Wehrle, 39–47. Stuttgart: J.B. Metzler (Springer Nature).

Waldenfels, Bernhard. 1997. *Topographie des Fremden. Studien zur Phänomenologie des Fremden*, volume 1. Frankfurt a.M.: Suhrkamp.

Waldenfels, Bernhard. 1998a. *Grenzen der Normalisierung. Studien zur Phänomenologie des Fremden*, volume 2. Frankfurt a.M.: Suhrkamp.

Waldenfels, Bernhard. 1998b. *Sinnesschwellen. Studien zur Phänomenologie des Fremden*, volume 3. Frankfurt a.M.: Suhrkamp.

Waldenfels, Bernhard. 1999. *Vielstimmigkeit der Rede. Studien zur Phänomenologie des Fremden*, volume 4. Frankfurt a.M.: Suhrkamp.

Waldenfels, B. 2000. *Das leibliche Selbst. Vorlesungen zur Phänomenologie des Leibes*, ed. R. Giuliani. Frankfurt am Main: Suhrkamp.

Walther, Gerda. 1923. *Zur Phänomenologie der Mystik*. Halle: M. Niemeyer.

Wehrle, Maren. 2022. Normality as Embodied Space: The Body as Transcendental Condition for Experience. In *The Husserlian Mind*, Routledge Philosophical Minds, ed. Hanne Jacobs, 195–207. London: Routledge.

Wehrle, Maren. 2024. Normality, as a Concept in Phenomenology. In *Encyclopedia of Phenomenology*, eds. N. de Warren and T. Toadvine. Cham: Springer. https://doi.org/10.1007/978-3-030-47253-5_185-1

Zahavi, Dan. 1994. Husserl's Phenomenology of the Body. *Études Phénoménologiques* 10(19): 63–84.

Zahavi, Dan. 2021. Applied Phenomenology: Why it is Safe to Ignore the Epoché. *Continental Philosophy Review* 54: 259–273.

Zahavi, Dan. 2023. Empathy, Alterity, Morality. In *Empathy and Ethics*, eds. S. Ferrarello and M. Englander, 489–500. Lanham, MD: Rowman & Littlefield Publishers.

Zahavi, Dan. 2025a. *Phenomenology: The Basics*, 2nd edition. New York: Routledge.

Zahavi, Dan. 2025b. *Being We: Phenomenological Contributions to Social Ontology*. Oxford: Oxford University Press.

Phenomenology in Action

Contents

M. Wehrle, *The Method(s) of Phenomenology*, https://doi.org/10.1007/978-3-662-71777-6_3

3

What do we do when we practice phenomenology? This can be summarized with a view to historical and contemporary phenomenology as follows: We describe typical experiences of concrete, situated, and historical individuals or groups and try to capture the general structures of these experiences, or of any possible experience at all. We are thereby directed towards the experience of things or the way of experiencing itself. We can therefore focus either on an experience or on that which is experienced, individually or in their necessary coexistence. Philosophically, we inquire back to the formal and genetic conditions of the possibility of this specific experience or of experience in general.

Phenomenology, if it is to remain relevant, up to date, and valid, must constantly expand and test its descriptions and determinations against current experiences. To do justice to the experience of an ever-changing world, the praxis of phenomenology itself must be adapted and renewed from time to time. Merleau-Ponty emphasizes this in his preface to the *Phenomenology of Perception* (1945), which reads like a phenomenological manifesto and a passionate plea for the method of phenomenology. He refers directly to Husserl, when he describes the methodological steps of phenomenology as description, eidetic and transcendental questioning. Going beyond Husserl, he understands these methodological steps as part of a necessarily *situated and engaged phenomenology*.

With Husserl, Merleau-Ponty emphasizes that for phenomenological *description*, that is, for being able to "see the world and to grasp it as a paradox", a certain distance is needed, or in Merleau-Ponty's words a "rupture" of "our familiarity with it" (Merleau-Ponty 2012, p. lxxvii). However, he considers the idea of a disinterested observer—one who has 'bracketed' all prejudices and implicit prior assumptions—to be illusory, as our being and thinking always remain situated and thus bound to a concrete time and place. Nonetheless, Merleau-Ponty makes clear that phenomenology cannot do without a *determination of the general* or eidetics, i.e., a grasp of the facts, structures, or things that go beyond specific contexts and times. But he points out that the determination of such general essences must remain bound to what is: the essence thus attains the status of an always only provisional a priori, i.e., one that is potentially temporary. Finally, he emphasizes that the *transcendental inquiry back to* the conditions of the possibility of experience is incessant. And he emphasizes, that this very inquiry leads to the insight that our concrete being-in-the-world, our temporal, spatial, and cultural situation, are the necessary conditions for experience and knowledge.

■ ■ Phenomenology as Lived Practice

Phenomenology is thus defined by Merleau-Ponty as a method that must orient itself to the things to be investigated and must prove itself ever anew. Phenomenology is therefore never just a theory but above all a lived practice (cf. Depraz 2012). It is a practice, whose method(s) must constantly adapt, legitimize, and optimize themselves in the confrontation with their objects of investigation. The last part of this introduction therefore deals with contemporary phenomenology in action. It looks at the question, what do researchers today do when they practice phenomenology? In the following, I will distinguish between different forms of 'applied' phenomenology, or phenomenology in action.

In the first part, *Contemporary Phenomenology*, the focus is on forms of phenomenology that deal with contemporary phenomena and problems. They are paradigms of 'situated phenomenology' in Merleau-Ponty's sense of the word, where 'situated' refers to the fact that they deal with concrete societal and cultural objects (technology), circumstances, and problems (oppression, racism) descriptively and critically. These approaches combine various humanities and social-science perspectives and often integrate empirical research.

In the second part, *Interdisciplinary Phenomenology*, the focus is on phenomenological research that a) uses empirical results and case studies for the description and determination of their objects of investigation (e.g., temporality, embodiment, self- or world-consciousness) or b) integrates qualitative research methods into phenomenological research.

In the third part, *Phenomenology in other disciplines*, the focus is on the influence of phenomenology on other disciplines, such as psychiatry, sociology, nursing sciences, or neurosciences. Here, the benefits and potential problems of the application of phenomenological methods in these fields are discussed.

3.1 Contemporary Phenomenology

Especially since the 1980s, various streams of phenomenology have developed, such as postphenomenology or critical phenomenology, that connect to 'classical' phenomenology in various ways but also differ from it. Much contemporary phenomenology also connects in various ways to other philosophical and scientific disciplines, such as philosophy of mind, cognitive science, sociology, poststructuralism, and political theory, to name just a few. Increasingly, contemporary phenomenology also refers to empirical research and case studies. Yet, despite the divergences between these streams and between them and their classical forebears, they all share the same subject of investigation or the same research questions: How do subjects generally or specifically experience and understand themselves and the world, and what are the general, special, necessary, or contingent conditions of this experience? Anthony Vincent Fernandez speaks in this regard of three layers of phenomenological research, that focus on three different subject matters: *existentials, modes,* and (the problem of) *prejudices* (cf. Fernandez 2017). In the following, I take this as my orientation, when I differentiate between three lines of investigation that lead to different methods, or better, to different methodological foci.

- First, is *the general philosophical question about the necessary or general structures of experience, cognition, or being* in general. This would theoretically correspond to a transcendental or a general ontological question. Phenomenological investigations of this level aim to uncover the structure of human existence in general or the framework through which any meaning is revealed to us.
- Second, is *the question about specific forms and manifestations of concretely situated experience*. Investigations of this level focus on the concrete modes of situated experience, i.e., the different ways in which the world can be experienced or

3

understood (e.g., in different material circumstances, social contexts, or historical epochs).

— Third, is *the question about the elimination of prejudice and the epistemological
claim of impartiality*. Investigations of this level focus on whether—or to what
extent—impartiality can be achieved by methodological precautions of one
kind or another. These range from Husserl's method of bracketing to critical
reflection on subjective habits, prejudices, and assumptions.

▪▪ Basic and Applied Debates

Contemporary philosophical phenomenology includes debates of two kinds: foundational and applied. Debates on the foundation of phenomenology generally deal
with the goals, methods, and subject matter of phenomenology. Applied debates,
on the other hand, typically deal with the description of certain features or aspects
of human existence. The latter can refer to general structures or conditions of
human existence (first level, *existentials*), such as corporeality or intersubjectivity.
Or they can refer to specific features of human existence (second level, *modes*),
such as those that have been ignored or downplayed in the phenomenological
canon, like gender (Oksala 2016; Young 2005), sexual orientation (Ahmed 2006),
or race (Alcoff 2006; Lee 2014).

Today, we see an increase in phenomenological research that falls into the category of *applied phenomenology* (next to historical research on phenomenology
and phenomenological contributions to theoretical debates in the philosophy of
mind and perception). However, this does not mean that foundational questions
and criticism do not also factor into these discussions. For example, the concrete
investigation of aspects of human existence that were ignored in the canonical
texts (second level, *modes*) can raise fundamental philosophical questions about
goals, methods, and topics (first level, *existentials*) that were also overlooked
(Oksala 2016). Moreover, critical phenomenology that engages with the question
of biased or impartial knowledge (third level, *prejudices*), in turn questions the
determination of supposedly eidetic or essential structures of existence (first level,
existentials) (Oksala 2022). In the following, I will present two examples of contemporary phenomenology that illustrate one—or combine several—of the above-
mentioned layers of investigation. Despite their differences in subject matter and
methodological focus, we will encounter in all of three examples, the 'classic' phenomenological methods and aims introduced in (▶ Chap. 2), that is, *describing
without prejudice, determining the general, or inquiring back to (general or historical) conditions*.

3.1.1 Critical Phenomenology

Many current phenomenological approaches draw on the methods, concepts, and
results of historical or classical phenomenology but also critically question and
develop them further. They do this by:

(a) shifting the focus of description from supposedly general or exemplary experiences to previously unnoticed, marginalized, or specific forms of experience,
(b) critically addressing the required impartiality of the description based on this shift to previously overlooked experiences,
(c) subjecting the status of the supposedly general and transcendental determination of experiential structures to a critical examination based on concrete descriptions and case studies, and
(d) inquiring-back to the concrete, i.e., the historical and material, conditions of these specific experiences.

The result is the establishment of new phenomenological areas of several distinct kinds. The first, which follows the model of Simone de Beauvoir (and Merleau-Ponty), can be understood as a **situated and committed phenomenology**. It describes the experiences of concrete subjects or groups of subjects, such as women in the patriarchal society of France in the 1940s (Beauvoir 1949), considering their material and historical circumstances and thus the conditions of their experiences. The focus is then no longer on the possibility of experience in general, but on the practical possibilities and impossibilities of the experience of these specific, situated individuals.

■ ■ **Genetic and Genealogical Description**
This involves either a concrete genetic-phenomenological investigation (according to the development and conditions of the particular subject) or a genealogical investigation (according to the external historical and material conditions). Both can be understood as a concrete form of critique of knowledge. The genealogical direction of analysis, therefore, does not aim at individual factors (past experiences, individual developments, or habits), but at social circumstances, structures, discourses, or power relations in the sense of Michel Foucault (cf. Oksala 2016; Heyes 2020). In both cases, the question concerning the conditions and limits of the given experience is central.

Critical and political phenomenology combine phenomenological descriptions of experience from an internal perspective with genealogical determinations from an external perspective, and show their necessary intertwinement. The former describes experience and action from the first-person perspective, i.e., how a certain situation is experienced by subjects, how subjects act and interact in this situation, and how they collectively *institute* meaning. The latter describes the material, historical, social, or discursive factors that provide the framework conditions that determine which forms of subjectivity are possible. In the words of Merleau-Ponty, the genealogical perspective refers to the fact of *being situated* in a world with already *instituted* meanings and norms; while the phenomenological perspective refers to the active *being-in-situation* of embodied subjects, i.e., how these subjects take up their situation, relate to it, shape, and change it. Decidedly critical or political phenomenological approaches go beyond a purely descriptive level and seek to connect the phenomenological description with normative and political questions.

▪▪ Political Phenomenology

In recent years, political phenomenology has moved to the center of (applied) phenomenological studies more generally (cf. Leghissa and Staudigl 2007; Bedorf and Herrmann 2020; Herrmann et al. 2024; Staudigl 2025). Political phenomenology is a subfield of political theory that seeks to highlight and establish the relevance of the phenomenological approach for political theory. On the one hand, it considers the 'political' phenomenologically, and on the other hand, it identifies relevant political concepts in historical phenomenology. It addresses questions about why politics becomes necessary at all and how it arises in intersubjective experience, or what constitutes a political experience or action. In short, when, why, and how does experience become political or gain political relevance (political experience)? Are there typical political ways of being or realms of being (political ontology)? Political phenomenology thereby identifies political phenomena and analyzes them with phenomenological concepts such as 'intersubjectivity', 'institution of meaning', 'appearance', 'existence', 'worldliness', etc. At the same time, it examines the extent to which various paradigms of methodological reflection in phenomenology are relevant for approaching the political. This includes, for example, the investigation of eidetic structures and types of experience, the hermeneutic analysis of our being-in-the-world, and genetic analyses that allow us to uncover the social and historical situatedness of the self, others, and the world, in order to understand the space of experience itself as the result of political struggles. In this context, political philosophers such as Hannah Arendt play a central role. Her phenomenological orientation and relevance is becoming increasingly clear (Loidolt 2018). The aim of a contemporary political philosophy is therefore not merely to help reformulate or add to central concepts in political theory, but also to establish a political phenomenology in a more systematic way by connecting first-person experience with normative political principles (Bedorf and Herrmann 2020).

▪▪ Critical Phenomenology

Critical phenomenology (Weiss et al. 2020, cf. also Magrì and McQueen 2022) also understands its critique as political. It aims, for example, to expand the canon of authors and concepts in classical phenomenology by bringing previously marginalized forms of experience to the fore. In doing so, it seeks to put the (implicit) assumptions of classical phenomenology, its methods, concepts, and general descriptions to the test. This concerns, for example, the question of whether the aspects of embodiment determined as general (e.g., in Husserl and Merleau-Ponty) really include all possible embodied subjects and circumstances or merely reflect a partial view that was considered an unquestioned norm (standard) at the time of determination (on this, see ▶ Chap. 2, ▶ Sect. 2.2, Critique of Essentialism). Critical phenomenology combines theoretical critique with political activism. Descriptions of oppression, violence, and discrimination are intended to give voice and visibility to marginalized people and their experiences by denouncing these conditions and motivating change. It draws on descriptions and general concepts of 'historical' phenomenology, such as those found in Husserl (e.g., the distinction between lived body and physical body, intentionality, horizon, lifeworld, spatiality, temporality, etc.), Merleau-Ponty (e.g., body schema, habitual and actual body, intentional arc, motor habit, situated spatiality, institution, etc.) Sartre (e.g., existence, situation, being-for-itself/in-itself/for-others, analysis of the objectifying gaze, etc.) or Levinas (e.g., radical alterity, the third party, etc.) (cf. Bedorf 2010). These concepts are in turn linked with discourse-oriented, sociological, or postcolonial approaches, and thereby expanded, or critically modified.

■■ **Methodological Debates**

Methodologically, critical phenomenology aims to distinguish its approach from that of classical phenomenology. When it comes to the *transcendental dimension of phenomenology*, for example, critical phenomenology inquires back to the conditions of givenness, just as classical phenomenology. However, the conditions it seeks are not the general structures of consciousness, but the historical and political structures of intersubjectivity. Rather than identifying transcendental structures that apply to all possible subjectivity, it aims to investigate contingent conditions and social structures, such as, for example, colonialism, anti-Black racism, or heteropatriarchy (cf. Guenther 2021, p. 6). These concrete structures "shape our experience, not just empirically or in a piecemeal fashion, but in what we might call a quasi-transcendental fashion", as Lisa Guenther puts it (Guenther 2020, p. 12). Social structures can therefore be seen as *transcendental* insofar as they refer not only to worldly conditions but also to inter-subjective sense-making. As such, they represent styles or ways of seeing, hearing, behaving, or relating that are constitutive of experience. In this sense, the transcendental epoché is still of relevance to critical phenomenology, as it leads to the discovery of the intersubjective constitution of the lifeworld, and thus its historical and political dimensions, as Johanna Oksala argues (Oksala 2022, p. 141f.) However, social structures are merely *quasi-transcendental* insofar as they are neither features of a transcendental subjectivity, nor essential or universal. Nonetheless these institutionalized and politicized historical, that is, empirical, structures operate in a self-evident, and thus almost necessary way, because their development and contingency has been forgotten (cf. Doyon 2024, p. 196). Critical phenomenology thus focuses on how quasi-transcendental structures like heteronormative gender norms, ableism, or racism shape specific forms of embodiment, experience, and affection, and thus the way one experiences, moves, behaves, and expresses oneself (cf. Guenther 2013; Al-Saji 2017, 2024).

The attitude of critical phenomenologists to the eidetic method or the search for universal structures ranges from one of extreme caution to one of outspoken rejection. In taking this more skeptical stance, they (a) point to the limits inherent in the practice of identifying generalities, that is, they question the possibility of eidetic variation, (b) problematize the aim of the method as it tends to negate differences and thus oppose the normative aim of critical phenomenology (cf. Oksala 2022), and (c) question the very existence of such universal structures. These criticisms of classical methods are relevant for the phenomenological project as a whole. However, they must not stand in opposition to it. The fact that there are contingent quasi-transcendental structures that shape experience differently, does not mean that there are no basic generalities or similarities. On the contrary, without basic structures of embodiment or subjectivity, one would not even be able to experience or identify these differences. In the example of the experience of the other (see ▶ Chap. 2, ▶ Sect. 2.3) we have seen that the two-sided nature of embodiment common to all animal beings (that they are *Leibkörper*) is crucial to being able to perceive the other as (other) subject. Husserl's minimalist account of common experiential or subjective structures can in this sense be helpful for making the differences in situation, embodiment, and related questions of (dis-)ability, gender, race, and oppression, visible and comparable. (cf. Doyon 2024, p. 202). In turn, a critical stance on eidetic phenomenology helps us avoid assuming false universalities and reminds us of the limits and contingency of our own reasoning capacities.

Critical phenomenology thus carries forward the phenomenological project as critical attitude and praxis that aims to see the world anew, while also going beyond mere description by understanding itself as a political praxis. As Lisa Guenther puts it: "[C]ritical phenomenology is a struggle for liberation from the structures that privilege, naturalize, and normalize certain experiences of the world while marginalizing, pathologizing, and discrediting others. [...] [T]he ultimate goal of critical phenomenology is not just to interpret the world, but also to change it" (Guenther 2020, p. 16).

▪▪ Phenomenology of the Alien and Feminist Phenomenology

Even before the establishment of a decidedly 'critical phenomenology', similar approaches in phenomenology were being developed by the German phenomenologist Bernhard Waldenfels. He brought phenomenology, especially French phenomenology, into a fruitful dialogue with postmodern theories, such as those of Jacques Derrida, Michel Foucault, and others (cf. Waldenfels 1983, 1987). In his phenomenology of the alien, Waldenfels, inspired by Husserl, Merleau-Ponty, Michel Foucault, and especially Emmanuel Levinas, develops a decidedly critical and ethical phenomenology of responsiveness and alterity. Here, questions of order, normality, normation, and exclusion are addressed (cf. Waldenfels 1990, 1994, 1997–1999). Parallel to this, feminist phenomenology was established in the 1990s; it attempts to strengthen the perspective of embodied experience within feminist philosophy, as well as subject experience to critical analysis (cf. Stoller and Vetter 1997; Fisher and Embree 2000; Stoller et al. 2005; Landweer and Marcinski 2016).

▪▪ Canonical Examples of Critical Phenomenology

Simone de Beauvoir's analyses of the discourse on—and the situated experiences of—women in a patriarchal society in *The Second Sex* (1949), can be read as an early example of a critical or political phenomenology. Soo too can Frantz Fanon's poignant descriptions of the experience of the colonized subject in *Black Skin, White Masks* (1952), and Iris Marion Young's canonical essay *Throwing Like a Girl* (1980). In each of these texts, the neutrality or universality of supposedly general determinations of the structures of consciousness or being are questioned in light of concrete experiences. For example, is Sartre's ontological determination of being-for-others, which expresses itself under the objectifying gaze of the other subject, universally valid?

■ ■ The Violence of the Gaze

According to Sartre, we become aware that the world exists not only for-us, but also for other subjects, through the gaze of the other. The sudden awareness of being seen is accompanied by an explicit object consciousness or 'thetic self-consciousness', as Sartre calls it. In this, we experience ourselves as objects in the world, which can be looked at, seen, and judged. What we are (our properties, our value) thus turns out to be primarily determined by other subjects. We are dependent on their recognition and acknowledgment. So far so good. But what does this seemingly neutral circumstance look like in the lived experience of a black person in the context of French (post-)colonial society? In the chapter 'The lived experience of the Black Man' of his book *Black Skin, White Masks* ([1952] 2008, 89–119), Fanon takes us into his perspective: Starting with the exclamation 'Dirty N****', he describes what this gaze, this immediate attribution, means for him. At first, he tries to reject the attribution. When this fails, he takes the path of rational argumentation to defend his equality and thus his status as subject. When this also fails, as does the attempt to establish a positive counter-identity, he finally capitulates under the burden of external determination. This intense description painfully reveals that the subject-object relation described by Sartre is, in reality, neither reciprocal nor antagonistic in a neutral way, but highly asymmetric and dependent on given power relations.

Not every concrete subject has the same ability to objectify the Other and thus co-determine what the other is (what properties he has as an object or being). And not everybody can escape this objectification, this gaze, by assuming the subject position and returning the gaze. The colonized subject is completely denied subject status; it remains an object. This constant objectification is manifested in a loss of self-evidence. Fanon describes how seemingly banal actions require constant attention and reflection, as he does not want to stand out, be seen as different or even dangerous. This is accompanied by a loss of individuality, as the subject is reduced to his skin color, race, or group affiliation. Thus, he cannot develop or change his identity himself. It is predetermined by the colonial Other, for example, by the then-current Western anthropological and historical research, which defined 'people of color' as primitive and underdeveloped.

> ▶ **Example: The colonial gaze**
>
> "Dirty nigger! Or simply, Look, a Negro! I came into this world anxious to uncover the meaning of things, my soul desirous to be at the origin of the world, and here I am an object among other objects.
>
> Locked in this suffocating reification, I appealed to the Other so that his liberating gaze, gliding over my body suddenly smoothed of rough edges, would give me back the lightness of being I thought I had lost, and taking me out of the world put me back in the world. But just as I get to the other slope I stumble, and the Other fixes me with his gaze, his gestures and attitude, the same way you fix a preparation with a dye [...]
>
> And then we were given the occasion to confront the white gaze. An unusual weight descended on us. The real world robbed us of our share. In the white world, the man of color encounters difficulties in elaborating his body schema. The image of one's body is solely negating. It's an image in the third person. All around the body reigns an

3

atmosphere of certain uncertainty. I know that if I want to smoke, I shall have to stretch out my right arm and grab the pack of cigarettes lying at the other end of the table. As for the matches, they are in the left drawer, and I shall have to move back a little. And I make all these moves, not out of habit, but by implicit knowledge. [...]

Beneath the body schema I had created a historical-racial schema. The data I used were provided not by "remnants of feelings and notions of the tactile, vestibular, kinesthetic, or visual nature", but by the Other, the white man, who had woven me out of a thousand details, anecdotes, and stories. [...]

Maman, look, a Negro; I'm scared!" Scared! Scared! Now they were beginning to be scared of me. I wanted to kill myself laughing, but laughter had become out of the question.

I couldn't take it any longer, for I already knew there were legends, stories, history, and especially the historicity that Jaspers had taught me. As a result, the body schema, attacked in several places, collapsed, giving way to an epidermal racial schema [...]. In the train, it was a question of being aware of my body, no longer in the third person but in triple. In the train, instead of one seat, they left me two or three. I was no longer enjoying myself. I was unable to discover the feverish coordinates of the world. I existed in triple: I was taking up room [...]. I was responsible not only for my body but also for my race and my ancestors. I cast an objective gaze over myself, discovered my blackness, my ethnic features; deafened by cannibalism, backwardness, fetishism, racial stigmas, slave traders, and above all, yes, above all, the grinning *Y a bon Banania* [...].

Disoriented, incapable of confronting the Other, the white man, who had no scruples about imprisoning me, I transported myself on that particular day far, very far, from myself, and gave myself up as an object. What did this mean to me? Peeling, stripping my skin, causing a hemorrhage that left congealed black blood all over my body. Yet this reconsideration of myself, this thematization, was not my idea. I wanted quite simply to be a man among men. I would have liked to enter our world young and sleek, a world we could build together." (Fanon 2008, pp. 89–92) ◄

■ ■ Existence Before Essence

Just like Fanon, Iris Marion Young examines the existence of specific subjects and concrete forms of intentionality. However, her subjects are girls in America in the 1980s, and her concrete forms of intentionality are those of bodily movement, with a specific focus on the way that girls throw balls. Is there a typically female style of movement, and if so, why and how does it emerge? Do we have to think of general terms like 'existence' in a gender-specific way? Before Young begins her analysis of the motility of girls, she defines—in relation to Simone de Beauvoir—what she means by female existence. 'Femininity' is not a mysterious quality or essence (in the sense of being) that all women have because of their biological femaleness. Rather, 'femininity' is "a set of structures and conditions which delimit the typical situation of being a woman in a particular society, as well as the typical way in which this situation is lived by the women themselves" (Young 1980, p. 140).

This also means that not *every* woman has to be 'female' or throw in a supposedly feminine way. The structures and behaviors that are considered typical for the situation of women (or other subject groups) are therefore not a priori necessary but historically changeable and contingent. With Sartre, one could say, existence (actions and projects) comes before essence. But with Beauvoir, one must add, every existence is concretely situated. This situation in turn provides the framework and conditions for what we can or must do. The situation and the associated activities and projects shape our physicality as well as our character (who we are). However, this situation can also be transformed, by one's own or others' actions or via external structural or material changes. Such a changed situation in turn opens new ways of existence, allowing one to do things differently or to do other things. Young, like Beauvoir, thus assumes that the way we are-in-the-world, our existence, is significantly shaped by our concrete situation.

To describe and determine the typical female movement pattern, Young combines Merleau-Ponty's eidetic general descriptions of bodily intentionality with Beauvoir's concrete application of phenomenological and existentialist concepts to the situation of women. Young agrees with Merleau-Ponty that there is a general level of description, applicable to any possible human existence, that captures the relation of the lived body to its world. However, she emphasizes that there is a particular style of bodily behavior that is typical for female (or other specific) existence(s); "this style for her is composed of certain *modalities* of the structures and conditions of bodily existence in the world" (Young 1980, p. 141).

Beauvoir's portrayal of the existence of women in patriarchal society provides the framework for these developing modalities. The concrete situation of women and girls is therefore characterized by a fundamental tension between *immanence* and *transcendence*. On the one hand, women, like men, are characterized by their transcendence—an active orientation towards the world, in which they freely and responsibly pursue their projects. On the other hand, they are defined by culture and society as the other of man, his non-essential counterpart. In this respect, they are more object than subject and are reduced to the sphere of immanence, i.e., to a background domestic and caring role, as opposed to a publicly visible creative role. Culturally and socially, women are thus denied subjectivity, autonomy, and creativity, even though these are considered characteristics of human nature in general. In patriarchal society, they become characteristics of men alone. Drawing on this analysis, Young's thesis is "that the modalities of feminine bodily comportment, motility, and spatiality exhibit this same tension between transcendence and immanence, between subjectivity and being a mere object" (Young 1980, p. 141).

■ ■ Embodied Social Norms

Why, and to what extent, do women and girls move differently in space, take up less space, maintain distance, move more hesitantly, or trust their physical abilities less? Why do they not use their whole body when throwing? Young, who takes these questions as her starting point, makes clear that the answer cannot be based on anatomical reasons alone. It is the result of their concrete situation, including gender-specific roles, expectations, tasks, and upbringing. Our body, with which, and through which, we are in and to the world, always also embodies the concrete social circumstances and norms of our life world, which have passed into our flesh and blood through repeated practice. And, as such, these circumstances and norms are no longer thematized but take on a kind of self-evidence (cf. Wehrle 2016, 2017).

3

> ▶ **Example: Throwing like a girl**
>
> "The three modalities of feminine motility are that feminine movement exhibits an ambiguous transcendence, an inhibited intentionality, and a discontinuous unity with its surroundings [...].
>
> 1. [...] While feminine bodily existence is a transcendence and openness to the world, it is an *ambiguous transcendence*, a transcendence which is at the same time laden with immanence [...] The lived body as transcendence is pure fluid action, the continuous calling forth of capacities, which are applied to the world. Rather than simply beginning in immanence, feminine bodily existence remains in immanence, or better is overlaid with immanence, even as it moves out toward the world in motions of grasping, manipulating, and so on. In the previous section, I observed that a woman typically refrains from throwing her whole body into a motion, and rather concentrates moti[o]n in one part of the body alone while the rest of the body remains relatively immobile. Only a part of the body, that is, moves out toward a task while the rest remains rooted in immanence.
> 2. [...] Typically, the feminine body underuses its real capacity, both as the potentiality of its physical size and strength and as the real skills and coordination which are available to it. Feminine bodily existence is an *inhibited intentionality*, which simultaneously reaches toward a projected end with an "I can" and withholds its full bodily commitment to that end in a self-imposed "I cannot". [...]
> 3. [...] The third modality of feminine bodily existence is that it stands in *discontinuous unity* with both itself and its surroundings. I remarked earlier that in many motions which require the active engagement and coordination of the body as a whole to be performed properly, women tend to locate their motion in a part of the body only, leaving the rest of the body relatively immobile. Motion such as this is discontinuous with itself. That part of the body which is transcending toward an aim is in relative disunity from those which remain immobile. The undirectedness and wasted motion which is often an aspect of feminine engagement in a task also manifests this lack of body unity [...].
>
> In summary, the modalities of feminine bodily existence have their root in the fact that feminine existence does not experience the body as a mere thing—A fragile thing, which must be picked up and coaxed into movement, a thing which exists as looked at and acted upon. To be sure, any lived body exists as a material thing as well as a transcending subject. For feminine bodily existence, however, the body is often lived as a thing which is other than it, a thing like other things in the world. To the extent that feminine existence lives her body as a thing, she remains rooted in immanence, is inhibited, and retains a distance from her body as transcending movement and from engagement in the world's possibilities." (Young 1980, pp. 145–148) ◀

Methodologically, the general structure of the intentionality of bodily movement serves as a starting point here. Against this background, the specificity and otherness of female subjectivations become clear. The 'inhibited intentionality' described by Young, which characterizes a girl's behavior (here: throwing) in a patriarchally organized society, thus becomes visible in comparison to generally determined structures of movement. But how general and essential is Merleau-Ponty's description of the bodily 'I-can' or Sartre's description of existence as a project? Isn't there a risk here of elevating a typically male behavior to universality and understanding the female in comparison as a deviation or inferior manifestation? Young herself later criticized her analysis as too unreflective, as it contains an implicit normative evaluation that takes male throwing as the norm. Should hesitation in movement or consideration for others (by taking up little space) always be regarded negatively? Must every movement necessarily be uniform and fluid? Is all attention to the body as an object problematic? These questions can only be answered in individual cases and with reference to a particular context.

The bottom line is: Intentionality, understood as the free 'I-can' and exploratory orientation towards the world, is by no means a neutral description that applies to all bodily subjects. It seems to be either an inductive generalization from concrete experience, in this case, the experience of male phenomenologists, or a mere ideal of optimal movement. However, this criticism is only directed at the quality of a specific orientation; intentionality as a structure of experience, as either 'consciousness of something' or bodily directedness towards the world (Merleau-Ponty), which applies to every possible bodily subject (or even organism), is not questioned as such.

■ ■ **The Eidetics of Inhibited Intentionality**
How one is intentionally directed to the world can therefore be more or less free or inhibited, but the fact remains that every subjective experience is directed to the world. That is, all consciousness is characterized by the structure of intentionality. It is on the basis of such a general determination, that differences in specific orientations can be distinguished from each other: an unhindered, free, and exploratory form on the one hand, and a suppressed, constrained, or impaired form on the other. Without the assumption of such a common essence, which of course must constantly be checked and possibly adjusted, no differences could be described at all and thus no criticisms could be formulated. A minimal eidetic determination of the experiences of certain subjects and their living conditions is therefore the prerequisite for any form of ethical or political evaluation, as demanded by critical theory, feminist theory, and so-called critical phenomenology.

■ ■ **Critique of Privileged Generalization**
However, the way in which these concepts and structures are described, and the way in which particular experiences and subjects are selected or rejected as objects of analysis, can and must be criticized. If one wants to identify and determine general and necessary structures and aspects of experience, these must include all kinds of experience, especially those that are not usually considered. They must be diverse and plural. Which determinations are general and necessary, and which are only due to my subjective perspective, my research interests, or my blind spots? Critical and political analyses remind phenomenology to take its commitment to unbiased description seriously. And they show it the limits of this commitment: they show how, despite the best of intentions, one's own certainties, privileges, and norms often seep in and influence the description.

▪▪ Queer Phenomenology

Another example of how the self-evidence of the phenomenological-philosophical perspective can be critically questioned is the 'Queer Phenomenology' developed by Sara Ahmed in her book of the same name (Ahmed 2006). Ahmed starts from the descriptions of objects, space, and movement by Husserl, Merleau-Ponty, and Heidegger, to reveal the concrete conditions that apply to these seemingly universal determinations. All these descriptions emphasize the importance of familiarity, concordance, availableness, habit, or 'home', which make up for a successful orientation in the world. But is the experience of a self-evident orientation and situation essential for every subject? What role do discordance, resistance, and disorientation play here?

Using the **leitmotif of orientation**, Ahmed describes and shifts classic analyses of perception and space, revealing their hidden social meanings. For Ahmed, the role of orientation is not just a spatial one. Living somewhere or staying somewhere refers to lingering in a place and time: If orientation is a matter of the way in which we arrange and settle ourselves in space—the way in which we inhabit it—then it becomes clear that orientation requires time. Time is needed to occupy the space, to get used to it, or to make it our own. Even if orientations seem to be about where we are in the *present*, they also point us to the *future*. This is what Ahmed calls the possibility of (or even hope for) a change of direction. It consists in the fact that we do not always know where certain paths will lead us: There is therefore always the risk of deviating from the straight path. But this is exactly what makes a new future possible, and such a future might also include getting lost, losing our way, or becoming queer.

Ahmed applies the concept of orientation to both sexual orientation and social, or ethnic orientation. Sexual orientation, Ahmed says, also requires time and work, and is always open to possible changes of direction. This means that one does not simply have a sexual orientation any more than one simply has a spatial orientation: Being heterosexual or *straight* is something we become. We are encouraged to turn to those 'objects' prescribed to us by heterosexual culture, and, at the same time, to turn away from other 'objects'. The queer subject within heterosexual culture is thus the one who deviates from the norm and is socially marked and made visible as such.

Racism can also be described as an orientation. Racism assigns or denies certain bodies particular directions, places, and movements So, on the one hand, we are racialized, due to the way we (are able to) occupy space, and on the other hand, the space itself is already an effect of racialization and is thus already occupied by racism. Ahmed is interested in how non-white bodies can orient themselves in a 'white society', i.e., can 'be at home'. In her descriptions, it becomes clear that not all spaces or objects are equally accessible to everyone. Bodies that do not conform to the 'white' standard of certain spaces are denied entry, which causes disorientation.

What Ahmed wants to show with her queer phenomenology is that it is not so easy to get to the things themselves. This is because neither 'the things' nor the spaces they occupy—that is, what is present, close, accessible, or familiar to us—

are random or neutral. We do not acquire our orientations by finding things here or there. Rather, certain objects are available to us because of paths, or 'lines' as Ahmed calls them, that we have already taken: Our biographies follow a certain pattern, through which we are also guided in a certain way (birth, childhood, adolescence, marriage, reproduction, death). The concept of 'orientation' allows Ahmed to show how life is guided in certain directions and not others, precisely by the demand to follow what is already given to us. So, this is not just about general temporal, genetic, or spatial aspects, but about the social meanings and orders that are intertwined with them. For a life to count as a good life, for example, it must set out in a certain direction and reach milestones that align with the social norms of the given society. A queer life, according to Ahmed, is one that deviates from these social landmarks and life courses (cf. Ahmed 2006, p. 21). Ahmed advocates confronting *phenomenology with its own self-evidence* through and with concrete orientations. In this context, moments of disorientation are to be collected, described, and thematized so that we can think in a different direction, which could lead us to the limits of social agreement, of the common, shared, or general.

> ▶ **Example: The hidden horizon of Husserl's desk**
>
> "The background to the object, which allows it to be put to work, depends upon work that is repeated over time that is often 'hidden from view'. Perhaps where Husserl's gaze fails to wander is into other spaces, such as the space of the kitchen—that is, as spaces that are often associated with the 'work' that tends toward the body in terms of caring for it and sustaining it. Does Husserl's gaze avoid wandering there insofar as those spaces are shaped by concealed labor; as the labor that gives him the capacity to 'think' about the writing table? In a way, a queer phenomenology is involved in the project of 'turning the tables' on phenomenology by turning toward other kinds of tables. Turning the tables would also allow us to return, a loving return we might even say, to the objects that already appear within phenomenology, such as Husserl's table, now so worn. Such tables, when turned, would come to life as something to think 'with' as well as 'on'." (Ahmed 2006, p. 63) ◀

Ahmed's description starts with typical objects of historical phenomenology, such as Husserl's desk or the table in general, and puts them into concrete contexts. She thus 'queers' them, i.e., robs them of their self-evidence. In doing so, she thematizes the material and social conditions that precede a philosophical description but usually remain hidden and unnoticed. Through the *noematic guideline* (table) and the *concrete variation of a general concept* (orientation), she succeeds in positively thematizing the differences, contingencies, and deviations, without ever losing sight of the general that connects them. Although queer descriptions and objects lead us to our limits, they still manage, literally, to bring us to the table to make orientation as such phenomenologically describable. The goal of such a **phenomenology and politics of disorientation** for Ahmed is to maintain astonishment about the queer forms of experience and social coexistence, and to show new possibilities and directions.

3

> ▶ **Example: The social order of tables**
>
> "[F]ar away from home, my partner and I are on holiday on a resort on an island. Mealtimes bring everyone together. We enter the dining room, where we face many tables placed alongside each other. Table after table ready for action, waiting for bodies who arrive to take up their space, to be seated. In taking up space, I am taken back. I face what seems like a shocking image. In front of me, on the tables, couples are seated. Table after table, couple after couple, taking the same form: one man sitting by one woman around a 'round table', facing each other 'over' the table. Of course, I 'know' this image-it is a familiar one, after all. But I am shocked by the sheer force of the regularity of that which is familiar: how each table presents the same form of sociality as the form of the heterosexual couple. How is it possible, with all that is possible, that the same form is repeated again and again? How does the openness of the future get closed down into so little in the present?
>
> We sit down. I look down, acutely aware of inhabiting a form that is not the same as that repeated along the line of the tables, although of course my partner and I remain in line insofar as we are a couple. The wrong kind of couple, however-it has to be said. Being out of line can be uncomfortable. We know this. This case of discomfort is enabled by a sense of wonder. Rather than just seeing the familiar, which of course means that it passes from view, I felt wonder and surprise at the regularity of its form, as the form of what arrived at the table, as forms that get repeated, again and again, until they are 'forgotten' and simply become forms of life. To wonder is to remember the forgetting and to see the repetition of form as the 'taking form' of the familiar. It is hard to know why it is that we can be "shocked" by what passes by us as familiar." (Ahmed 2006, pp. 82–83) ◀

Although Ahmed's is a *situated and descriptive phenomenology*, her descriptions certainly have a *transcendental philosophical significance*. Here too one could speak of an a priori: The given circumstances, discourses, and social norms already determine life and thus the practical possibilities and the style of experience in advance (before they are ever reflected upon). However, this a priori is not transcendental in the classical sense, but **historically changeable** (cf. Aldea and Allen 2016) or 'quasi-transcendental', as Guenther has put it (Guenther 2020, p. 12). Here connections to genealogical approaches, which go back to Friedrich Nietzsche and Michel Foucault and ask about the historically-discursively relative conditions of possibility of morality, knowledge, and power, become apparent.

▪▪ Phenomenology as Critique

Even if not every phenomenology explicitly reflects on concrete social circumstances and power structures, ultimately every phenomenology should be critical according to its own method, i.e., it should reflect on its own starting position, take a critical distance from it, and remain open to other perspectives. Phenomenology thus already has an inherent critical potential. It represents an immanent critique of experience, i.e., it criticizes its own experience, its conditions, influences, and limits (cf. Aldea 2016). Only such a critique makes it possible to describe the experience of other subjects from their own perspective (or to let them describe it), to address and communicate with others (second-person perspective), instead of merely evaluating them from the outside (third-person perspective), according to already established normative criteria. Such a critique goes hand in hand with the *insight into the intersubjective dimension of all meaning* and the unavoidable transcendence of others. The actual lesson of phenomenology is therefore that we are dependent on others, both theoretically and practically. Theoretically, we need others in order to move from the merely subjective perspective to one of objective validity. Practically, we need others to realize our possibilities, to attribute and experience meaning, and to form a personal identity. It is the task of critical phenomenology in particular to show that (a) a few perspectives concretely determine what is considered objective or normal, and that (b) existential vulnerability and dependence unfortunately affect some more than others due to their physiological, material, or social situation.

Methodological self-criticism remains a challenge for any phenomenology that wants to describe without prejudice, determine the general, and question conditions. In this context, a plurality of perspectives and intersubjective cooperation are indispensable.

3.1.2 Postphenomenology (Philosophy of Technology)

Since the 1980s, a new field of study calling itself 'postphenomenology', has emerged as a phenomenological subdiscipline within the philosophy of technology. Postphenomenology has set for itself the goal of focusing again on the description of things. In this case, however, the things are technical artifacts and technologies (cf. Müller 2020), as well as the way in which humans relate to them, or through them to the world. Therefore, it also explicitly initiates an empirical turn in the philosophy of technology (Ihde 1979, 1990, 1993, 2009; Achterhuis 2001; Verbeek 2000, 2011). The representatives of postphenomenology, which has become very influential in North America and the Netherlands, want to distinguish themselves from classical phenomenology, especially from Heidegger's reflections on the essence of technology, with the prefix 'post'. Instead of transcendental, metaphysical, or general statements about technique, engineering, or technology, it aims at the description and empirical investigation of individual technologies, as well as their concrete development and use. It employs phenomenological concepts, such as 'intentionality', to describe human-technology relationships. Peter-Paul Verbeek, inspired by the French sociologist Bruno Latour, emphasizes that 'subject' and (technical) 'object' are relational categories that can only be determined in and through their mediation. The phenomenologically descriptive approach is thus linked and extended by, Bruno Latour's (postmodern) network theory and the empirical-social constructivist approach of *Science and Technology Studies*.

Don Ihde, who coined the term 'postphenomenology', suspected that classical phenomenology has not adequately followed its guiding principle to return 'to the things themselves', and he saw postphenomenology as an attempt to do so. According to Ihde, classical phenomenology overlooks the crucial role that technology or technologies play in phenomenological descriptions of experience, namely, the way in which every experience is technically mediated. 'To the things themselves', here means to start with concrete (material) technologies and artifacts and from there to determine how these things mediate and shape our experience, our understanding of the world, and our moral judgment (cf. Verbeek 2011).

■■ Eidetics of the Human-technology Relation

Despite this clear demarcation, postphenomenology applies classical phenomeno-logical descriptions and concepts, such as 'embodiment', 'body schema', 'inten-tionality', 'lifeworld', 'hermeneutics', 'alterity', etc., to describe the general structures of the human-technology-world relationship. Postphenomenology, one could say, applies classical phenomenological methods that fall into the area of static phenomenology or constitution analysis. It takes the given object (techno-logical artifact or program) as a guideline (intentional object) and determines the way we are related to it (intentional act). Yet it no longer primarily locates this intentionality in consciousness but, like Heidegger or Merleau-Ponty, generally understands it as existential directedness towards the world. Thus, Ihde (1990) dis-tinguishes between various technology-world relationships such as the *embodied relation*, the *hermeneutic relation*, and the *alterity relation*.

> ▶ **Example: Human-technology relations**
>
> "1. *Embodied Relation:* I see–through the optical artifact–the world. This seeing is, in however small a degree, at least minimally distinct from a direct or naked seeing. [...] I call this first set of existential technological relations with the world *embodiment relations*, because in this use context I take the technologies *into* my experiencing in a particular way by way of perceiving *through* such technologies and through the reflexive transfor-mation of my perceptual and body sense. In Galileo's use of the telescope, he embod-ies his seeing through the telescope thusly: Galileo–telescope–Moon. Equivalently, the wearer of eyeglasses embodies eyeglass technology: I–glasses–world [...]. The technol-ogy is actually *between* the seer and the seen, in a *position of mediation*. But the referent of the seeing, that towards which sight is directed, is "on the other side" of the optics. One sees *through the* optics. [...] First, the technology must be *technically* capable of being seen through; it must be transparent [...]. This is a material condition for embodi-ment. Embodying as an activity, too, has an initial ambiguity. It must be learned or, in phenomenological terms, constituted. If the technology is good, this is usually easy. The very first time I put on my glasses, I see the now corrected world. [...] But once learned, the embodiment relation can be more precisely described as one in which the technology becomes maximally "transparent". It is, as it were, taken into my own perceptual-bodily self experience thus: (I–glasses)–world. [...]
>
> 2. *Hermeneutic Relation:* [...] you [...] see the thermometer nailed to the grape arbor post and *read* that it is 28°F. You would now "know" how cold it was, but you still would not feel it. [...] Instead, you read the thermometer, and in the immediacy of your reading you *hermeneutically* know that it is cold. There is an instantaneity to such reading, as it is an already constituted intuition (in phenomenological terms). But you should not fail to note that *perceptually* what you have seen is the dial and the numbers, the ther-mometer "text". [...] In the Three Mile Island incident, the nuclear power system was observed only through instrumentation. Part of the delay that caused a near meltdown was *misreadings* of the instruments. There was no face-to-face, independent access to the

pile or to much of the machinery involved, nor could there be. An intentionality analysis of this situation retains the mediational position of the technology: I–technology–world (engineer–instruments–pile). […]

3. *Alterity Relation*: I have suggested that the computer is one of the stronger examples of a technology which may be positioned within alterity relations. But its otherness remains a quasi-otherness, and its genuine usefulness still belongs to the borders of its hermeneutic capacities. Yet in spite of this, the tendency to fantasize its quasi-otherness into an authentic otherness is pervasive. Romanticizations such as the portrayal of the emotive, speaking 'Hal' of the movie *2001: A Space Odyssey*, early fears that the 'brain power' of computers would soon replace human thinking, fears that political or military decisions will not only be informed by but also made by computers—all are symptoms revolving around the positing of otherness to the technology. […] In spite of the temptation to accept the fantasy, what the quasi-otherness of alterity relations does show is that humans may relate positively or presentientially *to* technologies. In that respect and to that degree, technologies emerge as focal entities that may receive the multiple attentions humans give the different forms of the other. For this reason, a third formalization may be employed to distinguish this set of relations: I → technology–(–world)." (Ihde [1990] 2014, pp. 539–547) ◄

In these cases, Ihde differentiates between various qualities of perception or forms of consciousness, such as foreground or background consciousness, focus or horizon consciousness, in a manner similar to Husserl (cf. Hua XXXVIII) or Aaron Gurwitsch (cf. 2010) in their theories of attention and the field of consciousness. Technological mediation is therefore more or less transparent or opaque. The technical object can either be a quasi-counterpart—like a humanoid robot—and as such explicit, or it can be almost completely embodied—like a virtual reality headset—and thus part of our lived and active bodily existence or body schema, through which we directly perceive and act. Here Ihde and other postphenomenologists often refer to Merleau-Ponty's description of habituation and the extension of the body schema.

> ▶ **Example: Technical extensions of the body schema**
> "Without any explicit calculation, a woman maintains a safe distance between the feather in her hat and objects that might damage it; she senses where the feather is, just as we sense where our hand is. If I possess the habit of driving a car, then I enter into a lane and see that 'I can pass' without comparing the width of the lane to that of the fender, just as I go through a door without comparing the width of the door to that of my body. The hat and the automobile have ceased to be objects whose size and volume would be determined through a comparison with other objects. They have become voluminous powers and the necessity of a certain free space. […]
>
> The blind man's cane has ceased to be an object for him, it is no longer perceived for itself; rather, the cane's furthest point is transformed into a sensitive zone, it increases the scope and the radius of the act of touching and has become analogous to a gaze. In the exploration of objects, the length of the cane does not explicitly intervene nor act as a middle term: the blind man knows its length by the position of the objects, rather than the position of the objects through the cane's length. The position of objects is given

3

immediately by the scope of the gesture that reaches them and in which, beyond the potential extension of the arm, the radius of action of the cane is included.

To habituate oneself to a hat, the spatiality of one's own body and motricity an automobile, or a cane is to take up residence in them, or inversely, to make them participate within the voluminosity of one's own body. Habit expresses the power we have of dilating our being in the world, or of altering our existence through incorporating new instruments." (Merleau-Ponty 2012, pp. 144–145) ◀

▪▪ Hybrid Form of Intentionality

Peter-Paul Verbeek (2008) also describes other forms of human-technology-world relationship, e.g., the hybrid form of intentionality. Here, technologies are not only incorporated, but literally merge with our organic body, so that they can no longer be distinguished from it. This is the case with implanted visual aids, pacemakers, or internet-capable chips. Strictly speaking, one could argue that this is not a new form of intentionality (as a mode of directedness), but rather depending on the technology, a qualitative change of this directedness itself (which can influence several modes, such as perception, memory, thinking, imagining etc., and thus the entire form of existence). Furthermore, Verbeek speaks of a **composite intentionality**, which occurs when human perceptions and actions are combined with certain technologies. Here too, it would be more descriptively accurate to speak of an expanded intentionality, as it is not the directionality itself that changes, but its quality and range. In this context, Helena de Preester argues that it is useful to distinguish between technologies that merely extend the body, but remain external to it, such as a leg prosthesis, and technologies that are incorporated directly into the body, such as a pacemaker (De Preester 2011; cf. also Oudshoorn 2020). However, as Federica Buongiorno emphasizes, in digital embodiment, extension and incorporation are equally in play, since they are both required by digitally mediated forms of interactions (Buongiorna 2019).

In the age of the internet, it is becoming increasingly difficult to discuss technology in the form of things or technical artifacts, i.e., to view technologies or virtuality as separate things or realms of being. This is because digital technologies are almost completely integrated into our everyday activities. In fact, one could say that this digital infrastructure shapes and constitutes what Husserl calls the lifeworld: the immediate, practical, and unquestioned sphere of our daily lives. Intelligent devices and environments thus constitute a highly personalized domain of reality, a domain that does not exist separately from, or merely alongside, a material or 'real' reality but is dynamically integrated into one's lifeworld and personal identity (cf. De Mul 2010; Durt 2020).

Smart technologies like ICT's (*Internet Communication Technologies*), the 'Internet of Things' or Generative AI assistants, which operate on the basis of self-learning algorithms or large language models, not only present and communicate information, but act and decide for us. Therefore, this digital network can no longer be viewed as a composition of mere things or technological tools. Rather, these communicating things and smart environments completely reshape our experiences. They help us navigate our environment, direct our attention, select information, write, communicate, and 'think' for us. They also predict our behavior, based on data of past personal behavior or general language use (by computing probabilities). Thus, they ultimately shape our perception, emotions, behavior, and beliefs alike.

■■ **New Research Questions**

Against the backdrop of these new technological conditions of experience, new research questions arise. In what way is reality extended, supplemented, mixed, or even replaced by the virtual? At what level is the influence of smart technologies on our experience most pronounced? Do personalized algorithms merely shape our conscious beliefs, opinions, and preferences, or do they shape our actions and habits as well? Will personalized smart environments or generative AI change the way we perceive time and space, associate, anticipate, or learn in general?

These questions call for a consideration of typically genetic-phenomenological topics such as temporality, association, or habit, which investigate how coherence, identity, evidence, and meaning, (i.e., a 'meaningful world') arise for us in and through experience at all. Such genetic topics have only recently begun to be addressed by phenomenology (cf. de Warren and Cavallaro 2024) and postphenomenology (cf. Rosenberger 2013; Gerlek and Weydner-Volkmann 2025), although they are crucial for understanding the dynamic connection between subject and object. The description and analysis of an increasingly digital-technological lifeworld and its effects on the experiencing subject, seem to be a logical further development of phenomenological philosophy of technology. There are clear links, not only with Heidegger's time analyses and Merleau-Ponty's investigations into situated spatiality, the body schema, and the habitual body, but also with Husserl's analysis of inner time consciousness and his descriptions of attention and normality, habituality and typification, as well as various forms of intersubjectivity.

Social-phenomenological perspectives, such as Alfred Schutz's description of the social structures of the lifeworld, could also be helpful here, for example, to investigate how generative and socially shared practices, habits, and knowledge stocks are formed. (Schutz and Luckmann 1973; cf. de Boer 2022). And with the help of Hannah Arendt's political phenomenology, more precisely her distinction between the private and the political-public sphere (1960), the role of social media could further be analyzed, for example, with regard to current problems such as hate speech or 'post-truth' discourse (cf. Behrendt et al. 2019).

A genetic, generative, or social phenomenology, which focuses on temporal and associative syntheses, the acquisition of habits and typical beliefs, can help to explain how and why we come to experience something as real or illusory, normal or abnormal, and how this could be influenced by smart technologies. Genetic phenomenology points out that our sense of reality and normality is fragile and requires constant updating, testing, or even resistance from the outside world and the experiences of others. While we in the analog world are confronted with experiences that deviate from our expectations, that surprise or irritate us, smart environments tend to erase this corrective function by turning the world into a tailor-made comfort zone. What does it mean for our belief in reality, when our habits and beliefs are no longer challenged by the outside world or other subjects who are not like-minded? What happens to our development opportunities when we are only confronted with information that matches our previous preferences, confirms them, and thus preserves them?

▪▪ Return of the Transcendental Question?

To answer such questions, we need a phenomenology that thinks about the conditions and possibilities of its own technological lifeworld. For this reason, current voices in the philosophy of technology have advocated for a reintroduction of the transcendental question into the philosophy of technology. Now that digital technology has become a necessary and self-evident part of our everyday life, it itself becomes a condition of the possibility of experience, i.e., it becomes necessary to gain access to the world. This includes not just the analog world, but also digital information, communication, and virtual experience spaces. With this, digital technology loses the character of a tool or thing that we can freely pick up and use or else leave alone, and whose use we can control. It rather becomes a condition of (at least some) experience with its own forms of organization and rules. It is a condition, however, that can no longer be directly experienced. Heidegger pointed this out in his essay on the question of technology (1953), when he described the essence of technology not as an instrument, but as a kind of unconcealment, i.e., access to reality.

Thus the transcendental question, after having been criticized for years for its ostensibly absolute, overly abstract, and technology-hostile character (represented by Heidegger's critique of technology) again finds a place in the (post-)phenomenologically influenced philosophy of technology. After a long phase in which researchers focused on the descriptive and empirical microanalysis of individual technologies, there is now a willingness to talk about technology 'with a big T' (cf. Lemmens 2021) or move beyond one-sided debates referring to either ontological (essentialist) or empiricist approaches (cf. Blok 2024). Reflecting on the role of digitized or AI technology as a whole is especially necessary in view of global problems of the Anthropocene (the geochronological epoch in which humans have the greatest influence on geological, biological, and atmospheric processes), such as climate change, species extinction, global conflicts, and economic crises. What role does the digital technological infrastructure play for the cause, the course, and the possible responses to such crises, and how does what we create in turn change our thinking and acting or even the essence of being human itself?

However, one should not forget that technology, then as now, is not the only, or even the most important, transcendental condition for the possibility of experience. Technology alone does not determine what and how we experience. Other conditions must also be taken into account, including natural, biological, material, linguistic, cultural, social, and normative factors. In this context, one should particularly focus on the interrelations of these areas. So instead of absolutizing technology, it is phenomenologically necessary to first concretely describe our situatedness with and through technology, and only then—and with great caution—make general or even transcendental determinations. In this context, a cooperation between postphenomenology and the various forms of critical phenomenology could be helpful, as well as a dialogue between phenomenology in general and *Science and Technology Studies* or *Technofeminism* in particular (cf. Wajcman 2004; Zeiler 2020).

3.2 Interdisciplinary Phenomenology

Phenomenology as a method and philosophical movement is characterized from the outset by its interdisciplinarity. It critically analyzes empirical experiments, results, and case studies and integrates them into its own descriptions. Historically, this has taken place particularly with psychology, psychiatry, and neuroscience. Husserl's initial development of phenomenology would itself be unthinkable without his critical engagement with the theoretical and empirical psychology of his day, especially that of his teacher, Franz Brentano. Husserl, and many other phenomenologists after him, have also sought to deal with pathological cases in the field of psychiatry or neurology to concretize and problematize the concept of 'normal' lived experience.

Merleau-Ponty's (1945) discussions of famous cases from the history of psychology and neurology, as well as with certain phenomena such as the phantom limb, synesthesia, or hallucinations, are well known.

▪▪ The Concept of the Body Schema

One psychological concept that plays a particularly central role in the phenomenology of Merleau-Ponty is that of the **body schema** (cf. Goldstein and Gelb 1918). This concept is supposed to explain why our body, its position and location, are immediately given to us—why we do not have to explicitly determine our position or location in space or identify individual body parts as such before we are able to use them. Merleau-Ponty writes: "I hold my body as an indivisible possession and I know the position of each of my limbs through a *body schema* [*un schéma corporel*] that envelops them all" (Merleau-Ponty 2012, pp. 100–101). However, as he goes on to emphasize, this unity is not the "result of associations established in the course of experience", as the psychology of his time would have it, but rather a "global awareness of my posture in the inter-sensory world" (p. 125). The body schema is therefore a holistic form of organization that includes our environment. It gives us not only an immediate 'knowledge' of our size, location, and position, but also certain habits and abilities in relation to our environment. We know, for example, whether we can fit through a certain door, whether we can lift a certain object, how we should move or behave in a certain situation. Such practical knowledge literally has its place in our body; it is not thematic as such but is automatically retrieved as the situation calls for it.

This means not only that the body is more than the sum of its parts but that the unity of the body also includes its (past and current) experiences and abilities. Furthermore, it seems to break the boundaries between

- Inside and outside (as it is related to, and includes, the environment),
- Subject and object (as external things can be integrated into the body schema, like the blind man's stick in example 3.1.2), and
- Past and future (in every movement, the body uses previously acquired skills, which in turn reach into the future).

3

Merleau-Ponty makes this clear by reference to the phenomenon of the phantom limb. In that case, the practical field and the habits of the lost limb are still somehow present. However, they are not present in the form of explicit memories or as the result of a faulty judgment, as the psychology of the time assumed. Nor are they present in the form of actual physiological nerve stimuli from the stump, as these are not sufficient for a phantom limb to occur (e.g., it may not occur at all or only in conjunction with a psychological stressor). Nonetheless, the acquired habit or practical field is still present, although as an absence, as the actual body (due to the missing limb) is no longer able to realize it.

The unity of the body schema is not static or predetermined but must constantly update itself in experience and is therefore constantly acquiring new abilities. However, as was evident in the case of the phantom limb, this can take time or fail altogether: "The subject still remains open to the same impossible future, if not in his explicit thoughts, then at least in his actual being" (Merleau-Ponty 2012, p. 85). The body schema in Merleau-Ponty's phenomenological definition is therefore neither the sum of current information about the body nor a kind of internal global representation of the body. Rather, it points beyond its current state and its material boundaries. The body schema is, "in the end, a manner of expressing that my body is in and toward the world" (p. 103).

▪▪ Interdisciplinary Application

The phenomenological description of bodily experience from the perspective of the first or second person proves to be enlightening in many interdisciplinary studies of pathologies and diseases. Here, changes in embodiment are examined with reference to (a) the *body schema* as the operative (non-thematic) bodily being-in-the-world or (b) the *body image*—in which we 'have' our body as an object, i.e., perceive it, imagine it, or judge it. Although both forms of bodily self-consciousness are closely related, as Husserl emphasized, the distinction between them is helpful, for example, to describe the effects of a disease on bodily experience. When we ask about the body schema, we ask how we perceive the world with and through our body, and how this is susceptible to change. This can manifest itself, for example, in a perception that events are happening too slowly or too quickly, or that they pose some kind of obstacle or threat. When we ask about the body image, we ask how we perceive our body as a body, how we judge it or what feelings we associate with it. Changes in the body image are highly influenced by our co-subjects, social norms, and expectations. To what extent do I feel observed, and why? Is my body considered too slow, too large or small? Is it deviant, 'disabled', or abnormal? To what extent does this make me insecure or prevent me from participating in social life?

In some pathologies, such as deafferentation (see the case of Ian Waterman, in Gallagher and Cole 1995; cf. Gallagher 2005), where a person, for example, loses the proprioceptive sensation of their body from the neck down after poisoning, the operative functions of the body schema almost completely fail. Coordinated movement is no longer possible because the immediate feedback of the body (in Husserl's terms, 'kinesthetic sensation') is missing. The person only learns to walk again, slowly and laboriously, through the help of explicit visual perception of their own body. Here, a connection must be reestablished via the detour of the body image with movement intentions on the one hand and executed movements on the other.

> ▶ **Example: Pathology of the body schema: The case of Ian Waterman**
>
> "IW suffers from an acute sensory neuropathy in which large fibers below the neck have been destroyed by illness. As a result IW has no proprioceptive function and no sense of touch below the neck. He is still capable of movement and he experiences hot, cold, pain, and muscle fatigue, but he has no proprioceptive sense of posture or limb location [...].
>
> To maintain his posture and to control his movement IW must not only keep parts of his body in his visual field, but also conceptualize postures and movements. Without proprioceptive and tactile information he neither knows where his limbs are nor controls his posture unless he looks at and thinks about his body. Maintaining posture is, for him, an activity rather than an automatic process. His movement requires constant visual and mental concentration. In darkness he is unable to control movement; when he walks he cannot daydream, but must concentrate constantly on his movement. [...]
>
> IW learned through trial and error the amount of force needed to pick up and hold an egg without breaking it. If his attention is directed toward a different task while holding an egg, his hand crushes the egg [...].
>
> In terms of the distinction between body image and schema, IW has lost the major functional aspects of his body schema, and thereby the possibility of normally unattended movement. He is forced to compensate for that loss by depending on his body image (itself modified in important aspects) in a way that normal subjects do not. [...] IW, as a result of extreme effort and hard work, recovered control over his movement and regained a close-to-normal life. He did not do this by recovering proprioceptive sense, but by rebuilding a partial body schema and by using body image to help control movement." (Gallagher and Cole 1995, pp. 374–375) ◄

The conceptual distinction between body image and body schema is helpful for analyzing this case and making clear the precise nature of Waterman's motor difficulties. In turn, according to Shaun Gallagher, the case sheds light on normal and abnormal relationships between body image and body schema. Since Waterman's movements are controlled more by conscious attention than by a pre-personal body schema, they indicate an extraordinary, perhaps uniquely high, degree of intentional and personal control. However, they also show several limitations. For example, the movements do not have a holistic and fluid structure, and experiential integration with the surrounding world does not occur immediately.

3

▪▪ Bodily Consciousness and Consciousness of the Body

In other pathologies, such as eating disorders, changes in, or problems with, the body image seem to be in the foreground. Patients are very concerned with their external appearance and often seem to perceive this in a subjectively distorted way (compared to the perception of others or objective assessment) (cf. Rosen 1990). Phenomenologically inspired studies, however, suggest that this is more about a lack of connection between the lived body (*Leib*) and the corporeal body (*Körper*). A so-called 'alien hand experiment', showed that bulimic people tolerate a dissonance between their bodily experience and the perception of their body more than subjects who do not suffer from an eating disorder. In the experiment, the subject's gloved writing hand was placed in a specially constructed box, where it was not directly visible to them. The subject was then instructed to draw a sequence of shapes. A mirror placed above an opening in the box presented what appeared to be a reflection of the subject's hand. In fact, the mirror could be manipulated by the researcher—without the knowledge of the subject—to show either (a) the subject's own hand or (b) the researcher's hand (also gloved). As the subject drew various shapes, what they saw in the mirror alternated between their own hand and that of the researcher. The participating subjects (non-bulimic men, non-bulimic women, and bulimic women) were asked about their experiences during the experiment. Their statements were then sorted and interpreted according to the above phenomenological categories.

When bulimics saw hand movements that they had not initiated—movements that in reality belonged to the alien hand—they did not question the correctness of what they were seeing. They did not, for example, ask whether this was some kind of trick. Rather, they questioned their control of their own hand (Sørensen 2005). One bulimic participant expressed her experience as follows: "The hand just went on, but it was like we were two creatures: There was the hand doing what it liked to do, and there was me just looking speechless at it" (Sørensen 2005, p. 80). This suggests that a dissonance between lived body and perceived body was quite normal for these subjects and is closely associated with a feeling of loss of agency. Non-bulimic participants, by contrast, were more likely to interpret the dissonance as a trick than a lack of agency.

❯ For Further Study

Bodily Sensing and New Phenomenology

Other phenomenological approaches try to describe a non-objective bodily self-experience Dorothée Legrand, for example, has recently argued for an integrative approach that gradually connects various forms of bodily self- and world-consciousness, starting with a pre-objective and implicit body experience, which differs in content both from the experience of the world (intentional directedness towards something) and also from the experience of one's own body as a perceived body. She describes this as a vague background experience of the extension or voluminousness of one's own body (Legrand 2011).

In Germany, Hermann Schmitz (cf. 1965–1978) developed yet another approach, which he referred to as 'New Phenomenology'. This approach emphasized a **level of bodily sensing**, that is more fundamental than perception through the five senses (seeing, touching, hearing, smelling, and tasting). Schmitz describes this bodily sensing as an interplay between narrowness and breadth, each associated with experiences of tension and swelling. Paradigmatic for such an interplay is inhaling and exhaling. Inner bodily sensing does not mean that this is somehow an isolated immanent sphere. Rather, corporeality is thought of here as a sounding board, i.e., it does not stop at the boundaries of the body but transcends itself into the environment through its movements and gaze. At the same time, it literally takes in the outside, through so-called 'incorporation', which includes glances, gestures, moods, atmospheres, and feelings (Schmitz 1990, p. 116, cf. Schmitz 2019). Schmitz's approach has subsequently been applied to the phenomenology of feelings (Landweer 2020a, 2020b; Nörenberg 2020, 2021), and to the phenomenological sociology of the body, of sports (Gugutzer 2020, 2024) and of eating disorders (cf. Marcinski 2020). The New Phenomenology has also produced attempts, starting from concrete descriptions (based on personal experience as well case studies, second-hand accounts, and literary examples) to identify general structures of bodily sensing, which are typical for certain feelings, such as shame or guilt, or which change in typical ways, for example, in eating disorders or specific diseases.

■ ■ Phenomenology of Illness and Bodily Doubt

The interplay of *Leib* and *Körper*, that is, the reciprocal connection of an operative (implicit) and thematic bodily awareness, also plays a role in the phenomenological description of illness. If due to an illness or an accident, for example, the immediate *availability* (*Zuhandenheit*) of things, as Heidegger (1927) termed it, is lost. This means, that everyday tasks suddenly transform into mere general possibilities, that are no longer personally relevant or doable for me. In this experience of 'I-cannot (anymore)' (e.g., climbing stairs), the body, through which we are towards the world, turns into an explicit topic: an objective, material and vulnerable body, which I can only inadequately understand and control.

In her *Phenomenology of Illness*, Havi Carel (2016) uses phenomenological terminology (from Husserl, Merleau-Ponty, Heidegger, Sartre, et al.), to describe her own experience living with a permanent airway-narrowing lung disease. In her account, the body schema can change so much through the course of an illness that there is a loss of confidence in one's own abilities—a 'bodily doubt', as she calls it. This in turn forces one constantly to make the body a topic in itself (i.e., to thematize the body as an object). And this forced attention to one's own body (as an object) leads to a sense of alienation from it. The body is no longer a vehicle that remains in the background; it intrudes into the foreground where it is experienced as unfamiliar or even uncanny (cf. Leder 1990; Svenaeus 2000; Toombs 1987; Slatman 2014; Ratcliffe 2008, 2014).

▶ **Example: A phenomenology of breathlessness**

"Trapped. That is what breathlessness feels like. Trapped in the web of uncertainty, bodily doubt, practical obstacles, and fear. The deepest fear you can think of. The fear of suffocation, of being unable to breathe, the fear of collapsing, desaturated to the point of respiratory failure. [...] Perhaps you have never been so breathless. If you are

3

healthy, you probably haven't. So no, it is not like running for the bus; it is not like hiking in high altitude; it's more like what I imagine dying is like. [...] One aspect of such breathlessness is aptly termed by medics 'air hunger'—the air is rushing in and out, but the reduced surface area of the lungs means that the oxygen isn't coming in fast enough and the CO_2 isn't removed fast enough. The result is the worst sensation I have ever felt and one that is very hard to describe, unless you've held your breath for far too long and feel your chest is about to explode. [...]

What is the phenomenology of this total sensation? Like pain, you cannot ignore it under any circumstances. [...] The psychological impact is enormous. The sense of bodily doubt and insecurity gives rise to [...] despair, fearfulness, anxiety, depression, loss of hope. [...] The world shrinks and becomes hostile. The sense of possibility that accompanies objects disappears. A bicycle is not an invitation for an afternoon of fresh air and freedom. It is a relic of days bygone. Hiking boots now sit leaden in a cupboard. They are no longer 'something to be worn when going for a hike'. [...] The physicality of every action needs to be calculated, considered, configured to suit your body's limitations [...]. Groceries have to be judged by their weight: a pint of milk: yes; four pints: no. [...] Strolling along on a beautiful summer day is censored by the gradient, amount of oxygen left in the tank, temperature, and fatigue. Everything becomes potentially debilitating, frustrating, a *problem*." (Carel 2016, pp. 109–111) ◄

A phenomenology of illness aims to capture the subjective experience of illness from the first- or second-person perspective, in contrast, or in addition, to the medical determination of illness (*disease*), based on measurable symptoms and objective classifications. It intends to capture both the subjectivity and specificity of disease experiences and the eidetic (essential) features of disease experience in general. S. Kay Toombs, for example, has sought to define essential features that apply to every experience of being ill, such as the experience of a loss of bodily wholeness, of security and control, of freedom of action, and of a familiar world (Toombs 1992).

It is important here, as with the philosophical determination of general structures, that these supposedly essential structures are constantly tested against concrete case examples and experience reports. Illness is neither a logically general structure nor a categorical a priori. The meaning of an illness depends on the subjects who experience it as a form of suffering or as something restrictive and threatening. Here, the **relationship between diagnosed disease and the experience of this disease** must be reflected upon again and again. Not every diagnosed disease or change in the organism is actually (or immediately) experienced. And not every deviation from health norms, such as average blood pressure, leads to the experience of being ill or impaired. At the same time, there are many ailments and symptoms that (still) cannot be assigned to a diagnosable disease. Here, a systematic phenomenological description can help to relate measurable changes and objective causes with typical changes in experience more systematically.

▪▪ Phenomenological Psychopathology

In its theoretical orientation, phenomenological psychopathology (► Sect. 3.3.1) contributes to the problematization, description, and understanding of (the limits of) experience. It sees itself as a fundamental science of psychiatry and investigates, both theoretically and empirically, the basic structures of subjective experience and their modifications in mental illness. Already during the lifetimes of Husserl and Heidegger—and under their influence—Karl Jaspers founded the so-called Hermeneutic (*Verstehende*) psychopathology (1913). From this perspective, mental illness is no longer seen merely as a biological phenomenon, but as an expression of existential contexts. Influenced by Heidegger's hermeneutic phenomenology, Jaspers emphasized that understanding is a central instrument for grasping human existence and thus redefines the foundations of psychiatry methodologically and anthropologically. More recent phenomenological psychopathology and psychiatry are still influenced by Heidegger's analysis of 'Dasein' (Binswanger 1922; Blankenburg 1958, 2012; Holzhey-Kunz 2014), Husserl's analysis of time, and Merleau-Ponty's study of the body, and understand themselves as applied phenomenology. See, for example, the research group at the University Hospital Heidelberg around the psychiatrist and philosopher Thomas Fuchs, or the group practicing applied phenomenological psychopathology at the *Center for Subjectivity Research* under the direction of Dan Zahavi at the University of Copenhagen. Here, phenomenologists, in collaboration with psychiatrists, have developed a questionnaire for the diagnosis of early schizophrenic symptoms, called *EASE— Early Anomalies of Schizophrenic Experience*, whose validity is also being researched quantitatively (Nordgaard Frederiksen and Henriksen 2019). The questionnaire, which is based on phenomenological categories, aims to detect what Karl Jaspers called 'ego disturbances', i.e., changes in implicit and explicit self-experience, as well as the experience of the environment and other people.

Although phenomenological psychopathology is still a marginal phenomenon within clinical psychiatry, it has in recent years gained in influence and relevance. This is evident from, among other things, the publication of a handbook for phenomenological psychopathology by University of Oxford Press (Stanghellini et al. 2019). In current theoretical and empirical research, categories of experience such as 'body', 'space', 'temporality', and 'intersubjectivity' are particularly central. They find special application in the analysis of the schizophrenic self and intentionality disorders and in the experience of body and time in melancholy or depression. Thomas Fuchs, for example, who works theoretically, empirically, and therapeutically, investigates the altered experience of time in patients with schizophrenia and describes it, following Husserl's theory of inner time consciousness and Merleau-Ponty's concept of the 'intentional arc', as a disorder at the level of protention (i.e., the immediate anticipation of the next impression, such as a note of a melody). Fuchs thereby distinguishes between implicit and explicit temporality.

– *Implicit or lived time* is based on the protentional-retentional linkage and the affective dynamics of conscious life. If this basic implicit temporal unity is not given, there are fundamental disturbances in perception; for example, in the form of a fragmented perception of time, in which certain sounds, voices, or movements are experienced as sudden or as 'coming out of nowhere'. According to Fuchs, such basic disturbances of temporality are found in patients with schizophrenia.

3

— *Explicit, experienced, or autobiographical time* represents the dimensional time of future, present, and past. On this level, disorders can result in desynchronization, e.g., when one's own temporality is experienced as being too slow, or too fast compared to previous experiences (on an individual level) or compared to experiences of other subjects (on an intersubjective level). The former can occur, for example, in depression; the latter, for example, in mania or manic phases.

According to Fuchs, within these different orders of time, a variety of disturbances can emerge, which are particularly evident in mental illnesses.

> ▶ **Example: Disorders of implicit temporality in schizophrenia**
>
> "I am not able to feel myself at all. The one speaking now is the wrong ego [...]. When I watch television it is even stranger. Even though I see every scene properly, I do not understand the story as a whole. Each scene jumps over into the next, there is no coherence. Time is also running strangely. It falls apart and no longer progresses. There arise only innumerable separate now, now, now— quite crazy and without rules or order. It is the same with myself. From moment to moment, various 'selves' arise and disappear entirely at random. There is no connection between my present ego and the one before." (patient of Bin Kumura, quoted in Kobayashi 1998, p. 114, quoted in Fuchs 2013).
>
> "You are dying from moment to moment and living from moment to moment, and you're different each time." (Chapman 1966, quoted in Fuchs 2013, p. 13).
>
> The two patients are describing a weakening and temporal fragmentation of self-experience which, as I will argue in the following, should be considered as a generative disturbance in schizophrenia. Especially symptoms like thought disorder, thought withdrawal or thought insertion, passivity experiences and, finally, the 'loss of natural self-evidence' [cf. Blankenburg 1969/2001, 1971, author] may be regarded as resulting from a fragmentation of the intentional arc, which is fundamental to all our perceiving, thinking and acting as well as to our self-realisation. [...] The continuity of the intentional arc disintegrates, creating temporal gaps which, in severe cases, are experienced as thought blockages or thought withdrawal. Of course, this transition from simple disturbances of concentration to thought blockages and interferences, and finally to inserted thoughts, can no longer be explained as a mere disturbance of attention or comprehension at the level of semantic combinations. Rather, the disturbance must be localised at the transcendental level where the temporal coherence of conscious awareness is constituted. [...]
>
> "When I move quickly it's a strain on me. Things go too quickly for my mind. They get blurred and it's like being blind. It's as if you were seeing a picture one moment and another picture the next." (McGhie and Chapman 1961; quoted in Fuchs 2013, p. 86)
>
> "My feeling of experience as my own experience only appears a split second delayed." (Parnas et al. 2005, p. 245, quoted in Fuchs 2013, p. 86)
>
> A failure of the constitutive temporal synthesis will create micro-gaps of conscious experience. Through the retentional function, the just-past experience is still appropriated, but only behind time. Moreover, if protention is disturbed, the disactualization of unsuitable associations or impulses will also fail. Disturbing thoughts or physical movements can then intrude into the gaps of the intentional arc—but they, too, will only be

experienced in the retentional mode, that is to say, in retrospect. They appear in consciousness as 'erratic blocks' so to speak, which come to patients as a surprise—of course not in the way suddenness is normally experienced (which I have examined at the level of explicit time), but in a form whereby consciousness is surprised by itself. The subject is then no more actively directed towards the future, but is left with focusing on what just turned up in his consciousness, or on the sensory feedback of his just-past movement. This 'transcendental delay' may be regarded as the essence of the major schizophrenic self-disturbances. The unforeseen fragments of thoughts or movement which the patient encounters in retention, he can only experience as radically alien to the ego and external. (Fuchs 2013, pp. 84–87) ◄

■■ **The Special Case of Normality**

A phenomenology of mental pathology or diversity, of illness, pain, or injury, but also of aging and physical impairment, begins with a description that determines typical structures of experience and then proceeds to describe modifications of those structures. Here, the pathology, disease, disability, or impairment is usually understood as a deviation from normal experience. This is justified insofar as 'normal' here refers to the previous state of the subject (before the disease, accident, etc.). Caution is required, however, when assuming an intersubjective standard of normality (such as average blood pressure or historically variable standards of health or fitness). Is the experience of a person, for example, who is physically disabled (or differently abled) from birth not normal? Does the person actually feel restricted, or does his condition simply fail to correspond to the statistical average?

As already explained in ▶ Chap. 2, ▶ Sect. 2.2, **normality does not constitute an eidetic category**, i.e., it is not synonymous with the essence of experience or 'the human' in general. Normality is a relative category, which phenomenologically refers either to my previous experience or to the experiences of other subjects. Pathological experiences or non-normal bodies are therefore not insignificant but essentially belong to human experience. What is normal or pathological can thus never be determined once and for all (or a priori), since it changes as people and their environments change. This becomes particularly clear in the example of aging. Aging is a necessary and typical characteristic of all life, so associated changes and restrictions are not necessarily pathological, even if they are experienced as painful or debilitating or are characterized by a performance-oriented society as a 'deviation'. (cf. Beauvoir [1970] 1972; Stoller 2016; Wehrle 2020a)

Normality, concretely thought, is therefore **not the same as the determination of transcendental structures of experience**. The latter, if correctly determined, are necessary conditions of the possibility of experience in general and therefore of all possible modifications within experience. All experiences, even pathological ones, exhibit a minimum of temporal, associative unity, sense, consciousness, intentionality, and bodily directedness. In this sense, normality, understood as minimal concordance or coherence of experience, can be considered a transcendental condition. Specifically, pathological experience can then be qualitatively distinguished from normal experience, for example, in the form of an overemphasis on one aspect of experience or the lack of integration between temporal levels of experience,

3

between passive and active levels of experience, or between individual and inter-subjective experience. However, phenomenology can only describe experience against the background of normality as coherence, self-evidence, or harmony; while pathologies, especially psychopathologies, reside in a border area where common terms and realities disappear. When it comes to such radical differences in experiencing, the phenomenological method itself is put to the test and faces its limits. Moreover, to account for the 'edges of experience', that is, limit experiences such as childbirth or being sexually assaulted while unconscious, a combination of phenomenology with other methods and perspectives, such as feminist, social, or political theory, might be helpful, as Cressida Heyes argues in her book *Anaesthetics of Existence: Essays on Experience at the Edge* (cf. Heyes 2020).

▪▪ Describing Pathologies Without Prejudice

Even though most phenomenological descriptions of pathologies do not pose transcendental philosophical questions—what makes experience, reality or truth possible?—and therefore do not require a transcendental epoché or reduction, the phenomenological claim of impartiality remains relevant. In attempting to provide concrete descriptions and typifications that can be helpful in diagnosis and therapy, two pitfalls lurk. First, there is a tendency to make unreflective assumptions about what is normal and what is pathological. Second, as Merleau-Ponty pointed out, there is a temptation simply to infer from the pathological what is supposed to be normal or vice versa. However, this is never justified because illness or injury do not simply entail that a particular area or a specific function of the body has failed, which in the normal subject remains intact (cf. Bredlau and Welsh 2022). Rather, a pathology changes the entire way I am directed towards myself, others, and the world, i.e., how I perceive, think, or feel. There is a complete reorganization of the organism, through which some functions become more relevant or take on new tasks. In the case of vision impairment, for example, the fact that I cannot see the surrounding world, also significantly changes how I experience the world through touch. Conversely, touch takes on a completely different role and quality as soon as vision is lost. Thus, in order to describe pathologies without prejudice, one needs to describe them not as mere deficiencies or deviations from a supposedly normal state, but as holistic phenomena that change one's whole way of existing.

❯ For further study

Phenomenology and Normality

Normality is phenomenologically determined by Husserl and Merleau-Ponty as a modality of experience; it is therefore not content-specific. Questions around who or what is considered normal at any given time, are historically contingent and determined by social and cultural norms. This should be bracketed in the phenomenological investigation or made thematic as a noematic guide and critically questioned. Normality, not as noematic, i.e., content-specific, but as noetic investigation is not oriented towards the question of what counts as normal (object of this sort), but what it means to experience normally. Here, phenomenology assumes that normal experience is *concordant* (with reference to previous individual or intersubjective experience) and *optimal* (in relation to the environment, actions, and needs of the individual or in relation to an intersubjective community) (cf. Steinbock 1995; Heinämaa and Taipale 2019, Wehrle 2024). To what extent concordance, coherence, and orientation are actually necessary for the experience and well-being of embodied subjects must always be critically questioned. So too must the standards for what is considered optimal experience for an individual or society (cf. Wehrle 2015, 2016, 2021).

However, almost all subjects with pathologies suffer from permanently fragmented or disconnected, self- and world-experiences, and try to actively make sense of their experience (i.e., regain some form of 'normality') or to establish it for themselves in a different way (than the majority). Although the distinction between normality and pathology is relative and possibly only gradually distinguishable in experience, it cannot be completely abandoned. How else would care, therapy, and treatment be possible if suffering cannot be designated as such?

A descriptive approach to phenomenological psychopathology can start from basic (minimal) general experiential structures and then determine the typical self- and world-experience of depressive, anorexic, or schizophrenic subjects, without either making the difference between normal vs. pathological central or evaluating it normatively. However, even here, a provisional notion of 'normal experience', worked out together with the affected parties, is relevant to defining the goal of possible treatments or societal changes. This does not mean that the patients should become 'normal' again in the sense of adhering to a social standard of normality or social average, but simply, that they can live and socially participate in a 'better' way (pain-free, unrestricted, unburdened, worry-free, etc.).

This implies that general determinations of experience (including those of phenomenology itself) serve as provisional orientations that must always be problematized by new insights or empirical results. When dealing with pathologies or diseases, the social and cultural dimension, i.e., the situation of the affected parties, must also be reflected upon. The definitions and classifications of pathologies and diseases are always historical, but so too is experience itself. Experiential reports and empirical results in interdisciplinary phenomenology are therefore not primarily there to confirm general concepts and theories, but to test and critically question them. Most interdisciplinary phenomenology does not, however, apply qualitative methods by itself, but only integrates existing results of empirical research into its analyses. It uses **pathological cases or case studies as examples**, to concretize, substantiate, or test its phenomenological analyses. Such real examples can serve as **concrete eidetic variations**, which help to check a supposedly general structure of experience against real variations.

However, it is not pathological experiences alone that are helpful for these purposes. Bodily experiences that require a special ability, competence, or expertise, such as dance or sport, can be helpful too. Such 'positive' and highly specialized experiences and forms movement can constructively challenge, expand, or clarify phenomenological thinking.

3

▪▪ Possibilities of the Moving Body

As highly trained specialists, dancers and athletes present concrete variations of the movements, sensations, and interactions that are possible for embodied subjects (although not for everyone equally). While pathological cases involve physical or mental deviations that are not desired by the subject and are usually perceived as obstructive and limiting, the specialized movements of dancers and athletes have been brought about through deliberate practice and active training of the body. They illuminate and concretize possibilities of experience in a positively perceived sense and therefore represent concrete eidetic variations of what a moving body can be (cf. Ravn 2021). Because of their specialized nature, they also highlight experiences that are not immediately present in everyday life (Legrand and Ravn 2009). While pathological cases focus on specific physical changes of the body or mind that can be measured and tested by medical science, this is not the case with studies that investigate 'positive' bodily habits or skills.

Furthermore, both pathological cases and those of athletic or artistic practice involve forms of embodiment and corporeality that are culturally and socially determined. Dance, for example, is an expression of a certain culture and thus associated with more or less explicit rules and social norms that co-determine the framework of possible execution. This is even more obvious for forms of dance that developed out of rituals and local traditions tied to a specific time and place. In the same way, how we experience and judge certain diseases is partly dependent on social and cultural framework conditions. Therefore, in all of these cases, it makes sense to **combine phenomenological description with genealogical or sociological perspectives**.

Self-collected experiential reports or experiential data, first-person case studies, etc. can serve phenomenology as *factual variations* (Froese and Gallagher 2010, p. 86) in contrast to imagined eidetic variations (▶ Chap. 2, ▶ Sect. 2.2), and can thus be helpful in determining both concrete features and general structures of experience. Based on such factual variations, a mutual verification can take place, between already established phenomenological concepts and invariant structures of experience on the one hand, and the concrete experiential reports from qualitative studies (surveys) on the other (▶ Sect. 3.3.1).

3.3   Phenomenology in Other Disciplines

There is hardly an approach within philosophy that has found such wide application and so many interdisciplinary connections as phenomenology. Already during Husserl's lifetime, phenomenology was a starting point and source of inspiration for **psychology and psychiatry**, as can be seen in the phenomenological psychopathology or existential *Daseinsanalysis* of Karl Jaspers ([1913] 1997; cf. Fuchs et al. 2013), Ludwig Binswanger (1922; cf. Hoffmann and Knorr 2019), Wolfgang Blankenburg (2012; cf. Heinze 2019) and later of Henri Maldiney (1991; Thoma 2019). In contrast with classical psychoanalysis where the focus is on the unconscious, here the focus is on the loss of natural self-evidence or common sense, which is associated with psychophysical pathologies. With this, psychiatrists such as

Blankenburg, for example, tried to capture difficulties or inabilities to 'naturally' engage in everyday social interactions, or pragmatically interact with the environment. This loss of natural self-evidence, analyzed by Blankenburg within a single-case study about the experience—both inside and outside of clinical contexts—of the patient Anne Rau (Blankenburg [1971] 2012, plays out at the level of intentional thinking as well as that of bodily, habitual, and intuitive interaction. Phenomenological psychopathology thus tries to recognize and describe this loss of self-evidence in the experience of self, world, and other on different levels (temporality, perception, action, thinking, judging, communication, etc.).

▪▪ Adaptation of Phenomenological Key Concepts

To explore, for example, abnormal experiences of the self or of time, space or other people, it is necessary to ask some quite specific, yet open, questions. Typically, a 'semi-structured interview' is chosen for this purpose. This is an interview that is based on a fixed set of questions, where the order of the questions is not binding, (as it is in a structured interview). With the help of such a semi-structured interview, it is possible to identify relevant areas of experience and to show possible changes in these experiences. As a starting point and guide for this interpretation, phenomenological distinctions and concepts must already be taken as a basis. Therefore, since there is not a complete bracketing of pre-assumptions, the approach is most similar to hermeneutic philosophy (cf. Sass 2019). But one can also identify an *eidetic orientation* within phenomenological psychiatry and psychopathology, as it starts from general determinations and areas of experience. However, the qualitative investigation of the patients' abnormal experiences can and should also contribute to the refinement of these basic concepts. In the case of psychotic disorders, such a refinement can even prove to be revolutionary. The researchers must strive to understand what, at least at first glance, does not seem conceivable at all, and thus come to new variations of experience and concepts.

▪▪ Hermeneutic Circle

Here we can see both that the knowledge of the essence of experience is experiential, and that all knowledge of facts includes an a priori understanding of the essence. Thus, there cannot always be a strict separation between a philosophy that provides the definitions and concepts, and one that tries to understand facts. Instead, in the connection of psychiatry and philosophy, we encounter a hermeneutic circle, a 'hyperdialectic', i.e., a back and forth between theory and evidence, between essence and existence or facts.

Recent Phenomenological psychopathology therefore focuses on essential structures of subjectivity and their potential or factual deviances, for example, the role of the self in mental illnesses. One of the most important hypotheses here is that schizophrenia, for example, is characterized by a disturbance of the (implicit) basic self or selfhood (cf. Sass and Parnas 2003; Parnas 2003; Parnas and Henriksen 2014; Henriksen and Nordgaard 2016). The investigation of such phenomena can inspire phenomenology to question the universality of described structures or to broaden the notion of what we refer to as consciousness. At the same time, it suggests the need to distinguish between different aspects of basic self-experience (e.g., between *agency* and *ownership*) that were not previously distinguished (Zahavi 2005). Recent research also emphasizes the relevance of social constituents for psychopathologies. Referring to Blankenburg's case study of Anne Rau, Samuel Thoma et al. point to the fact that schizophrenia typically appears in adolescents, a decisive stage of ego development, where young adults must situate themselves in the familial and social context; therefore, it is crucial to also investigate the familial and social contexts of patients (cf. Thoma et al. 2022).

3

> **For further study**

Hermeneutic aspects of psychopathology

While phenomenological psychopathology focuses primarily on disturbances of implicit self-consciousness (i.e., the pre-reflective structures of self-perception such as temporality and embodiment), hermeneutic phenomenology focuses on the consequences of such disturbances for explicit self-consciousness. This is necessary insofar as a comprehensive investigation of a possible self-disturbance includes not only implicit consciousness or behavioral processes, but also the personal level of being a subject.

As persons, we are bodily, but also social and rational beings, who must give these aspects of our being a place and a meaning. Therefore, the concept of the person is broader than the concept of the self as it is typically used in phenomenological psychopathology. While the self, in its minimal form is merely a continuous and consistent implicit self-reference, the concept of the person also includes the biological, social, and ethical aspects of human life. Moreover, it refers to aspects of human identity that we do not directly experience, such as the person we want to be in the future, our ambitions, or our hopes and dreams. Together these aspects belong to the temporal and narrative horizon of the person. Accordingly, they also significantly influence the experience of illness and suffering.

Identity in its full personal form can be understood as a kind of self-narration in which we actively participate in creating the **narrative**, *storyline*, or *plot* of our life. We do not simply live our lives but want to give meaning to them. So, we tell stories about ourselves and others to link events and behaviors and integrate them into a meaningful whole. Such a narrative identity is a way of answering so-called 'Who?' questions: 'Who is that?', 'Who are we?', 'Who said that?', 'Who did that?' However, this narrative self always remains fragile (cf. Ricœur 1990), and, in the context of mental illnesses, is radically questioned. To be able to address and treat these aspects of mental illness, it is important to integrate hermeneutic methods into psychiatry. As René Rosfort aptly puts it, it is a special feature of mental illnesses that they question our identity or even threaten to dissolve it:

"The questions that accompany severe mental suffering often provoke a sense of losing or having lost oneself. […] Why do I feel the way I do? Is my reaction normal? Am I to blame for what is happening to me? Is it because of something that I have done or because I am actually not who I think I am? These questions do not arise with the same existential urgency when it comes to a broken leg or kidney disease […]. The person's identity is more radically at stake in mental illness due to the lack of determinate experiential givenness or an explicit cause (e.g. the pain of hitting one's toe or the feeling of sadness because of a disparaging remark)." (Rosfort 2019, p. 244)

▪▪ A Sociology of the Everyday

Phenomenology has also had a long and fruitful connection with sociology, starting from Husserl himself and continuing in the social phenomenology of Alfred Schutz ([1932] 1972; Schutz and Luckmann 1973). This particular form of inquiry understands itself as sociology of knowledge of the everyday, or inquiry into the lifeworld. Rather than addressing merely epistemological questions or focusing on established sciences and theoretical ideas—as in a classical sociology of knowledge—the phenomenological approach understands knowledge in a broader sense: as practical know-how, which operates as a stock of knowledge, including codes of behavior, manuals, and maxims. In this sense, it comprises not only the knowledge of scientists or a cultural elite, but also of nurses, mechanics, cashiers, and ordinary people (cf. Overgaard and Zahavi 2009). For Schutz, experiences in the lifeworld are shaped and guided by a social repertoire or stock of such (practical) knowledge. In the familiar lifeworld we thus encounter objects not primarily in their individuality or singularity, but according to their acquired type, that is, as a 'tree', 'house', 'animal', or 'person'. This is especially relevant in social interactions where we most often do not address people as individuals, but according to their supposed type, for example, as postal worker, waiter (functional types), as man or women, as native or foreigner (identity types). These types come with certain assumptions, behavioral scripts, and expectations built in. In this sense, one follows a socially approved behavioral pattern or script (how to behave in a restaurant, when posting a letter, etc.), which both facilitates and automatizes social interactions, but can also lead to problematic biases and prejudices. This happens especially when such typified interactions dominate interpersonal relations, and the respective 'types' are no longer questioned or adjusted in intersubjective experience (cf. Schutz [1932] 1972, p. 185). This is difficult as these types or this social background knowledge belong to our 'natural attitude', as Schutz puts it, following Husserl; that is, we take them for granted without questioning their validity (Schutz 1962, p. 74, cf. Overgaard and Zahavi 2009, p. 105). In this sense, Schutz distinguishes between different ways one can relate to others, in which these types can be established, stabilized, adjusted or corrected: First, we can relate to others in the way of a face-to-face encounter. Second, we can relate to both our predecessors (upon whom I cannot act, but whose actions influence me and can be interpreted by me) and our successors (to whom I can orientate my action, but with whom I cannot communicate directly).

▪▪ Lifeworld and Intersubjectivity

In line with Husserl, Schutz understands sociology as an investigation not into (already established) institutions, social classes, or socio-economic structures, but into intersubjective meaning-making processes. The task of such a phenomenological sociology is thus to give an account of how experiencing and acting individuals together constitute the structures of meaning that make up social reality. A phenomenological sociology must therefore refer to the meaning-constituting activities of the social world. These include one's everyday experience of, and with, other persons, one's understanding and stabilization of pre-given meanings, and possibly one's initiation of new meaningful behavior (Schutz [1932] 1972). A phenomenological approach to sociology in the vein of Schutz can thus be characterized by a rehabilitation of the lifeworld or the everyday, and an emphasis on the individual person or subject, or better, on intersubjectivity. As Søren Overgaard and Dan Zahavi poignantly put it,

> » [A] society cannot be reduced to the sum of its individual members; but on the other hand, the phenomenologists maintain that there is no society without individual subjects. [...] A community of *no one* is hardly a *community*. An impersonal 'system' will never yield a society. For that, we need the *interpersonal*—and without the *personal*, there is no interpersonal. (Overgaard and Zahavi 2009, p. 112)

■■ Social Constructivism and Phenomenology

In the 1960s, Thomas Luckmann and Peter Berger took up Schutzian ideas in their well-known treatise 'The Social Construction of Reality' (1966), which served as inspiration for a distinct sociological approach: *Social Constructivism*. They broadened and radicalized Schutz's account by investigating not only the distribution or constitution of meaning, but also its societal conditions, and by showing how social knowledge constructs and maintains a reality, i.e., determines what subjects experience as real (Berger and Luckmann [1966] 1991, p. 28). However, it should be noted that a (radical) social constructivism differs in crucial aspects from phenomenology. For example, it focuses mostly on language, culture, and communication while treating our ostensibly objective experience of the world, ourselves, and others as a byproduct of social practices, negotiations, and conventions. Phenomenology by contrast does not do away with objectivity but instead attempts to show how objectivity—in the experience of the transcendence of external objects and other persons—shows itself within subjective experience. Although, Husserl emphasizes that objectivity relies on intersubjectivity, this does not primarily refer to concrete social interactions, but the transcendental necessity of the existence of other (transcendental) subjects, and thus a potential plurality of perspectives. Only when what I experience can in principle and potentially be experienced by others, can I be sure that it is not merely 'subjective' (cf. ► Chap. 2, ► Sect. 2.3). Therefore, objectivity calls for others who share with us the same essential structures of (transcendental) subjectivity (i.e., intentionality, minimal self, temporality, embodiment, affectivity, etc.).

■■ Ethnomethodology

Starting in the 1960s, another phenomenologically inspired approach looked at how social structures develop and are maintained out of social interactions: the *ethnomethodology* of Harold Garfinkel. Garfinkel completed his PhD under Talcott Parsons at Harvard in 1952 but developed his account in close discussion with phenomenologists like Alfred Schutz and Aaron Gurwitsch, while also drawing on the thought of Husserl, Merleau-Ponty, and Heidegger. Garfinkel applied phenomenological concepts to empirical research to better understand the construction of our shared social order. Contrary to his doctoral supervisor Talcott Parsons, Garfinkel understood action not as a product of a pre-existing social order (internalized by the agents) but as the place where order develops intersubjectively. He thus aimed to develop a method that helps to reveal the organization of the everyday, i.e., to demonstrate how actors accomplish this organization through actions and experience in concrete situations.

One of Garfinkel's early attempts to do this came in the form of his famous 'breaching experiments'. Here, participants would encounter unexpected situations or events in everyday settings that would lead to confusion or frustration. For example, he asked his students to pretend to be lodgers in their parent's home instead of family members. Such irritating situations were meant to violate the taken-for-grantedness of the social organization, and by this, make the implicit background expectations of the participants explicit. Reactions to the situation ranged from making jokes about it to attempts to find explanations for it, that is, attempts to 'normalize' it, or make sense of it again (cf. vom Lehn 2016, p. 75).

In his version of a phenomenological sociology, Garfinkel tried to 'see sociologically' (Garfinkel [1948] 2006) in addressing the organizational actions of individuals as phenomenon of investigation, and to study how these actions reflect their 'natural attitude' or background knowledge and make sense of their lifeworld. The starting point was the assumption that experience is always already a kind of (social) interpretation, i.e., ordered in a certain way. These orders are in turn interactively created, confirmed or questioned by the subjects. The order, the 'ethnos', is made by the actors themselves, but without their explicit awareness. Ethnomethodology is developed as a method to make these various orders—or the ordering and meaning-giving activity itself—explicit and to turn them into objects of investigation. Later, Garfinkel's insights and methods were applied and extended to an interpretative conversation analysis with the goal of discovering how participants create social order and organization in linguistic interactions such as everyday talk (cf. Heritage 1984). Garfinkel's approach thereby led to a hermeneutic turn within sociology and also contributed significantly to the establishment of empirical qualitative social research (cf. Francis and Hester 2004; vom Lehn 2016).

■■ Phenomenological Anthropology

In the 1970s, phenomenology also began to influence anthropology, or anthropological ethnography, through the work of Clifford Geertz (cf. Desjarlais and Throop 2011; Zigon and Throop 2021). In *The Interpretation of Cultures* (1973), he attempted to show how different cultural or religious perspectives frame experience. To do this, he applied the phenomenological sociology of Alfred Schutz to interpret the results of his ethnographic studies of indigenous groups in Bali. For example, he used Schutzian concepts to describe and differentiate, how people relate to their environment (*Umwelt*), to contemporary others (*Mitwelt*), predecessors (*Vorwelt*), or successors (*Folgewelt*). Although phenomenology has never been at the center of his work (Katz and Csordas 2003, p. 277), he also drew on concepts from the tradition of hermeneutic phenomenology such as those from Paul Ricoeur. With Ricœur, Geertz shared the assumption that human actions have a symbolic structure, that is, can be read and interpreted like written works through the methods and practices of textual interpretation (cf. Vendra 2020, p. 52; Breyer 2013). Since the 1980s, Geertz's hermeneutic study of subjective experience has been seen as a promising response to the crisis of representation within anthropology,

3

at a time when approaches that define culture as a form of objective or collective representation have been coming under increased scrutiny.

A more thoroughgoing use of phenomenological concepts and methods was made by Geertz's colleagues at Harvard, working under the mentorship of Arthur Kleinman and Byron Good. Members of the so-called *Harvard Group*, who worked with Geertz, had detailed knowledge of continental philosophy, which they applied in their studies. These include pioneering works on illness and disease (Kleinman 1988), and on medical rationality and experience (Good 1994). Here, phenomenological thinking is applied effectively to theorize the subjective experience of being ill and the objectified description of having a disease. These works laid the foundation for a phenomenological anthropology that was later developed more systematically by pioneering anthropologists like Thomas J. Csordas, Robert R. Desjarlais, Tim Ingold, Michael D. Jackson, Cheryl F. Mattingly, Jason Throop, and Jarrett Zigon (cf. Schnegg 2023a, p. 63). These thinkers put phenomenological concepts like 'embodiment', 'temporality', 'empathy', 'affectivity', etc. to ethnographic use. For example, Thomas Csordas, who understands embodiment as the existential ground for culture (Csordas 1994), has investigated embodiment and embodied experience with regard to phenomena such as ritual healing in the indigenous Navajo tribe of North America. And Jason Throop, who draws on the phenomenological concept of empathy, has investigated the personal, cultural, and moral significance of pain on the island of Yap (*Waqab*), in the Federated States of Micronesia. His studies have identified differing cultural phenomenological orientations implicated in the experience and expression of empathy (Throop 2008).

However, these field studies show that using phenomenological concepts to organize or interpret ethnographic data, like field notes, video or audio recordings, etc., is not a one-way street. Rather as Michael Schnegg puts it, phenomenology does not remain unchanged when tested by ethnographic situations; the concepts "will come back differently from their encounter with anthropology and 'the field'" (Schnegg 2023a, p. 61; cf. Bubandt and Wentzer 2023). In this sense, ethnography can become "a means to stabilize, broaden and diversify phenomenological concepts, and thus to develop them further" (Schnegg 2023a, p. 61; Schnegg and Breyer 2022, Mattingly 2019). Nonetheless, as Schnegg emphasizes, to develop the full critical potential of a phenomenological anthropology, anthropologists can profit from re-reading the original phenomenological texts to discover new ideas and concepts that have not been recognized, and to engage with contemporary phenomenological approaches like critical phenomenology.

■■ Six Ways to Apply Phenomenology to Anthropology

In his paper, Schnegg (2023a) illustrates how such an engagement and application can take place. He starts with an example from his field studies in arid northwestern Namibia, where he had been trying to understand how Damara pastoralists (‡*Nūkhoen*) get to know their environment and how, in particular, they cope with the most distressing weather-related phenomenon in their world, that is, rain. (Strong rain falls after a long dry period.) Schnegg then lays out the six phenomenological approaches that he deems most relevant for anthropology and shows how they can help to understand the situation and interpret data (from interviews with the Damara people). Each of these six approaches sheds light on a different aspect of the phenomenon as it appears to the pastoralists. Together, they complement each other and provide a comprehensive description of the ethnographic situation.

—   The first and most basic approach draws on Husserl's concept of intentionality (*of-ness*). Applied to Schnegg's field study, this means that, for example, the appearance of rain (as intentional phenomenon) can be characterized by co-perceptions, is given in abundances, and thus consists of inner- and outer horizons. This helps to explain why the phenomenon appears different to the investigator (as positive) than to the pastoralist (as a deadly threat). In anthropology, one can therefore apply and extend such a study of appearance (here: rain) to longer temporal intervals and understand how environmental concepts are created (differently) (cf. Schnegg 2023b).

—   The next phenomenological approach is indebted to Heidegger's concept of Being-in-the-Word (*in-ness*). Considering being-in-the-world-as-pastoralist (i.e., looking at the totality of the context in which they are embedded) can make clear how the appearance of rain is embedded in the overall being-in-the-world of this indigenous population, and how this in turn differs to the being-in-the-world-as-anthropologist (as a Western, academic ethnographer) (Schnegg 2023a, p. 77).

—   A third approach is related to Merleau-Ponty's phenomenology of embodiment (*embodied-ness*). It directs attention to the way in which phenomena always also appear through the body. Knowing the weather includes, for example, feeling the cool, humid air on the skin, as the body anticipates rain (as before it rains the wind direction changes, it gets colder, and this coldness and moisture in the air is felt) (Schnegg 2023a, p. 78).

—   A fourth approach makes use of Waldenfels' responsive phenomenology (*responsive-ness*). Here one is reminded that meaning is primarily an attempt to "get a grip on the alien, the insecure and the chaotic that irritate us" and thus a response to the demands of a situation. The weather situation affects everyone, but it affects the ethnographer and the pastoralist in different ways. What does the change of clouds, wind, and sun mean? How should one react to the changes? For the pastoralist, the environment contains alienness and danger, and poses demands, to which they must respond. The ethnographer has different knowledge and habits and thus different registers (pastoral, religious, scientific), from which the phenomenon emerges differently, and that forecloses our possible responses. Waldenfels' approach thus helps to explain how we know and respond situationally and how this differs between different people at different times (Schnegg 2023a, p. 81; Leistle 2017).

—   A fifth approach is indebted to Herrman Schmitz's New Phenomenology (*in-betweenness*). With this one can analyze atmospheres and emotions between people, objects, and practices. The weather situation—the view of the sky when opening a window, the sky that grows dark, the wetness of the wind—creates an atmosphere that affects the pastoralist. He is worried, frightened, fearful; his body is alert and tense, ready to take action (e.g., to protect the animals). However, this also shows how two people, present at the same time and place, can be

3

surrounded by different atmospheres. And it shows why the ethnographer might not be receptive to the atmosphere of the pastoralist, as they differ in experiences, knowledge, and aims (cf. Schnegg 2024, 2025).

— The sixth approach comes from Edith Stein and her theory of empathy (*withness*). This multilayered approach comprises three steps: (1) recognizing an emotional expression from the other (or the environment), (2) being pulled in by the experience of the expression and urged to responsively engage with it, and (3) attempting to reflectively understand the other (or the environment) anew because of the experienced expressions (Schnegg 2023a, p. 84). These steps, which have already been fruitfully applied within anthropology (Throop 2008, 2010), allow one to expand the concept of empathy beyond the human and to clearly demarcate its limits (Schnegg and Breyer 2022). Schnegg describes, for example, how the pastoralist goes through all three steps when empathizing with his goats (regarding the chance of heavy rain), but only step one when it comes to the wind (Schnegg 2023a, p. 86).

▪▪ A Critical Phenomenological Anthropology

In conclusion, we can see from Schnegg's systematic review of how to apply phenomenology to anthropology, that phenomenology provides universal concepts for theorizing experience—concepts that help to make differences visible. However, these concepts are not by themselves enough for understanding the different experiences he and the pastoralist are having in particular situations. For this, anthropology must add the concrete historical, cultural, social, political, and economic context. In the formula of Schnegg: "*what* we experience in a situation is a function of *how* we experience it plus the *context* in which the experience takes place" (86). Here, we clearly see possible links with critical phenomenology (cf. ▶ Sect. 3.1) or feminist and post-colonial analysis. We see, for example, how analyses of inhibited intentionality (Young), normative frames of orientation (Ahmed) the objectifying or post-colonial gaze (Fanon) could be used to embed first-person descriptions within existing contexts and socio-economic structures, and thus help to develop a critical phenomenological anthropology. One example that Schnegg gives is how the formerly self-evident practice of food sharing (among the Damara pastoralists) becomes something people are ashamed of. This "reveals how discourses and institutions, including neoliberal and partly Christian ideologies of the self, change what is 'normal' and, with this, the 'gazes' the subject must face" (Schnegg 2023a, p. 91). In line with critical phenomenology, these discourses and institutions can be conceptualized as quasi-transcendental structures that circumscribe the concrete possibilities of experience of the Damara pastoralists.

▪▪ Ethnographic Field Work and the Event

Rather than ask how phenomenological concepts can be applied to anthropology, one might ask what makes anthropology unique (and different from armchair phenomenology) and what phenomenology could learn from it. For anthropologists Christopher Stephan and Jason Throop, this is the fact that the empirical field of anthropology is grounded in the singularity and particularity of the event. Events for them are more than measurable facts; they are necessarily personal, that is, they open up horizons of possibility for a subject to take up (cf. also Romano 2009). A paradigmatic example would be the event of 'birth'. Ethnographic practice is characterized by the concrete interpersonal encounter (between ethnographer and interlocuters), as an in-between that cannot be reduced to mere transcendental structures or customary modes of interaction. In this sense, there are uncontrollable and unexpected moments with the interlocutors, where the usual anticipations of the ethnographer are disrupted and new horizons of understanding emerge between ethnographer and interlocutor. In their fieldwork in Ottawa, Canada on Charismatic Protestant experiences of spiritual healing, Stephan and Throop describe an open interview with a woman named Debra in which she tries to describe how she felt after experiencing an extraordinary conversion to the charismatic Christian movement. Here, one situation stood out, where, after a long silence, Debra shook the hand of the ethnographer to show what she meant (that her knowledge was not like 'book understanding' but rather experiential, a shared bodily understanding or an agreement) (Stephan and Throop 2023, p. 348). As Stephan and Throop argue, the event—how it affected both parties, how it stood out in the entire field study—is what is foundational for anthropological research. Only on the grounds of this shared event can one make general conceptual distinctions. However, the particular event can never be reduced to a mere illustration of a general structure or concept, i.e., between, say, 'knowing that' and 'knowing how' (cf. Ryle 1946). Rather, events like this show the limits of concepts in capturing the indeterminacy of the event and its excess of meaning. Although, we see that the basic commonality of embodiment makes such an understanding possible (through the handshake), this at the same time shows the differences between the experiences and embodiment of ethnographer and interlocutor.

▪▪ The Ethnographic Epoché

Throop (2010, 2012, 2018), and before him other anthropologists (Jackson 1995; Bidney 1973), have spoken of an ethnographic epoché, which, unlike the phenomenological epoché, happens passively. Being affected by certain unfamiliar events can shed light on latent assumptions, orientations, habits, and dispositions, which are normally taken for granted. Rather than bracketing, or self-consciously reflecting on, one's prior prejudices and assumptions, the ethnographic epoché relies on engaged participation in the world of the indigenous group being studied. This aspect of engaged or participatory science, as 'being there', can already be found in Geertz (Geertz 1988), who points to the highly situated nature of ethnographic description. In line with Waldenfels, one can call the ethnographic epoché a *responsive* one, as it presupposes openness towards the other in a shared situation, where there is a direct intersubjective and intracorporeal encounter (Stephan and Throop 2023, p. 340). Here, one can point to a difference or complementariness between *phenomenological anthropology* on the one hand and *sociological ethnography* on the other. While the former tries to unsettle the assumptions of their mostly Western and privileged study participants, (see, for example, the study of how police officers typically identify and treat juvenile delinquents, (Cicourel 1976)), the latter aims not to shake but to *restore the foundations* of the social world of their interlocutors (Katz and Csordas 2003, p. 276).

■■ Prejudices and Participatory Understanding

The call of phenomenology—to return to the things themselves—must not be misunderstood in this context as a naive call to return to a supposedly immediate and directly accessible experience (of one's own or of another culture). Nor should it be equated with a hostility to theory. One should be cautious not to suppose that a confrontation with another culture by itself leads to a break with the natural attitude. For this to occur, the ethnographer must inhabit a special responsive, and thus ethical, attitude. Not for just anyone does an experienced deviation from normality motivate critical reflection or the opening of new horizons. After all, such a deviation might just as easily lead to a devaluation of the other culture or a defense of one's own normality, culture, origin, or nationality, as it has throughout much of the history of anthropology from the Enlightenment to its culmination in racial doctrine under Hitler and National Socialism. Contemporary phenomenological ethnography therefore tries both to reflect critically on its own methodological presuppositions, expectations, and observations and to establish a direct and engaged contact or 'existential inside view'. The latter is intended to open new ways of understanding 'alien' or unfamiliar cultures, for example, through empathetic understanding or practical co-experiencing. In field work, one is confronted with one's own prejudices about the culture or subject groups to be studied, not only in advance or in hindsight, but during the observation itself, i.e., performatively. In the attempt to participate and co-live in the everyday life of the subjects to be studied, the researcher's own starting position and presuppositions are made explicit—for example, by being surprised or irritated. In the ethnographic investigation itself, a kind of intersubjective and intercultural constitution of meaning takes place, which determines both the other and one's own culture in mutual contrast. Hermeneutically speaking, it is only in the confrontation with the other that one's own pre-understanding becomes apparent: in trying to understand others, I come to understand myself differently.

■■ Ethnography, Psychopathology, and the Lack of Self-evidence

Both phenomenological psychiatry or psychopathology and phenomenological sociology or anthropology try to describe the self-evidence of world experience or its lack. Both do this in conversations with, or through reports from, other subjects, i.e., from a *second-person perspective*. It is no longer one's own experience that is the starting point of the description (first-person perspective), but the observed, expressed, or articulated and reported experience of other people. If the challenge of cultural and social research lies in the fact that the researchers and the researched represent two different worlds or normalities (e.g., different cultures), in psychopathology it lies in the fact that a common basis for description is often lacking altogether. As the German psychiatrist Wolfgang Blankenburg emphasized, a distinction must be made here between the method of reduction or epoché, i.e., a temporary methodical bracketing of self-evidence (i.e., the natural attitude), and the concrete pathological loss of the same. Patients with schizophrenia, for example, must desperately strive to maintain a minimum of common sense, or fight against the terror or the groundlessness of their own existence (Blankenburg 2012, pp. 97, 133, 93, 90). The challenge of both disciplines—and of the classical phenomenological method—lies in recognizing and describing commonalities as well as differences. However, contrary to the theoretical phenomenologist, psychiatrists and ethnographers must enact a responsiveness and empathy towards the other and their experiences. They must accept the radical difference or alienness, and work with and through it.

▪▪ Describing Without Prejudice?

In this context, 'to describe without prejudice' does not mean to negate a theory, but to ground it in experience. A critical distance towards one's assumptions is crucial, whether it is methodologically induced or initiated by concrete intersubjective experiences. In the case of ethnography or anthropology, this includes presuppositions about what makes a 'human' or a 'culture' and what constitutes relevant categories of analysis. In psychiatry, for example, a critical approach to the distinction between normality and pathology is required. Also, we see that in both disciplines, description is always situated and cannot (and maybe should not) be neutral, as it relies on intersubjective interaction and empathy, and is also shaped by historical, social, and economic background. Although minimal structures or conditions can be identified that apply to all people (embodiment, temporality, spatiality, language, etc.) or cultures (tools, tradition, rituals, etc.), the pure essence or the original of a culture or psychopathological phenomenon cannot be determined a priori once and for all. After all, it is always specific, culturally, socially, and historically situated people who study other specific, culturally, socially, and historically situated people. Especially in the doctor-patient relationship, the asymmetry between psychiatrists and patients, researchers and researched, becomes clear. There remains a power imbalance between those investigating and those investigated, which can take on stigmatizing, imperial, or racist traits, as the post-colonial critique within ethnography and anthropology has shown. This occurred for example, when twentieth-century Western anthropologists studied so-called 'primitive' peoples and either devalued them as uncivilized or idealized and romanticized them as 'noble savages'. A similar danger lurks when in psychiatry deviant experiences and behavior are too quickly pathologized or the real suffering from a mental illness is idealized as creative genius.

▪▪ Transcendental Questions and Critique of Methods

Is research in these areas transcendentally relevant? According to Husserl, the transcendental arises when we no longer ask how something is given to us, but how anything can be given to us at all, that is, when the conditions of the possibility of givenness as such are investigated. For psychiatry, we can tentatively answer this questions with a 'yes'—transcendental questions are implicated—since it deals with the investigation of borderline cases of experience where any temporal and content coherence in self- and world-reference is lost. Where are the limits of experience and of the self? Where does experience altogether dissolve? Here, a look at psychopathologies is instructive. For the fields of sociology, ethnography, and

3

anthropology, by contrast, the answer is 'no'—they need not concern themselves with the search for a priori transcendental necessities. However, these fields point us to the concrete genealogy of expressions and sense (as *quasi-transcendental structures*) and by this remind us of the limits of our own presuppositions, as these are relativized in view of history, other cultures, and foreign situations. Phenomenology, ethnography, and psychopathology can thus test and correct each other, to meet the *imperative of describing without prejudices*. In doing so, one should not only question one's own preconceptions, but also the historical-cultural conditions of one's field. Such a *genealogical critique of science* must go beyond a purely phenomenological investigation (e.g., by explicitly asking about the historical or economic, i.e., structural, conditions).

3.3.1 Phenomenology and Qualitative Research

How can we collect and include experiences, that is experiential reports and data, in the analysis of current research? And what is specifically phenomenological in these research practices it, apart from the thematic focus on experience itself?

In such qualitative social (psychological or anthropological) research, the subjects themselves, along with their experience and their behavior, are the objects of investigation. Qualitative research, which refers to phenomenology as a method, collects experiential data in the form of direct questioning (interviews or recorded experience reports, e.g., diaries or journals) and sometimes also includes the observation of behavior as background information. This approach usually goes beyond a one-time survey and instead focuses on a group over a longer period of time. This can be described as a kind of ethnographic approach or short-term field research (cf. Ravn 2021).

▪▪ Interpretative Phenomenological Analysis (IPA)

A common method used for this is Interpretative Phenomenological Analysis, or *IPA*, a hybrid method inspired by both sociology and phenomenology. A current study in the field of medicine and nursing sciences involving the Dutch phenomenologist Jenny Slatman can illustrate the use of this method (cf. Bootsma et al. 2021). The study focuses on suffering from chronic fatigue in cancer patients, and the role played in this experience by the loss and recovery of old habits and the acquisition of new habits. The aim of the study was not only to find out how chronic fatigue is associated with the loss of habits (i.e., how this is experienced by the subjects concerned), but also how to help cancer patients build new habits in therapy so that those affected can regain a sense of normality.

For this purpose, semi-structured interviews were conducted with a targeted sample of 25 participants who had suffered from severe CCRF (*chronic-cancer-related fatigue*) for at least three months. A topic guide on the lived experiences of the patients was used. This consisted of open questions based on research literature and clinical experience, and which were tested in advance at the Institute for Psycho-oncology, together with therapists, who had clinical expertise in the treatment of patients with CCRF. The topic guide covered the areas of experience (descriptions, sensations, cognitions, patterns, attributions, etc.), consequences (for daily life, the body, the feeling of self, etc.) as well as actions (in relation to oneself and others; mention of enabling and hindering factors, etc.). The IPA was then used to analyze the transcripts, by 'coding' the reports in six steps. According to the authors, the IPA is particularly useful for examining the multidimensionality (i.e., the dynamics), the influence of the context, and the subjective dimension of CCRF.

■ ■ Six Steps of Coding Experiential Reports

The *first step* of coding, according to IPA, consists of reading and rereading the transcripts, which serves to familiarize the researchers with the data. In the *second step*, the researchers begin to make initial notes on the relevant reports, a process referred to as 'open coding'. In the *third step*, researchers identify recurring themes, which are then used in subsequent interviews. In the above study, a selection of six categories (metaphors, beliefs, comparisons, responses, helpful and unhelpful responses) were divided into one of two classes: maladaptive (e.g., carry on, deny and resist) and adaptive (e.g., slow down, stop or reduce) responses. In the *fourth step*, the researchers look for connections between the emerging themes. In the above study, they designed a table with two general patterns in the coping process: *adaptation* (individual/social) to new circumstances and *letting go* (individual/social) of old habits. In the *fifth step*, researchers summarize the individual interviews and check them for completeness. In the *sixth step*, they conduct two team discussions to identify overarching themes that comprehensively describe both adaptive and maladaptive reactions. Thematic inconsistencies between the team members are discussed until a consensus is reached. Here, it is advantageous for the members of the research group to have a multidisciplinary background, i.e., philosophical, clinical and/or qualitative research experience in psycho-oncology.

> **Definition**
>
> The 'IPA' (cf. Smith et al. 2009), or Interpretative Phenomenological Analysis, is a method developed by psychologist Jonathan Smith, among others, that is used in the field of social and health research. In IPA, no pre-established hypothesis or theory is tested; based on the experience reports, meanings and structures are determined. For this, semi-structured interviews are used, i.e., interviews that specify certain areas of experience, but are otherwise kept open. After the transcription of the data, the researchers work with the text and comment ('code') it in several rounds. This is intended to provide insight into (a) the first-person perspective of the subjects (phenomenology) and (b) how subjects make sense of their experiences (hermeneutics). In the further course of the analysis, the researchers catalog these 'codes' and begin to look for so-called themes, i.e., recurring patterns of meaning (ideas, thoughts, feelings), which can then be integrated into overarching themes. Ideally, the process of commenting and coding is carried out by several researchers, who discuss and negotiate the findings.

3

As a result of the above study, five interconnected themes or typical reactions were identified that were equally relevant to all participants in the experience of CCRF as well as in the documented gradual adjustment to the new life circumstances: (1) discovering bodily and emotional boundaries, (2) communicating support needs, (3) reorganizing and planning activities and rest, (4) letting go of 'habitual identity' (Wehrle 2020b) and (5) recognizing and accepting CCRF.

■■ Genetic Levels of Habit Formation

As the authors emphasize, some of these themes or reactions correspond to the three levels of habit formation that can be distinguished in relation to Husserl and Merleau-Ponty (Wehrle 2020b). The first level of habit formation is defined as a style of experience that is based on direct passive reactions to repeated individual experiences. The fight against CCRF with habits and beliefs that are no longer 'adaptive' is a desperate attempt to continue on as before. This is reflected, for example, in the fact that patients neglect their own bodies. According to the research group, this is based on a primarily unconscious reaction to CCRF, the gradually intensifying experience of fatigue due to their developing cancer. The second level of habit formation refers in a mostly pre-reflective, but still active, way to previous bodily and practical experience (e.g., body memory). Topics such as 'discovering physical and emotional boundaries', 'communicating support needs' and 'planning and reorganizing activities and rest periods' are examples of habit formation at this level. Bodily experience and perception of the body are central in this phase; they are related to previous experiences and recorded by the patients in various self-observation processes, such as writing about experiences, recording activities, or taking care of their bodies. Although these processes are initially voluntary, they then turn into new bodily habits and thus become normal. The third level of habit formation is based on personal reflection; it aims to consciously change old habits and form and adhere to new behaviors and beliefs. This personal level of habit formation is reflected in the topics 'letting go of the accustomed identity' and 'recognizing and accepting CCRF'.

■■ Phenomenological Interpretation?

The phenomenological perspective can provide insight into the formation of new habits and beliefs and thus shed light on which reflective and pre-reflective processes would be most helpful in supporting a positive response to CCRF. The interpretative phenomenological analysis allows researchers to capture how subjects experience CCRF and react to it. The response to a chronic illness is a complex process that is never fully completed. However, typical elements of such a response can be determined with an eye to helping patients adjust to their new life circumstances.

IPA is also often used in nursing and health sciences as it is suitable for investigating how small subject groups in specific contexts experience a certain phenomenon (their disease, their sexuality, or other aspects of their lives). From a purely philosophical point of view, however, there is much to criticize about the understanding of phenomenology and its method, for example in the fields of psychology or pedagogy (cf. Zahavi 2018). For example, one can ask to what extent IPA really allows for a completely neutral and theory-free survey and whether this is even desirable in a practical context. In long-term research projects, it is not clear whether the orientation and focus of a qualitative study crystallizes solely from 'neutral' experience reports or whether it was influenced by certain phenomenological differentiations or previous experiences with patients. If it is the latter, this does not necessarily have to be understood as a bad thing or something to be criticized. Also, the orientation based on phenomenological concepts or results can lead to a new and revealing perspective on the experience of the subjects and the disease under investigation, which can complement other approaches. However, it is advisable to make this orientation and these assumptions explicit in advance and to justify their selection in order to ensure the transparency of the investigation.

Other phenomenological approaches, e.g., in educational science, are also influential in this context. On closer inspection, the methods or methodological recommendations adopted there, such as 'examine the experience as you experience it, independent of conceptualizations' or 'identify essential themes that characterize these experiences', etc. (cf. van Manen 1990, p. 31f.) only superficially share something with the philosophical questions and goals of phenomenology. This does not have to be a problem, as long as these approaches are transparent about how they apply or adjust concepts and methods of phenomenology to their purposes. However, some authors, like educational scientist Max van Manen, a Dutch-born Canadian scholar and professor emeritus from the University of Alberta, present their approaches as true to the original sources and as valid interpretations of philosophical phenomenology. Rather than putting phenomenological concepts and methods into practice, they then present a misguided, confusing, and overly complex version of the epoché or reduction. In van Manen's case, the result is nine different forms of reduction followed by even more methods and heuristic moves. The effect is to make the reader dizzy by even reading it! It is difficult to imagine such a convoluted tangle being mastered by practitioners such as nurses, doctors, or clinical psychologists (cf. Zahavi 2020).

▪▪ Better to Forget the Epoché?

This has prompted Dan Zahavi to ask whether every application of phenomenology must necessarily be transcendental or must strictly adhere to its original methods (cf. Zahavi 2021). Qualitative investigations offer a variety of possibilities for generating and interpreting data. The selection of qualitative research methods depends on the subject of investigation, i.e., on the researcher's access to the relevant individuals, groups, and fields, as well as their research questions and interests. Therefore, it seems paradoxical and almost unphenomenological that many qualitative research studies that refer to phenomenology insist that the application of the epoché, in the sense of transcendental reduction, must be at the forefront (cf. Allen-Collinson and Evans 2019; Giorgi 1975, 2008). Zahavi concludes that this is not always advisable, especially with empirical research and therapy.

It is misleading when, for example, researchers like van Manen (2017, p. 820; cf. Zahavi 2021, p. 260) explicitly demand the application of phenomenological methods such as eidetic variation or transcendental reduction in empirical research. Due to the various, sometimes incorrect, interpretations of these methods and the

3

lack of philosophical background on the part of the empirical researcher, this often leads more to confusion than to systematic results. Instead of getting lost in methodological discussions about the interpretation or applications of the epoché or reduction, Zahavi therefore advises us to 'forget' the epoché for pragmatic reasons. It would be more productive if one were to orient oneself instead to the results or the concepts and distinctions gained in philosophical phenomenology (such as embodiment or interplay between *Leib* und *Körper*, intentionality, life-world, etc.) and then apply, differentiate, expand, or empirically verify these where they are useful for practice (cf. Zahavi 2021).

■■ **Theory and Practice**

Terms like 'transcendental epoché' and 'reduction', as we have seen, are associated with very specific transcendental philosophical goals in Husserl. Their purpose is to free us from a certain natural dogmatism in which we simply accept the world as given, and to open up a series of fundamental epistemological and metaphysical questions. The execution of the transcendental reduction is intended to help the-matize and make understandable the self-evidence of the being of the world as a whole. Such philosophical reflection deals with the essential interconnectedness of subjectivity, reason, truth, and being; these are important transcendental philo-sophical ideas. However, it is not obvious why someone who wants to apply phe-nomenology *outside* of philosophy should constantly refer to these ideas. While such reflections may be relevant for a theoretical determination of experience within these disciplines, this is only partially true for the *practice* of the psychia-trist, the psychotherapist, the nursing staff, or the qualitative researcher. For them, other aspects of phenomenology may be more important, such as phenomenolo-gy's critique of scientism, its recognition of the importance of the lifeworld, its attempt to adopt an unbiased attitude, or its careful analysis of human existence, in which the subject is understood as an embodied, socially and culturally embed-ded being-in-the-world (cf. Zahavi 2021).

In a non-philosophical context, therefore, it is not important for phenomeno-logical research or practice to strictly adhere to Husserl's (or Heidegger's or Merleau-Ponty's or any one else's) cursory instructions. Far more important is that the application enables new insights or better therapeutic interventions, i.e., that it makes a valuable difference to the scientific community and/or the patients. The successful application of phenomenology is therefore not so much measured by the exact imitation of the methods described by Husserl, but rather by how these meth-ods are adapted and further developed according to their subject of investigation.

■■ **The Peculiarity of the Second-person Perspective**

It therefore seems appropriate to first reflect on the specificity of the subjects of investigation and on what is phenomenologically relevant in qualitative surveys of those subjects before opting for a particular philosophical method. This would cor-respond entirely to Husserl's criticism of the psychology of his time: Here he emphasized that one cannot simply use natural scientific methods, which were developed to study material things, to investigate the psyche, since the psyche is a very special kind of object. Similarly, a qualitative interview is phenomenologically neither a neutral analysis of the object of investigation, nor a description of one's own experience. Rather the *second-person perspective* characteristic of an interview necessarily implies a reciprocal relation between an I and a You (cf. Zahavi 2015). And yet this is not a personal, but a scientific, interaction, in which the researchers approach the subjects to be investigated with specific interests and questions. The interviewers are therefore just as involved in the production of knowledge and meaning as the subjects to be interviewed, and one can speak of a co-production of knowledge. In addition to recorded oral conversations or written reports, the investigation also includes unarticulated information in the form of gestures, facial expressions, or tone of voice, with which something is indicated. All of this is part of a reciprocal interaction and influences its dynamics. It is advisable to reflect on these phenomenological circumstances and make them as transparent as possible.

■ ■ Situated Analysis

Qualitative research can be considered situated inquiry in two ways. First, qualitative researchers deal with the concrete historically, culturally, and socially situated experience of their research subjects. Due to these contextualized conditions, the qualitative researcher cannot fulfill the scientific criteria of 'replicability' in the same way that quantitative researchers can. The latter use instruments and methods in a standardized way so that measurements are consistent over time and hence repeatable (Golafshani 2003). Qualitative researchers, by contrast, rely on subjective perspectives and experiences. While these would be considered undesirable distortions in quantitative analyses, since they 'disturb' the replicability of the objective data, they remain the proper research domain of qualitative analyses. Second, the qualitative researcher, like the research subjects, is herself situated 'in-the-world'—and thus part of the situation in which data is co-generated. Qualitative researchers must therefore be aware that their own history, biography, social class, ethnic affiliation, gender, etc. cannot be neutralized, but co-determine the interaction. These factors should therefore be explicitly addressed in the study. This does not mean that the situation determines whether and how one can generate data in the right way. As sports scientist Susanne Ravn emphasizes, one does not have to be a dancer to understand or investigate the experiences of dancers. Rather, it is about reflecting on the different positions that researchers take in relation to the subjects and practices being studied in the analysis. If one has a practical proximity of experience, e.g., because one dances oneself, this can also be used productively in qualitative research.

> ▶ **Example: Bodily self-perception in dance**
>
> In what way are dancers aware of their own bodies and embodiment while they dance? This question is posed by sports scientist Susanne Ravn and phenomenologist Dorothée Legrand in a recent qualitative research project (Ravn 2009; Legrand and Ravn 2009). Professional dancers make particularly interesting cases, since the experience of their own movement is of great importance for their training.
>
> Given the diversity of dance practices in the European context, different genres and styles of dance were included in the study. A total of 13 dancers with various backgrounds (ballet, contemporary dance, improvisation, etc.) from various European cities

participated in the research project. To integrate the local contexts and their influence on the dance practices into the study, the dancers were interviewed and observed on site. The short-term field research, typically lasting one week, was conducted in Copenhagen, London, Amsterdam, Malmö, Brussels, and Vienna. It included a formal interview, which was prepared based on the short-term field research. This was usually repeated twice with each of the dancers (Ravn 2009, pp. 118–120).

Susanne Ravn has a professional dance background herself, and this was used in the study, for example, by participating in some of the trainings. Using her observations during participation, the formal interviews were prepared. Dancers were asked to describe their practices both from within (as lived and experienced) and in relation to their external structures and contexts. Often, specific situations, such as training, were included in the questions. The researcher's familiarity with the subject matter required careful consideration of how to maintain an open and self-reflective attitude towards the subject matter. In addition, the data and analysis were discussed several times with other researchers who had no dance experience. These discussions were used particularly between the interviews and in preparation for follow-up interviews (Ravn and Hansen 2013).

In the subsequent phases of the analysis, overarching themes were first identified for each case individually. Coding categories were developed based on the dance practice and its contextual embedding. To verify the validity of the generated descriptions, the dancers were asked to either accept, comment on, and/or adjust the edited interview (Ravn 2009, pp. 141 ff.). The edited transcriptions, along with the complete original transcription and observation notes, were included in the case-specific analyses. It was particularly noticeable that the dancers each described in their own way how they had to feel their body in a certain way to be able to dance well. The specific way they were aware of their bodies was in turn dependent on the techniques and styles in which they trained and performed. For the ballet dancer, it was all about feeling 'aligned' and bodily in place. For one of the improvisers, it was absolutely necessary to feel 'weighted'. For a dancer who specifically referred to Body-Weather training (a Butoh-related dance practice), it was important to feel 'grounded', which was central to her expressive dance activities (Ravn 2009, 2017).

In the following phase of the phenomenological analysis, it was then checked whether certain structures of experience, despite the diversity of people and styles, were recognizable across dancers and dance practices. Specifically, the phenomenological analysis by Dorothée Legrand (2007a, 2007b) on the bodily self was used. As a result, it was noted that a generally shared 'form of experience of the subjectivity of the body' seems to be central to dancing. This is a special kind of pre-reflective, performative bodily self-awareness. Although it is a kind of perception, it does not aim at reification or objectification (Legrand and Ravn 2009, p. 405), as in the case of body image, where the body is the object of one's own perception or imagination. ◄

The involvement of researchers in the situation thus requires a (critical) self-reflexivity throughout the entire research process. The integration of qualitative research methods and phenomenological analysis calls for research methods that are sensitive to the contextual premises of the experiences associated with certain cultural and social practices. When investigating the experiences of dancers or athletes, for example, it is important to connect these experiences with the historical and cultural context of their practices. To what extent do rules, traditions, and norms play a role in—or form the framework of—these subjectively executed practices? An open-ended, non-objectifying, and self-reflective perspective on dance and sport is helpful here. At the same time, behavioral observations ought to be included in the design of such studies. These amount to short-term ethnographic field studies or participatory observations. Ideally, the results can then be critically evaluated with a cultural or sociological perspective on the given behavior.

▪▪ Guidelines for a Phenomenological Interview

Given all the possible challenges facing the application of phenomenology to diverse topics and fields—especially those arising from the investigation of subjectivity in all its concrete forms—are there some tentative guidelines that one can follow? Instead of drawing a neat conclusion, I will present five general guidelines for a phenomenologically inspired interview, drawn from the research of the applied phenomenologist Simon Høffding (cf. Høffding 2018):

1. *Try to go back to the 'things' themselves:*
   Create as open and detailed an experience report as possible, without presupposing existing theories, explanations, or beliefs on the topic.
2. *Try to identify typical structures of a specific experience (or part of subjectivity):*
   Although one must highlight the specificity of the subject under investigation, invariant or typical structures of experience can be identified. The phenomenological interview is therefore more than simple introspection. Although it includes descriptions of 'inner' experience, it does not stop there. The aim is to discover invariant phenomenological structures that apply to all descriptions of a specific experience (of illness, movement, etc.).

To meet these first two guidelines, Høffding suggests two stages of investigation, a descriptive and an analytical one, which should overlap and mutually influence each other:

a) In the first stage, interviews are conducted and descriptions of experience are generated by the researchers familiarizing themselves with the lived experiences of the subjects under investigation.
b) In the second stage, these descriptions are analyzed, and it is evaluated to what extent they can be generalized, to be able to make statements about structures of experience or subjectivity as such.

Here, it is explicitly intended that the phenomenological theory influences the interpretations of the descriptions. At the same time, however, further descriptions in the course of the analysis can question this theoretical framework. Descriptions of the second-person perspective and their phenomenological analysis are thus in a dialectical relationship—until a certain degree of consistency is achieved, i.e., all or most descriptions can be made clear under the conceptual framework developed

3

in this way. However, this leads to the question of how one can be sure that the analysis really hits the phenomenon one wants to investigate (in the case of Høffding's study, that of musical absorption), and not another (e.g., the experience of memories)?

For this, a third phenomenological guideline is relevant:

3. *Remind yourself of the irreducibility of subjective data*:
   Experiential reports cannot be completely objectified, which is why a different, non-quantitative, method is needed in the first place.

In this context, the question arises to what extent the description of an experience distorts it. However, this is only a problem if one understands the description as a kind of representation of the experience, which can be either adequate or inadequate to the experience. Instead, the description or articulation of the experience can also be interpreted as another kind of manifestation of the same experience. Every experience, such as, for example, having a headache, goes through various gradual or qualitative stages, from the first signs that are not perceived as such (the letters blur, concentration decreases), to the explicit articulation of, or reaction to, the pain (I decide to take a painkiller). In this context, Dan Zahavi argues, for example, that a **reflection on, or description of, an experience** should **not be seen as a distortion of a pre-reflective experience**, but rather as an **opening onto such an experience** (Zahavi 1999, pp. 181–189; 2005, pp. 89–96, 2011). Of course, this does not mean that descriptions cannot be faulty. However, faultiness alone is not a sufficient argument to disqualify a method, but only a reason to think about how this faultiness can be reduced and the method improved. Descriptions of experiences cannot be reproduced like other data in the strict sense. After all, experiences are not static data, but temporal occurrences.

The fourth phenomenological guideline is therefore:

4. *Keep in mind that research is embodied, situated, and enactive*:
   This emphasizes that questioning is also a bodily skill, a knack that one must practice. Here, the aspect of participant observation plays a role. Spending active time with the subjects to be studied can contribute to the contextualization and understanding of the descriptions. But this also means that no questioning or description can be neutral. Every investigation is always also interpretation; it reveals certain perspectives, while at the same time concealing others.

Does this mean that every experience report must be distorted or untrustworthy? Not necessarily. Validity can be checked, for example, based on internal phenomenological consistency. Such consistency refers to the possibility of finding an interpretation that can make all or most descriptions of the interviews understandable. The more descriptions that can be made understandable by means of a phenomenological interpretation, the stronger its consistency.

However, an external control must be added here, which leads to a fifth guideline:

5. *Make sure that you validate your results intersubjectively:*
   The results should be compared with other studies and discussed with other researchers.

This **methodological step of intersubjective validation** (Varela and Shear 1999, p. 10) or confirmation (Gallagher and Zahavi 2008, pp. 29–31) is, as Husserl himself emphasized, indispensable.

3.3.2 Phenomenology and Quantitative Research

As a philosophy of consciousness and subjective bodily experience, phenomenology is related not only to psychology and sociology with their qualitative research programs, but also to cognitive psychology and neuroscience, whose research programs are partially quantitative. Here, the question becomes how descriptions of experience relate to the neurological underpinnings of those experiences. In other words, how can experiential data be correlated with objective data?

■■ Naturalization of Phenomenology

For this to happen, the phenomenological investigation must be naturalized to some extent, that is, directly linked with physical, biological, or material processes. But doesn't phenomenology then lose its claim to impartiality, since this requires not assuming the truth of any scientific theory, including physicalism? And doesn't it sacrifice its transcendental claims, since these require taking the conscious and cognizing subject as primary? These worries have sparked a lively scholarly debate going back to the late 1990s (cf. Petitot et al. 1999). Some advocate a pragmatic attitude. After all, Husserl himself noted that all substantive results of transcendental phenomenology also have their validity on the concrete level (i.e., the natural attitude). Others see such a naturalized phenomenology—a phenomenology in the service of empirical research—as problematic. In any case, it should be noted that while phenomenology is critical of scientism, which has forgotten its reference to the lifeworld, it is by no means anti-scientific. Whether, or to what to extent, phenomenology can be naturalized remains an important, and as yet unresolved, question. Does naturalization only mean that experience and consciousness are always embodied and therefore necessarily associated with a biological, physiological, or material counterpart? Or does it entail that experience and consciousness—perhaps with more advanced technology—can ultimately be traced back to, or even reduced to, neuronal processes?

■■ Reductionism

The most common meaning of 'naturalization' is that of reduction. It is assumed that in principle, every phenomenon of consciousness can be reduced to something 'natural', i.e., material. Just as water can be reduced to its chemical components H_2O. Reduction presupposes a physicalistic worldview in which only that which is material, i.e., extended, causally effective, and directly measurable, is understood as real. Although this ultimately assumes a *monism* (there is only one form of being or reality) or an *identity theory* (the mental is identical with the material; the feeling with the neuronal state), the problem of *dualism* remains.

How do my subjective experiences and thoughts relate to the simultaneous neural activities? How can the meaning and quality of my experience be explained by neural activities? And why is consciousness needed at all if it can apparently be reduced to the material and functional level of the brain? This 'hard' problem of consciousness, as David Chalmers calls it (see Chalmers 1995), remains unsolved. It almost seems as if there are two layers of being or two worlds—that of the material, visible, and measurable, and that of the mental and ideal, a *res extensa* (extended thing) and a *res cogitans* (thinking thing), as Descartes called them. Only now it is not the *res cogitans* that controls the body, as Descartes had it; it is the body or brain that produces the illusion or effect of consciousness.

This form of naturalization thus essentially wants to reduce subjective experience to a sub-area of objectivity (here understood as material reality). However, this does not solve the problem of consciousness. After all, we still have experiences and feelings, even if they are declared scientifically irrelevant. This then leads to a double 'explanatory gap' (see Levine 1983): that between measurable brain activities and experiences on the one hand, and that between the everyday life of people and the science that excludes this domain as (unscientific) on the other.

▪▪ The Forgetting of the Lifeworld

This is exactly what Husserl criticized in *The Crisis of European Sciences*, written in 1938 (see CES/Hua VI), namely, that science has lost its connection to the lifeworld. Scientists have forgotten that they and their practice belong to the lifeworld. It is out of the lifeworld that their questions and problems—the very motivation to do science in the first place—emerge. The divergence of these two 'worlds' (the objective world and the lifeworld) led in the 1930s—and perhaps still leads today—to a wave of science skepticism and rejection, a flight to alternative truths and esotericism.

▪▪ Property Dualism

Another, more inclusive, concept of naturalization is represented by David Chalmers (2010). In his property dualism, naturalization is synonymous with the expansion of our conception of nature. Here, the realm of experience is included in a more comprehensive concept of nature, without reducing the experience merely to physical nature (objectivity). The basic equipment of the world (its ontology) is thus expanded to include experience, which is defined as a new type of 'property'. However, it follows from the method of phenomenology (the change of attitude) that conscious experience is not a thing or property that one has, but rather the prerequisite for things to be given to us at all and for us to be able to differentiate them according to properties. Consciousness is therefore not something that one 'has' alongside other things or properties, but rather the way in which we are or live. It cannot therefore be limited to the domain of entities or properties that can be categorized, but rather describes our entire bodily subjectivity as lived and experienced from inside and outside. Consciousness is in this sense neither something purely material (brain) nor purely ideal (mind) but must be attributed to the bodily subject or living organism as a whole (see Fuchs 2011, 2017).

Property dualism cannot, therefore, fully explain why this additional 'property' has emerged, how it correlates with material processes or purely functionally determined cognitions. Nor can it explain what its utility is. A phenomenological investigation of perception, however, can show that consciousness—not only in its explicit form, but especially in the form of an implicit self-reference—is necessary for a coherent, i.e., real and objectively appearing, object perception. We not only experience things, but also, albeit mostly implicitly, our experience of these things.

■■ Consciousness: Secondary or Primary Role?

Perception is thus not a simple 'registering' of data, but the result of a relation of temporal impressions and their successful integration in a unified experience. The spatial and content context in which the 'thing' is located, as well as our movements, planned actions, sensations, and previous experiences, play a role in this. In short: It could turn out that consciousness, contrary to popular theories in the philosophy of mind or cognitive science, does not play a merely secondary role. A phenomenological perspective could help to highlight differences between automatic registration, symbolic representation, or statistical calculation, and human perception, thinking or habitual action. These differentiations could in turn help to distinguish biological (human) from artificial forms of intelligence.

Phenomenology can offer a theoretical-methodological alternative by making clear how subjectivity and objectivity belong together. The objective is always that which is valid not only for me, but for all potential subjects, i.e., it is intersubjectively valid. At the same time, phenomenology distinguishes different attitudes in which we perceive the world and ourselves, e.g., in a personal or scientific attitude, from inside and outside, etc.: Only together do these attitudes or perspectives add up to 'sense' or a 'world'. The scientific view of the world as a context of material thingness is itself a (historically contingent) attitude that we adopt in relation to the world and ourselves, and not a reality *in itself*. To acknowledge this in all modesty does not mean to deny this reality, its transcendence and precedence, but to critically reflect on our access to it.

■■ Objective Knowledge and Experience

So far, the most significant progress in neuroscience has come in the accumulation of objective knowledge about the body (here: the brain). For example, new imaging techniques have allowed high spatial resolution of various regions of the brain. And devices for electrical and magnetic recording have produced high temporal resolution of brain activity. This has resulted in an impressive corpus of anatomical and functional data about the central nervous system. Unfortunately, this considerable amount of information says nothing about the behaviors or experience that the mental processes are supposed to underpin—at least not until they are directly or indirectly related to subjective data. It still has to be determined, for example, what it feels like to undergo these corresponding neural processes, and how and why this feels differently for different subjects. What use is neuroscience if it cannot answer everyday questions, if it has no relation to our experiences? A

3

random collection of recorded EEG data or a colorful image of the brain has neither meaning nor significance without context. Representations only have this when we know what they represent: a specific human experience or activity, a change in relation to past experiences and brain activities, or in comparison to other people performing the same action. Without this correlation, that is, without a lifeworld context, a question, a specific human problem (such as lack of attention) or human suffering (such as depression), these numbers or images are insignificant. This necessity to establish a connection between objective determination and subjective experience makes phenomenology an important partner in psychopathology, medicine, and bioethics.

How then can the perspective of subjective experience be integrated into the quantitative? How can qualitatively recorded experience data or experience reports be related to objectively measurable body data, such as brain activity? There are various possibilities here. For example, one could ask test subjects to directly describe their experience during a measurement. However, the use of *self-reports* or *introspection* remains underdeveloped and methodologically deficient. It is used only with great skepticism and restraint. In practice, it often reduces to a multitude of yes-no or multiple-choice questions. Another possibility is the indirect inclusion of experience in the form of a *study of behavior*. This is often preferred on the grounds that an objective observation of behavior can be more easily compared with the objective data of brain measurement. However, one should not forget that observable movements, for example, are only accorded the status of a 'behavior' (and not just a mechanistic reflex) when they are associated with lived intentions and experience. In this sense, it is almost impossible to completely exclude lived subjectivity from neuroscience neuroscientific research.

■■ Transcendental Questions

If, on the other hand, one assumes objective neurobiological processes to be the origin (or triggering cause) of behavior or consciousness, one has not solved the 'hard' problem of subjectivity but only shifted it. Consciousness or experience are then just further objective facts added to the others. However, as soon as one practices science or philosophy, i.e., investigates, measures or reflects, one has already presupposed consciousness. This points to the fact that, regardless of how the brain may have originated and why, neuroscience relies on researching subjects with consciousness and a brain, who in turn examine this brain in other subjects as an object. Philosophically, the well-known transcendental questions arise here; practically, this means that experience, perception, and consciousness are necessary to give meaning to neuroscientific data, even if this meaning is considered secondary and derived (Bitbol 2014).

■■ Neurophenomenology

In the 1990s, a new sub-discipline called 'neurophenomenology' was developed by Chilean biologist, philosopher, and neuroscientist Francisco Varela, which tries to counter these difficulties. First, it invites researchers to develop new methods for investigating subjective experience. Methods for obtaining experience data should be given the same priority as methods for obtaining objective data (Depraz et al.

2003). Neurophenomenology advocates a permanent interplay between subjective and objective sources of information, which should support each other, i.e., it tries to transfer one level into the other (Gallagher 2003). One consequence of this newly established balance of methods is that the objective level of measurable data no longer has ontological priority. Neurophenomenology therefore wants to bracket the assumption that only objective or directly measurable data can provide information about reality. It thus shifts the perspective, away from the search for an objective solution to the origin of subjectivity, towards an investigation of how the identification of general structures of experience, which many or all subjects share, can help to objectively grasp consciousness and world (Varela 1999).

Neurophenomenology also applies a kind of phenomenological reduction, as it calls it, or a phenomenological change of attitude: away from the (assumed to be self-evidently objective) things, towards the question of their *givenness*. Here, with Husserl, it should be recognized that the first- and third-person perspectives are not two different areas, but two attitudes within (possible) experience. Just as we perceive ourselves as both lived body and as physical body, we can now perceive the latter with the help of new technology. This allows access to ongoing processes in our own body, which were previously not self-experienceable. In addition to our experience, there is now an arsenal of data on metrics such as heart rate, temperature, or brain activity. However, these do not give direct access to the bodily processes, but a statistically mediated reproduction, as is particularly clear in the measurement of brain activity. In functional magnetic resonance imaging, brain activity is not directly measured. What is directly measured are the changes in blood flow in the brain (hemoglobin content), which in turn indicates metabolic processes, which are then associated with brain activity. The statistically calculated difference in blood flow before and during an experimental investigation is then represented as a brain image.

▪▪ No Priority of Objectivity

Neurophenomenology points out that both levels, the experienced and the externally measured, must constantly be related to each other. Phenomenology and cognitive science or neuroscience and their respective results are mutually dependent, according to Varela. An overall assessment can only be given if both sciences are ready for a mutual clarification of these levels. However, this means that neuroscience cannot leave its claim to objectivity unquestioned. What is the condition of the possibility of the experience (measurement) of brain activities? What can be measured exactly? And how does it relate to behavior and experience? Without a reference to subjective experience, the measurements make no sense, as the measurements represent the specificity of a certain behavior compared to a 'resting state', which thereby makes the underlying neuronal activities objectively visible.

▪▪ Experience as a Starting Point

However, in neurophenomenology according to Varela, lived experience should be the starting and ending point of neuroscientific research and thus serve as the guiding thread of the investigation (Varela 1996, 1999). This means, first, that phenomenal consciousness is not considered a mere explanandum but the *basis* for every

3

explanation. Second, neurobiological processes (like experiences) are not simply a part of what 'exists' but a specific class of phenomena that were selected because of their invariance in relation to an experimental situation. Third, the correspondence between neuroscientific phenomena and the contents of consciousness should not be interpreted in terms of a one-sided causality. Rather, it should be understood as a continuum of what shows itself, as a kind of joint manifestation of the lived body and the perceived body. This can be seen, for example, in the simultaneity of the experienced 'decision' to move one's own arm, on the one hand, and the empirical observation of this movement, on the other (Bitbol 2014).

The necessity of the connection between brain events, behavior, and experience is of course not new and, by itself, quite uncontroversial. What is new—and specifically phenomenological—about it is the claim that the levels are mutually conditioned. This means that so-called 'disciplined self-reports' of the test subjects must be an integral part of the validation of a neurobiological approach and not just random or heuristic information. This does not mean either that experience can be reduced to functional or physiological processes, or that experience is independent of these processes. Instead of making certain physical or philosophical assumptions, attempts should be made on both levels to identify invariants in the experienced and measured data in a methodologically sound way and to relate these to each other.

■ ■ **Neurophenomenology** *light*

In its actual implementation, neurophenomenology has become a sort of 'neurophenomenology light': An attempt is made to pragmatically include the dimension of experience in the empirical investigation of brain activities with the help of phenomenological expertise, without neuroscience necessarily having to critically question its own assumptions or procedures. For example, phenomenologists, as experts in the first-person perspective or 'I-perspective', are invited into the laboratories of cognitive scientists for short consultations. The task of phenomenology here is mainly to contribute to objective neuroscience.

In this context, phenomenological descriptions and concepts are used to clarify the function of various biological processes (Thompson et al. 2005), in order to specify the correlation between the technically advanced neuroscientific data set and the still vague experiential knowledge. This is done by determining mutual constraints, i.e., certain aspects (subjective as well as objective) that cannot be changed without causing changes on the other level as well. The application of phenomenology to neuroscience usually takes place in one of two ways. Either phenomenological concepts and distinctions are used in the design and composition of questions for neuroscientific experiments, which is sometimes referred to as *frontloading phenomenology* (cf. Gallagher 2003), or research subjects are trained to pay attention to particular experiential states so that they can capture and report their experience with greater detail and nuance during an experiment (Lutz 2002), for example in a survey or microgenetic interview (Depraz et al. 2003).

■ ■ Experienced and Measured Attention

For example, in a neuroscientific perception experiment, a strong correlation was found between the state of 'potential readiness' and the reaction speed measured with an EEG when performing a perception task (Lutz 2002). The research subjects wrote subjective assessments under phenomenological guidance before the actual experiment, i.e., they were instructed to pay attention to their subjective state before and during the trial runs of the experiment: Were they distracted or not? Were there inattentive moments? Or, did they apply a specific cognitive strategy during the trials? Based on these prior training reports, descriptive categories were defined in order to divide the trial runs into phenomenological clusters, e.g., perceived readiness or unreadiness. During the trials, further phenomenological distinctions could then be made, for example between a stable and a hesitant readiness and a state of non-readiness.

> ▶ **Example: Neurophenomenology and meditating brains**
>
> How can statements about the experience of participants be integrated in a reliable and systematic way into neuroscientific studies on attention using imaging methods? A neurophenomenological experiment involving the phenomenologist Evan Thompson has taken up this challenge by using test subjects with proven experience in meditation (cf. Garrison et al. 2013). To link objective measurement data and subjective experience data, a real-time fMRI (rt-fMRI) was used, which could give the participants feedback about their own brain activity during an ongoing task. This real-time feedback during a focused attention task showed that the posterior cingulate cortex, which is 'normally' activated in the state of mind wandering or 'thought wandering', was not active during meditation.
>
> In a first experiment, both meditators and non-meditators reported a significant correlation between the feedback graphic and their subjective experience of focused attention on the one hand or mind wandering on the other. However, when they were instructed to consciously try to influence their brain activity, only the meditators were able to do so. They voluntarily brought about a significant deactivation of the posterior cingulate cortex. These results were subsequently replicated in a separate group of meditators using a novel stepwise rt-fMRI discovery protocol, in which the participants had no prior knowledge of the expected relationship between their experience and the feedback graph (i.e., focused attention versus mind wandering). These results confirm that the use of real-time fMRI in neuroscientific research makes it possible to link objective measurements of brain activity with reports of parallel subjective experiences. At the same time, they show that the expertise of meditators in introspective perception can be generalized (since the effect occurred in all test subjects with meditation experience) and applied to new contexts, here the execution of an attention task. ◄

■ ■ A New Form of Introspection?

Also, in the survey or so-called microgenetic interview, the training of research subjects is at the center. This is supposed to allow a more differentiated access to a particular experience, especially to implicit or non-thematic processes within experience. Whether and how this is possible, however, is controversial within both philosophical phenomenology and empirical science. Philosophically, the question arises whether a new form of introspection is being developed here. This would contradict a classic phenomenological approach, which understands itself as eidetic and transcendental philosophy and not as introspection. After all, phenomenology does not want to look at the inner self but rather to view *the world from the inside out*. Furthermore, philosophical phenomenology is not so much interested in the specific experiences of the individual, but in the invariant **structures of experience in general**, or which of these structures are necessary and constitutive for the experience of a world. Scientifically, the inclusion of introspection also presents us with some problems. The first regards the demand for *transparency*. To what extent is the experience altered by experimental circumstances, specific questions, or the focus of the investigation? And to what extent is it altered by reporting and reflecting on the experience itself? The second problem relates to *validity*. To what extent can we trust self-reports? To what extent are experiences false, imagined, etc.? And the third problem relates to *generalization*. To what extent can we move from individual introspection to general structures of experience that can be correlated with objective data?

▪▪ What Do We Really Know about Our Experience?

In the scientific and psychological context, introspective experience reports are often disregarded, as they are not reproducible and therefore not verifiable due to the singular nature of the experience. Richard Nisbett and Timothy Wilson (1977) have shown in an influential study that people often tell more (about themselves) than they actually know (about themselves). They concluded from this that subjects do not have reliable introspective access to their own cognitive processes. A Swedish team of cognitive scientists (Johansson et al. 2005) confirmed these conclusions. In their study, participants had to choose between two pictures of female faces, with the attractiveness of the faces serving as the evaluation criterion. Immediately after the selection, the subjects were shown the selected (more attractive face) again, along with a request to explain the reasons for their choice. In some cases, a picture was presented that the subjects had not actually selected themselves. Surprisingly, the participants only recognized this trick in 20% of cases. In the remaining 80%, they therefore explained a choice they had not actually made.

It seems, then, that we know very little about how we experience and decide. This is not surprising for a phenomenologist, since so much of Husserl, Merleau-Ponty, Sartre, Beauvoir, Heidegger, and other classical phenomenologists is given to describing the passive, implicit and therefore non-thematic areas of consciousness and existence. Are all self-reports therefore unreliable and useless, or can subjects possibly be trained to capture and describe their own experiences more attentively and thus in a more accurate and more nuanced fashion?

▪▪ About Becoming Aware

A group of French phenomenologists and psychologists repeated the above experiment, with one seemingly small difference, to answer exactly this question. The researchers integrated a so-called elicitation interview between the two experimental steps (between the first selection of the picture and the explanation of the selection) for half of the research subjects. In this interview, neutral but precise questions were put to the participants, which were supposed to help them direct their attention retrospectively to the processes of the experience that had just taken place, so that they could describe it in a more differentiated way. The elicitation interview was therefore supposed to help make the subjects' implicit experiences conscious to them afterwards. What thoughts, associations, or feelings led to the decision? In those participants in the experiment who were given the elicitation interview, there was indeed a difference in the result, while in the 'normal' experimental group the result of the other studies was confirmed. The use of the elicitation interview even reversed the numbers: the wrong picture was now recognized in 80% of the cases (Petitmengin et al. 2013).

▶ **Example: Elicitation or microgenetic interview**

The elicitation interview is designed to help study participants become more aware of implicit aspects of their mental or physical actions (cf. Vermersch 1994). In cognitive science, it continues to be used to describe the microdynamics of experiences associated with cognitive process (Petitmengin 2006). Their purpose is to help subjects shift their attention from the content of the experience to the dynamics of the appearance of this content, which usually remains unrecognized, unnoticed, or in the phenomenological language, 'pre-reflective'.

The first step is to shift attention from the content to the complete act of consciousness. This is equated by Michel Bitbol and Claire Petitmengin (2013, p. 273) with the execution of the phenomenological reduction. However, this is misleading, as it does not relate to any transcendental considerations, i.e., philosophical questions about the conditions of the possibility of experience in the first place. Instead, it shifts the test subjects' attention to their own singular experience. Whenever the test subjects are distracted, for example, by commenting, justifying, explaining, or evaluating this experience, it redirects their attention to the level of description.

The second step is to help test subjects recall or 'evoke' the relevant experience, regardless of whether it is in the distant or recent past. Since these are implicit and pre-reflective processes, sensory triggers are particularly important to allow the emergence of the entire memory in all its qualitative, emotional, and cognitive dimensions. (A famous example is the so-called 'madeleine effect', named after the episode in Marcel Proust's multi-volume novel *In Search of Lost Time*, where the taste of a 'madeleine' pastry triggers a vivid memory of childhood in the main character.) In this context, criteria could be identified that indicate the effectiveness of a retroactive evocation act (Vermersch 1994/2014; Petitmengin 2006), e.g., the spontaneous use of the present tense, the decrease of visual focus, the slowing of the flow of speech, and the occurrence of gestures.

The third step is to direct the subjects' focus to the microprocesses of the given acts, i.e., the pre-reflective elements that usually take place in the background. This is done by shifting attention from the content of an inner image to the dynamics of its appearance, i.e., the genesis of this content. This might include, for example, the emergence of a new idea, an auditory perception, a feeling of surprise, a perceptual illusion, or a painful episode. For this purpose, subjects are asked questions of the type: 'How did it start?',

'What happened then?', 'What exactly did you do?', 'What exactly did you feel at that moment?'. This type of 'content-free' questioning is intended to enable a precise description without generating false memories.

The structure of an elicitation or microgenetic interview is iterative. It is intended to help the test subject to evoke the relevant experience several times, and to direct their attention to a diachronic network that is increasingly refined until the desired level of detail is reached. The goal is to identify a generically dynamic structure that is independent of the various contents of experience (Petitmengin 1999) — e.g., the typical structures or microprocesses that are essential in an experience such as surprise or the emergence of an idea. ◄

▪▪ Naive vs. Guided Description of Experience

Two things become clear here. First, naive descriptions of decision-making processes or experiences are generally unreliable. Second, these descriptions can be corrected and made more reliable through the use of an elicitation interview. Returning to the experiment that asked participants to select the more attractive of two faces, it is clear that the high recognition rate of the 'wrong' image among those participants who were given an elicitation interview shows that it is possible to avoid such misjudgments by directing focus to the decision-making process. Through the interview, a kind of memory of the experience of selecting the image becomes possible. And this memory is regularly refreshed and classified during the course of the interview. The high recognition rate demonstrates the efficacy of this process and thus also the reliability of the memories, which in turn speaks for the validity of the descriptions. Naive or untrained descriptions of the experience, even among participants who were not deceived, were, by contrast, both schematic and inaccurate. The descriptions also remained focused on the content of the choice, i.e., on the faces themselves. People stated, for example: 'I chose this person because they had a nice smile' (cf. Bitbol and Petitmengin 2017, p. 732).

Meanwhile, the 'guided' subjects provided very detailed descriptions of their experiences and decision-making processes. For example, they described the temporal sequence of exploring the features of the faces, the fleeting inner images evoked by the photographs, or the subtle inner feelings used as selection criteria. A difference was also evident in the length of the reports or the number of words used: unguided subjects described their experience with an average of 200 words, while guided subjects needed 3000 words on average. For Claire Petitmengin and Michel Bitbol, these detailed descriptions are the result of a redirection of attention: from the content of perception (face) to the 'how' of its givenness (acts and micro-processes). The interview thus has a similar function to that of the *descriptive epoché* in phenomenology, but now externally guided by questioning. Experiments in which subjects merely report their experiences in a naive and superficial way cannot therefore be considered a general discrediting of introspection. As this study shows, *guided* introspection can produce accurate and detailed descriptions.

▪▪ Phenomenology and Introspection

At this point, the following critical remarks are in order. Methodologically, a distinction must be made between phenomenologically inspired introspection and the method of philosophical phenomenology proper. Even though both processes involve a redirection of attention from the content of the given to the 'how' of its givenness, in the case of guided introspection, the 'given' does not refer to experienced things or the world, but to mental processes. Phenomenology, by contrast, begins *with things* and from there inquires back to the general structures and necessary conditions of experience and ultimately back to subjectivity in general. However, the elicitation interview starts with the *content of a mental process* and from there inquires back genetically to the individual micro-processes that have motivated this content. The becoming-aware thus aims at the concrete description of pre-reflective mental processes in the second-person perspective (of the test subjects). However, it does not stop there, because the descriptions of the test subjects are collected to determine a general, eidetic structure of the microgenesis—one that applies to all test subjects.

▪▪ Microphenomenology and Eidetics

Such a genetic microphenomenology attempts to describe concrete forms of experience in their typicality (or specific generality). For example, which microprocesses precede the experience of surprise or of having an idea? In contrast to eidetics in phenomenology, where a given experience merely serves as an arbitrary starting point for variation, this typification remains bound to particular experiences and their unique qualities. This makes the approach susceptible to premature generalizations (Who was / was not interviewed? How many were interviewed? etc.), and it risks steering the evocation of the experience too much in a certain direction, thereby promoting a subsequent rationalization of the experience. This does not even have to be triggered by the researchers themselves but can be due to a particular social or cultural situation. Therefore, it should be borne in mind that all descriptions of experience are implicitly shaped by language, conventions, and expectations.

The fact that introspective microphenomenology differs from the traditional phenomenological method or that it must struggle with the known problems of introspection does not mean, however, that it does not lead to important results, i.e., that it is not useful in research or therapy. Since every neuroscientific study is based on test subjects and direct or indirect experience reports, further methodological reflection and the development of a procedure for systematizing the experiential reports is urgently needed.

▪▪ Becoming Aware of What is Happening Within Oneself

Some studies also suggest that the elicitation interview can provide insight into the creation of illusions, for example in the context of the famous 'rubber hand illusion' (Moguillansky et al. 2013), where a contradictory combination of visually perceived object (a lifelike rubber hand) and felt touch (the real hand lying under the table) creates the impression that the seen rubber hand is one's own. The elicitation interview has also proved useful in the clinical field. For example, it enabled

3

patients to become aware of the early signs of an epileptic seizure. This confirmed on the experiential level what had already been anticipated on the neuronal level (Le Van Quyen et al. 2001), namely, that seizures do not 'strike like a bolt from the blue' but are visible results of a process that started long before. An awareness of this microgenesis of seizures could therefore be the key to a new cognitive therapy for epilepsy (Petitmengin 2006).

▪▪ Frontloading Phenomenology

However, phenomenology can also be integrated into quantitative research without the need for prior training of research subjects. In the approach advocated by Shaun Gallagher, known as *frontloading phenomenology*, the experimental design is guided by phenomenological insights, for example by phenomenological differentiations between body schema and body image or between the feeling of *ownership* (possession of one's body) and feeling of *agency* (initiation of bodily action). In this context, the hypothesis was tested whether action initiation (a) is conditioned by neuronal processes that control motor skills—so-called efferent signals, i.e., signals that the brain sends to the muscles to trigger movement –, or (b) is associated with higher cognitive areas of action intention. Roughly speaking, the neuronal correlates of *agency*, on the one hand, and *ownership*, on the other, were sought using magnetic resonance imaging (Chaminade and Decety 2002; Farrer and Frith 2002; Tsakiris and Haggard 2005).

▪▪ Sub-personal and Personal Level

A critical phenomenological interpretation of these experiments shows that the loss of the feeling of ability to act can have different causes and can be located at different levels, depending on the case. It can be located at either the motor or cognitive level, or both (cf. Gallagher and Zahavi 2008, p. 162f.). Here, a clear distinction must first be made between the *sub-personal level* of neuronal processes and the *personal* (or pre-personal) *level* of experience, before attempting to correlate both levels. For example, at the neuronal level, it may appear as if there is no difference between observing my own movements and observing those of someone else. Both activate the same brain regions, or neuronal frameworks, that is, so called 'mirror neurons'. In this context, it seems that one first sees an apparently 'naked intention' and only in a second step attributes an author (me or the other) to this intention. However, this distinction plays a crucial role at the level of experience, because except in very rare pathological cases, one's own movement is never confused with that of others. Just as consciousness is always consciousness of something—however minimal this 'something' may be—we always perceive movements as movements of someone or something (a living being, for example). Therefore, one cannot simply infer from the neurological level to the level of experience. If one wants to know what constitutes consciousness or the ability to act, it is not enough to consider only one of these two levels.

▪▪ Problems of Correlation

As was made clear above, the sub-personal and the personal level do not have to be similar (isomorphic). What is immediately given in experience, can presuppose various neurological or sub-personal processes. And yet a certain mutual conditionality is to be expected, i.e., there are so far no good reasons to assume that the connection between experience and neuronal activity is arbitrary, or that sub-personal processes and personal (thematic) experience are completely independent of each other. There are, for example, good reasons to assume that differences at the level of experience, such as between perception (presentation) and memory (reproduction or representation), are somehow also reflected in the neuronal area or in the type of sub-personal information processing, as it is called in cognitive science. Phenomenology can therefore not only inspire or test neuroscientific experimental research through its descriptions and concepts but can also benefit from it by using its results to refine, confirm, or refute philosophical concepts.

The so-called frontloading approach is therefore preferable in many cases to the more introspective method, as it is not always possible to train test subjects phenomenologically. Moreover, in some cases, it is not desirable for the test subjects to be informed in advance about what is going to happen in the experiment. For example, experiments on so-called 'change blindness' (where people do not recognize substantial changes in images or scenes), depend on the naivety of the test subjects. In other cases, test subjects may be unable to follow phenomenological instructions for various reasons, e.g., due to their age, or bodily or cognitive condition.

▪▪ Dimensions of Correlation

When searching for correlations between experienced and measurable data, one can start from either a specific neuronal structure or a phenomenologically identified category of experience. Here, one must think about how the relevant variable of experience should be identified—a posteriori, by comparing phenomenologically guided descriptions from test subjects, or a priori (*front loaded*), by letting phenomenological concepts and differentiations determine the design of the experiment (These can be action-guiding hypotheses or tasks that the test subjects are to perform while their brain activity is being recorded).

It is also important to ask what kind of correlation one is looking for. Are you looking for:

(a) A correlation of generic structures of experience, in which the peculiarities of individual experience are neglected in favor of determining a general structure? This is a correlation in the form of a *type*, i.e., a generally determined form or category of experience.

(b) A correlation of a specific singular experience and its corresponding neural process? This is a correlation in the form of a *token* i.e., a singular occurrence.

Finally, the question arises on what time scale a correlation is sought or expected. Methods such as the survey interview, which provide access to the micro-processes of experience, could be combined with new methods, such as real-time analysis of neuro-electrical signals, wearable MRI scanner, or even pro-active methods such as deep brain stimulation or neuromodulation (cf. Sergiou et al. 2020)—although ethical caution and discussion is needed here. This would allow immediate feedback from the test subjects (and researchers) about the fine dynamics of the ongoing neural activity. First- and third-person data could thus be combined in the experience of the test subjects themselves, as experienced from within and perceived from without.

▪▪ The Limits of Phenomenology

The latter constructively pushes phenomenology to its methodological limits. It raises the question to what extent we can still experience those *passive processes in consciousness* (or corporeality) that make our *consciousness of things* and the world possible. How can a non-objective, pre-reflective self-experience be described? While most phenomenologists would agree that every intentionality and world-directedness is accompanied by an implicit self-reference (cf. Zahavi 1999/2020), the question regarding the extent to which this can actually be experienced remains controversial. Precisely for this reason, it is important to seek methods that allow a self-experience beyond superficial status statements to be systematically and scientifically captured.

To what extent is this still phenomenology in the sense of a description of things or a determination of general or transcendental structures? Perhaps this question is simply wrongly posed. As Husserl was never tired of emphasizing, phenomenology must constantly subject itself to a metacritique, i.e., **methodological critique**, to live up to its claim of being prejudice-free. This includes going thematically and methodologically to the limits of what phenomenology is capable of. What are the limits of description (methodologically) or of consciousness itself (thematically)? Do we still experience the world and ourselves in sleep, delirium, or coma? And how can this then be described?

These are questions that Husserl himself repeatedly asked, for example in the manuscripts recently published as *Limit Problems* (Grenzprobleme) *of Phenomenology* (Hua XLII), as have many phenomenological researchers after him. Phenomenology can show us one thing, namely, that every experience, even the banal perception of things, always points beyond itself and thus contains aspects that are not actually perceived, i.e., not yet, no longer, or not explicitly experienced. And yet all these aspects and processes make our experience what it is. Starting from what we are currently actually perceiving, we can therefore inquire back (past experience), empathize (into the experience of others) and differentiate between (a) experiences that are thematically conscious, (b) those that can potentially be made conscious, and (c) those that may never—or only in borderline cases—be experienced (such as the functioning of internal organs or the brain). In the latter case, cooperation with the natural sciences and technology opens up risks, such as the objectification and medicalization of the body, but it also presents unique possibilities to perceive our consciousness and our bodies—and those of others—in new ways.

3.4 Returning to Experience: Method as Project

Within philosophy, and within interdisciplinary applications of the humanities and natural sciences, there are various beliefs about what constitutes a phenomenological method. Despite these differences, however, clear similarities can be identified that concern the research style, the direction of research questions, the attitude towards research, the area of investigation, and research practices and goals.

▪▪ Areas of Application and Methods
Whether in current movements, such as critical phenomenology or philosophy of technology, or in the application of phenomenology in cognitive and neuroscience, sports medicine, nursing studies, psychiatry, medicine, bioethics, or even in pedagogy or sociology — everywhere the detailed description, classification, explanation, or critique of experience lies at the center. This is done directly or indirectly through the first- or second-person perspective, i.e., through experience reports, behavioral observation, surveys, or direct interaction, such as in therapy.

From a theoretical point of view, questions arise about the relation between experience and physically measurable reactions (neuroscience) or between experience and cognitive functions (cognitive science). Can causalities, similarities, or mere correlations be established? Or can experience be completely reduced to brain activities or formal processing functions? Can phenomenological descriptions be naturalized or find empirical confirmation? In all these investigations, a careful and detailed description of the experience, i.e., the different forms of consciousness and experience, is both a necessary starting point and the goal. If neuroscience, psychology, or cognitive science is to be the answer, the question as well as the explanandum — that is, what needs to be explained —, must be clearly outlined. Phenomenology can be helpful in many ways, whether in setting up hypotheses, designing experiments and questionnaires, or interpreting data.

From a practical point of view, phenomenology can play a significant role in diagnosis, treatment, and therapy. The application of phenomenology in the clinical context is not only of interest from the perspective of the patients. Part of the task is precisely to apply a theoretical framework that allows us to grasp the fundamental structures of the changed life situation. How does one's own being-in-the-world change when living with schizophrenia, epilepsy, or cerebral palsy? How does a disease, a sudden, lifelong, or congenital disability, or a mental disorder affect the subject's relationship to herself, the world, and others? Should one distinguish between normal and pathological, healthy and sick, disabled and non-disabled subjects based on their experiences, or are these merely external attributions, and variations of a gradual spectrum of bodily or neuronal diversity? What phenomenology can offer here is genuine descriptions that include and make visible the multiple differing ways of being embodied and related to the world, rather than setting them aside as anomalous, deviating, or pathological, or using them only to demarcate what is supposedly normal.

3

▪▪ Historical and Cultural Situating of Experience

Furthermore, phenomenology can draw attention to how different times, material circumstances, or social and political contexts are experienced, or how experiences (of ourselves, the world, and others) change or are shaped by individual circumstances or social contexts. How does my experience (of myself, my environment, and other people) develop and change through sports, education, technology, media, or even persecution, imprisonment, oppression, or discrimination? How do experiences of people in different circumstances, with different origins, histories, physical conditions, habits, or opportunities differ? How do technologies mediate and shape our perception and habits? Can experience itself be racist or sexist, i.e., the way we perceive, move, and behave, without us being explicitly aware of it? These are just some of the pressing questions that contemporary phenomenology poses, consciously crossing the boundaries of academic disciplines, to get to the things themselves.

Practicing phenomenology means describing various forms of experience and subjectivity (or inter-subjectivity) in an as unbiased and differentiated way as possible using phenomenological methods or concepts. Depending on the orientation and focus, basic or applied questions are at the center. Sometimes impartiality or epistemic critique is more central, and sometimes practical openness or flexibility is. Sometimes attempts are made to determine general structures or to describe specifically situated experiences, and other times necessary or concrete conditions of this experience and subjectivity are sought. And sometimes practicing phenomenology means doing all of these things at once.

Literature

In the text, the cited volumes of Husserl's Collected Works in German (Husserliana) are only indicated with the siglum Hua and the volume number. The individual volumes are always listed in the bibliography. Where possible, a published English translation has been used. Where not possible, the texts have been translated automatically and subsequently edited by the author. The English translations of Husserl are indicated with the siglum CW, when they are published within the series Collected Works, or with the following abbreviations:

CES = The Crisis of European Sciences and Transcendental Phenomenology

Achterhuis, Hans, ed. 2001. *American Philosophy of Technology: The Empirical Turn*. Trans. R.P. Crease. Bloomington, IN: Indiana University Press.

Ahmed, Sara. 2006. *Queer Phenomenology: Orientations, Objects and Others*. Durham: Duke University Press.

Alcoff, Linda Martín. 2006. *Visible Identities: Race, Gender, and the Self*. Oxford: Oxford University Press.

Aldea, Andreea Smaranda, and Amy Allen, eds. 2016. Historical A Priori in Husserl and Foucault. Special Issue. *Continental Philosophy Review* 49(1): 1–11. https://doi.org/10.1007/s11007-015-9359-8.

Aldea, Andreea Smaranda. 2016. Phenomenology as Critique. Teleological-Historical Reflection and Husserl's Transcendental Eidetics. *Husserl Studies 32*(1): 21–46.

Allen-Collinson, Jacquelyn, and Adam B. Evans. 2019. To Be or Not to Be Phenomenology? That is the Question. *European Journal for Sport and Society* 16(4): 295–300.

Al-Saji, Alia. 2017. Feminist Phenomenology. In *The Routledge Companion to Feminist Philosophy*, eds. A. Garry, S. J. Khader, and A. Stone, 143–54. New York: Routledge.

Al-Saji, Alia. 2024. Touching the Wounds of Colonial Duration: Fanon's Anticolonial Critical Phenomenology. *Southern Journal of Philosophy* 62(1): 2–23.

Beauvoir, Simone de. (1949) 2011. *The Second Sex*. Trans. Constance Borde and Sheila Malovany-Chevallier. New York: Vintage Press.

Beauvoir, Simone de. (1970) 1972. *The Coming of Age*. Trans. Patrick O'Brian. New York: Putnam.

Behrendt, Hauke, Wulf Loh, Tobias Matzner, and Catrin Misselhorn, eds. 2019. *Privatsphäre 4.0: Eine Neuverortung des Privaten im Zeitalter der Digitalisierung.* Stuttgart: J.B. Metzler (Springer Nature).

Bedorf, Thomas. 2010. Der Dritte als Scharnierfigur. Die Funktion des Dritten in sozialphilosophischer und ethischer Perspektive. In Die Figur des Dritten: ein kulturwissenschaftliches Paradigma, ed. Eva Esslinger, pp. 125–136. Berlin: Suhrkamp.

Bedorf, Thomas, and Steffen Herrmann, eds. 2020. *Political Phenomenology: Experience, Ontology, Episteme*. New York: Routledge.

Berger, Peter L., and Thomas Luckmann. 1966. *The Social Construction of Reality: A Treatise in the Sociology of Knowledge*. Harmondsworth: Penguin.

Bidney, David. 1973. Phenomenological Method and the Anthropological Science of the Cultural Life-World. In *Phenomenology and the Social Sciences*, Northwestern University Studies in Phenomenology and Existential Philosophy, ed. Maurice Natanson, 109–140. Evanston, IL: Northwestern University Press.

Binswanger, Ludwig. 1922. Einführung in die Probleme der allgemeinen Psychologie. Berlin: Julius Springer.

Bitbol, Michel. 2014. *La conscience a-t-elle une origine? Des neurosciences à la pleine conscience: une nouvelle approche de l'esprit*. Paris: Flammarion.

Bitbol, Michel, and Claire Petitmengin. 2017. Neurophenomenology and the Micro-Phenomenological Interview. In *The Blackwell Companion to Consciousness*, 2nd edition, eds. S. Schneider and M. Velmans, 726–740. Hoboken, NJ: Wiley.

Blankenburg, Wolfgang. 1958. Daseinsanalytische Studie über einen Fall paranoider Schizophrenie. *Schweizer Archiv für Neurologie und Psychiatrie* 81: 9–105.

Blankenburg, Wolfgang. 1969. Ansätze zu einer Psychopathologie des "common sense". Confinia Psychiatrica 12: 144–163. Engl. Transl. First Steps Toward a Psychopathology of 'Common Sense'. *Philosophy, Psychiatry, & Psychology 8* (2001): 1071–1076.

Blankenburg, Wolfgang. (1971) 2012. *Der Verlust der natürlichen Selbstverständlichkeit. Ein Beitrag zur Psychopathologie der schizophrenen Alienation*. Berlin: Parados.

Blok, Vincent. 2024. Ecological Hermeneutic Phenomenology: A Method to Explore the Ontic and Ontological Structures of Technologies in the World. In *Phenomenology and the Philosophy of Technology*, eds. Bas de Boer and Jochem Zwier, 27–52. Cambridge, UK: Open Book Publishers.

Boer, Bas de. 2022. Attending to Your Lifestyle: Self-Tracking Technologies and Relevance. In Access and Mediation: Transdisciplinary Perspectives on Attention, eds. Maren Wehrle, Diego D'Angelo, and Elizaveta Solomonova, pp. 217–238. Berlin: De Gruyter.

Bootsma, Tom I., Melanie P.J. Schellekens, Rosalie A.M. van Woezik, Jenny Slatman, and Marije L. van der Lee. 2021. Forming New Habits in the Face of Chronic Cancer-Related Fatigue: An Interpretative Phenomenological Study. *Supportive Care in Cancer* 29(11): 6651–6659. https://doi.org/10.1007/s00520-021-06252-3

Bredlau, Susan, and Talia Welsh. 2022. *Normality, Abnormality, and Pathology in Merleau-Ponty*. New York: Suny Press.

Breyer, Thiemo. 2013. Handlung, Text, Kultur. Überlegungen zur hermeneutischen Anthropologie zwischen Clifford Geertz und Paul Ricoeur. *Research in Hermeneutics, Phenomenology, and Practical Philosophy* 5(1): 107–129.

Bubandt, Nils, and Thomas Schwarz Wentzer. 2023. *Philosophy on Fieldwork: Case Studies in Anthropological Analysis*. New York: Routledge.

Buongiorna, Federica. 2019. Embodiment, Disembodiment and Re-embodiment in the Construction of the Digital Self. *Humana Mente Journal of Philosophical Studies* 36: 310–330.

Carel, Havi. 2016. *Phenomenology of Illness*. Oxford: Oxford University Press.

Chalmers, D. 2010. The Character of Consciousness. Oxford: Oxford University Press.

Chalmers, David J. 1995. Facing Up to the Problem of Consciousness. *Journal of Consciousness Studies* 2(3): 200–219.

Chaminade, Thierry, and Jean Decety. 2002. Leader or Follower? Involvement of the Inferior Parietal Lobule in Agency. *Neuroreport* 13(15): 1975–1978.

Cicourel, Aaron V. (1968) 1976. *The Social Organization of Juvenile Justice*. London: Heinemann.

Csordas, Thomas J. 1994. *Embodiment and Experience: The Existential Ground of Culture and Self*. Cambridge, UK: Cambridge University Press.

Depraz, Natalie, Francisco Varela, and Pierre Vermersch, eds. 2003. *On Becoming Aware: A Pragmatics of Experiencing*. Amsterdam: John Benjamins Publishing.

Depraz, Natalie. 2012. *Phänomenologie in der Praxis. Eine Einführung*. Freiburg: Karl Alber Verlag.

De Mul, Jos. 2010. *Cyberspace Odyssey: Towards a Virtual Ontology and Anthropology*. Newcastle upon Tyne, UK: Cambridge Scholars Publishing.

De Preester, Helena. 2011. Technology and the Body: The (Im)Possibilities of Re-embodiment. *Foundations of Science* 16: 119–137.

Desjarlais, Robert, and C. Jason Throop. 2011. Phenomenological Approaches in Anthropology. *Annual Review of Anthropology* 40: 87–102.

Doyon, Maxime. 2024. *Phenomenology and the Norms of Perception*. Oxford: Oxford University Press.

Durt, Christoph. 2020. The Computation of Bodily, Embodied, and Virtual Reality. *Phänomenologische Forschungen* 1: 25–40.

Fanon, Frantz. (1952) 2008. *Black Skin, White Masks*. Trans. R. Philcox. New York: Grove Books.

Farrer, Chlöé, and Chris D. Frith. 2002. Experiencing Oneself vs. Another Person as Being the Cause of an Action: The Neural Correlates of the Experience of Agency. *Neuroimage* 15(3): 596–603.

Fernandez, Anthony Vincent. 2017. The Subject Matter of Phenomenological Research: Existentials, Modes, and Prejudices. *Synthese* 194: 3543–3562.

Fisher, Linda, and Lester Embree, eds. 2000. *Feminist Phenomenology*. Contributions to Phenomenology 14. Dordrecht: Springer.

Francis, David, and Stephen Hester. 2004. *An Invitation to Ethnomethodology: Language, Society and Social Interaction*. London: Sage Publications.

Froese, Tom, and Shaun Gallagher. 2010. Phenomenology and Artificial Life: Toward a Technological Supplementation of Phenomenological Methodology. *Husserl Studies* 26(2): 83–106.

Fuchs, Thomas. 2011. The Brain — A Mediating Organ. *Journal of Consciousness Studies* 18(7–8): 196–221.

Fuchs, Thomas. 2013. Temporality and Psychopathology. *Phenomenology and the Cognitive Sciences* 12: 75–104.

Fuchs, Thomas, Thiemo Breyer, and Christoph Mundt, eds. 2013. *Karl Jaspers' Philosophy and Psychopathology*. Berlin, Heidelberg, New York: Springer.

Fuchs, Thomas. 2017. Ecology of the Brain. The Phenomenology and Biology of the Embodied Mind. Oxford: Oxford University Press.

Gallagher, Shaun. 2003. Phenomenology and Experiential Design. *Journal of Consciousness Studies* 10(9–10): 85–99.

Gallagher, Shaun. 2005. *How the Body Shapes the Mind*. Oxford: Oxford University Press.

Gallagher, Shaun, and Jonathan Cole. 1995. Body Schema and Body Image in a Deafferented Subject. *Journal of Mind and Behavior* 16(4): 369–390.

Gallagher, Shaun, and Dan Zahavi. 2008. *The Phenomenological Mind. An Introduction to Philosophy of Mind and Cognitive Science*. New York: Routledge.

Garfinkel, Harold. (1948) 2006. *Seeing Sociologically: The Routine Grounds of Social Action*. Boulder, CO: Paradigm Publishers.

Garrison, Kathleen A., Dustin Scheinost, Patrick D. Worhunsky, Hani M. Elwafi, Thomas A. Thornhill, Evan Thompson, Clifford Saron, Gaëlle Desbordes, Hedy Kober, Michelle Hampson, Jeremy R. Gray, R. Todd Constable, Xenophon Papademetris, and Judson A. Brewer. 2013. Real-time fMRI Links Subjective Experience with Brain Activity During Focused Attention. *Neuroimage* 81: 110–118.

Geertz, Clifford. 1988. *Works and Lives: The Anthropologist as Author*. Stanford: Stanford University Press.

Gerlek, Selin, Weydner-Volkmann, Sebastian. 2025. Materiality and Machinic Embodiment: A Postphenomenological Inquiry into ChatGPT's Active User Interface. *Journal of Human-Technology Relations* 3(1): 1–15.

Giorgi, Amedeo P. 1975. An Application of Phenomenological Method in Psychology. *Duquesne Studies in Phenomenological Psychology* 2: 82–103.

Giorgi, Amedeo P. 2008. Concerning a Serious Misunderstanding of the Essence of the Phenomenological Method in Psychology. *Journal of Phenomenological Psychology* 39(1): 33–58.

Goldstein, Karl, and Adhemar Gelb. 1918. Psychologische Analysen hirnpathologischer Fälle auf Grund von Untersuchungen Hirnverletzter. *Zeitschrift für die Gesamte Neurologie und Psychiatrie* 41: 1–142.

Good, Byron J. 1994. *Medicine, Rationality, and Experience: An Anthropological Perspective.* Cambridge, UK: Cambridge University Press.

Gugutzer, Robert. 2020. Beyond Husserl and Schütz. Hermann Schmitz and Neophenomenological Sociology. *Journal for the Theory of Social Behavior* 50(2): 184–202.

Gugutzer, Robert. 2024. Strength as Phenomenon: A Pure Phenomenology of Sport. *Journal of the Philosophy of Sport* 51(3): 403–422.

Guenther, Lisa. 2013. *Solitary Confinement. Social Death and its Afterlives.* Minneapolis, MN: University of Minnesota Press.

Guenther, Lisa. 2020. Critical Phenomenology. In *50 Concepts for a Critical Phenomenology*, eds. Gail Weiss, Ann V. Murphy, and Gayle Salamon, 11–16. Evanston, IL: Northwestern University Press.

Guenther, Lisa. 2021. Six Senses of Critique for Critical Phenomenology. *Puncta* 4(2): 5–23.

Gurwitsch, Aron. 2010. *The Collected Works of Aron Gurwitsch (1901–1973), Volume III: The Field of Consciousness: Phenomenology of Theme, Thematic Field, and Marginal Consciousness.* Phaenomenologica 194. Eds. Richard M. Zaner and Lester Embree. Dordrecht: Springer.

Golafshani, Nahid. 2003. Understanding Reliability and Validity in Qualitative Research. *The Qualitative Report* 8(4): 597–606.

Heidegger, Martin. (1927) 1962. *Being and Time.* Trans. J. Macquarrie and E. Robinson. Oxford: Basil Blackwell.

Heinämaa, Sara, and Joona Taipale. 2019. Normality. In *The Oxford Handbook of Phenomenological Psychopathology*, eds. Giovanni Stanghellini, Matthew R. Broome, Anthony Vincent Fernandez, Paolo Fusar-Poli, Andrea Raballo, and René Rosfort, 284–298. Oxford: Oxford University Press.

Heinze, Martin. 2019. Wolfgang Blankenburg. In *The Oxford Handbook of Phenomenological Psychopathology*, eds. Giovanni Stanghellini, Matthew R. Broome, Anthony Vincent Fernandez, Paolo Fusar-Poli, Andrea Raballo, and René Rosfort, 157–164. Oxford: Oxford University Press.

Henriksen, Mads Gram, and Julie Nordgaard. 2016. Self-Disorders in Schizophrenia. In *An Experiential Approach to Psychopathology: What is it like to Suffer from Mental Disorders?*, eds. Giovanni Stanghellini and Massimiliano Aragona, 265–280. Cham: Springer.

Heritage, J. 1984. *Garfinkel and Ethnomethodology.* Cambridge: Polity Press.

Herrmann, Steffen, Gerhard Thonhauser, Sophie Loidolt, Tobias Matzner, and Nils Baratella, eds. 2024. *The Routledge Handbook of Political Phenomenology.* New York: Routledge.

Heyes, Cressida J. 2020. *Anaesthetics of Existence: Essays on Experience at the Edge.* Durham, NC: Duke University Press.

Høffding, Simon. 2018. *A Phenomenology of Musical Absorption.* Cham: Palgrave Macmillan.

Hoffmann, Klaus, and Roman Knorr. 2019. Ludwig Binswanger. In *The Oxford Handbook of Phenomenological Psychopathology*, eds. Giovanni Stanghellini, Matthew R. Broome, Anthony Vincent Fernandez, Paolo Fusar-Poli, Andrea Raballo, and René Rosfort, 111–117. Oxford: Oxford University Press.

Holzhey-Kunz, Alice. 2014. Daseinsanalyse Der existenzphilosophische Blick auf seelisches Leiden und seine Therapie. Vienna: Facultas WUV.

Husserl, Edmund. (1936/1976) 1970. *The Crisis of European Sciences and Transcendental Phenomenology* (**CES**). Northwestern University Studies in Phenomenology and Existential Philosophy. Trans. D. Carr. Evanston, IL: Northwestern University Press. German edition: Husserl, Edmund. 1976. *Die Krisis der europäischen Wissenschaften und die transzendentale*

Phänomenologie: Eine Einleitung in die phänomenologische Philosophie. Husserliana: Edmund Husserl—Gesammelte Werke VI (**Hua VI**), ed. W. Biemel. Dordrecht: Springer.

Husserl, Edmund. 2004. *Wahrnehmung und Aufmerksamkeit. Texte aus dem Nachlass* (1893–1912). Husserliana: Edmund Husserl—Gesammelte Werke XXXVIII (**Hua XXXVIII**). Ed. T. Vongehr and R. Giuliani. Dordrecht: Springer.

Husserl, Edmund. 2013. Grenzprobleme der Phänomenologie. Analysen des Unbewusstseins und der Instinkte. Metaphysik. Späte Ethik. Texte aus dem Nachlass (1908–1937). Husserliana: Edmund Husserl - Gesammelte Werke XLII (Hua XLII). Ed. R. Sowa and T. Vongehr. Dordrecht: Springer.

Ihde, Don. 1979. *Technics and Praxis: A Philosophy of Technology*. Boston Studies in the Philosophy and History of Science XXIV. Eds. R.S. Cohen and M.W. Wartofsky. Dordrecht: D. Reidel Publishing Company (Springer).

Ihde, Don. 1990. *Technology and the Lifeworld: From Garden to Earth*. Bloomington, IN: Indiana University Press.

Ihde, Don. 1993. *Postphenomenology: Essays in the Postmodern Context*. Northwestern University Studies in Phenomenology and Existential Philosophy. Evanston, IL: Northwestern University Press.

Ihde, Don. 2009. *Postphenomenology and Technoscience: The Peking University Lectures*. SUNY Series in the Philosophy of the Social Sciences. Albany, NY: SUNY Press.

Ihde, Don. [1990] 2014. A Phenomenology of Technics. In *Philosophy of Technology: The Technological Condition: An Anthology*, 2nd edition, eds. Robert C. Scharff and Val Dusek, 539–560. Malden, Massachusetts: Wiley Blackwell.

Jackson, Michael D. 1995. *At Home in the World*. Durham, NC: Duke University Press.

Jaspers, Karl. (1913) 1997. *General Psychopathology*, Volume 1. Trans. J. Hoenig and Marian W. Hamilton. Baltimore: The Johns Hopkins University Press.

Johansson, Petter, Lars Hall, Sverker Sikström, and Andreas Olsson. 2005. Failure to Detect Mismatches Between Intention and Outcome in a Simple Decision Task. *Science* 310(5745): 116–119.

Katz, Jack, and Thomas Csordas. 2003. Phenomenological Ethnography in Sociology and Anthropology. *Ethnography* 4(3): 275–288.

Kleinman, Arthur. 1988. *The Illness Narratives: Suffering, Healing, and the Human Condition*. New York: Basic Books.

Kobayashi, T. 1998. Melancholie und Zeit. Basel/Frankfurt: Stroemfeld.

Landweer, Hilge. 2020a. On the Spatiality of Emotions. *Gestalt Theory* 42(2): 165–180.

Landweer, Hilge. 2020b. Aggressive Emotions: From Irritation to Hatred, Contempt and Indignation. In *The Routledge Handbook of Phenomenology of Emotions*, eds. Thomas Szanto and Hilge Landweer, 441–454. New York: Routledge.

Landweer, Hilge, and Isabella Marcinski, eds. 2016. *Dem Erleben auf der Spur*. Feminismus und die Philosophie des Leibes. Berlin: Transcript Verlag.

Leder, Drew. 1990. *The Absent Body*. Chicago: The University of Chicago Press.

Lee, Emily S. 2014. Living Alterities: Phenomenology, Embodiment, and Race. New York: SUNY (State University of New York Press).

Leghissa, Giovanni, and Michael Staudigl eds. 2007. Lebenswelt und Politik. Perspektiven der Phänomenologie nach Husserl. Würzburg: Verlag Königshausen & Neumann.

Legrand, Dorothée. 2007a. Pre-reflective Self-as-Subject from Experiential and Empirical Perspectives. *Consciousness and Cognition* 16(3): 583–599.

Legrand, Dorothée. 2007b. Pre-Reflective Self-Consciousness: On Being Bodily in the World. *Janus .Head* 9(2): 493–519.

Legrand, Dorothée. 2011. Phenomenological Dimensions of Bodily Self-Consciousness. In *The Oxford Handbook of the Self*, ed. Shaun Gallagher, 204–227. Oxford: Oxford University Press.

Legrand, Dorothée, and Susanne Ravn. 2009. Perceiving Subjectivity in Bodily Movement: The Case of Dancers. *Phenomenology and the Cognitive Sciences* 8: 389–408.

Lehn, Dirk vom. 2016. *Harold Garfinkel: The Creation and Development of Ethnomethodology*. New York: Routledge.

Leistle, Bernhard, ed. 2017. *Anthropology and Alterity: Responding to the Other*. Routledge Studies in Anthropology. New York, NY: Routledge.

Lemmens, Pieter. 2021. Technologizing the Transcendental, not Discarding it. *Foundations of Science* 27: 1307–1315.

Le Van Quyen, Michel, Jacques Martinerie, Vincent Navarro, Paul Boon, Michel D'Havé, Claude Adam, Bernard Renault, Francisco Varela, and Michel Baulac. 2001. Anticipation of Epileptic Seizures from Standard EEG Recordings. *Lancet* 357: 183–188.

Levine, Joseph. 1983. Materialism and Qualia: The Explanatory Gap. *Pacific Philosophical Quarterly* 64: 354–361.

Loidolt, Sophie. 2018. *Phenomenology of Plurality: Hannah Arendt on Political Intersubjectivity*. Routledge Research in Phenomenology 7. New York: Routledge.

Lutz, Antoine. 2002. Toward a Neurophenomenology as an Account of Generative Passages: A First Empirical Case Study. *Phenomenology and the Cognitive Sciences* 1: 133–167.

Magri, Elisa, and Paddy McQueen. 2022. *Critical Phenomenology: An Introduction*. Cambridge, UK: Polity Press.

Maldiney, Henri. 1991. *Penser l'homme et la folie*. Grenoble: Editions Jérôme Millon.

Marcinski, Isabella. 2020. *Hunger spüren. Leib und Sozialität bei Essstörungen*. Frankfurt a.M.: Campus Verlag.

Mattingly, Cheryl. 2019. Defrosting Concepts, Destabilizing Doxa: Critical Phenomenology and the Perplexing Particular. *Anthropological Theory* 19(4): 415–439.

Merleau-Ponty, Maurice. (1945) 2012. *Phenomenology of Perception*. Trans. Donald M. Landes. New York: Routledge.

Moguillansky, Camila Valenzuela, J. Kevin O'Regan, and Claire Petitmengin. 2013. Exploring the Subjective Experience of the "Rubber Hand" Illusion. *Frontiers in Human Neuroscience* 7: 659. https://doi: 10.3389/fnhum.2013.00659

Müller, Oliver. 2020. Postphänomenologie: Über eine technikphilosophische Methode. *Phänomenologische Forschungen* 2: 165–184.

Nisbett, Richard E., and Timothy D. Wilson. 1977. Telling More than We Know: Verbal Reports on Mental Processes. *Psychological Review* 84(3): 231–259.

Nörenberg, Henning. 2020. Hermann Schmitz. In The *Routledge Handbook of Phenomenology of Emotion*, eds. Hilge Landweer and Thomas Szanto, 215–223. London: Routledge.

Nörenberg, Henning. 2021. Deontological Feeling: The Tranquil, the Familiar, and the Body. *Frontiers in Psychology* 12. https://doi.org/10.3389/fpsyg.2021.662675

Nordgaard Frederiksen, Julie, and Mads Gram Henriksen. 2019. Phenomenological Psychopathology and Quantitative Research. In *The Oxford Handbook of Phenomenological Psychopathology*, eds. Giovanni Stanghellini, Matthew R. Broome, Anthony Vincent Fernandez, Paolo Fusar-Poli, Andrea Raballo, and René Rosfort, 942–951. Oxford: Oxford University Press.

Oksala, Johanna. 2016. *Feminist Experiences: Foucauldian and Phenomenological Investigations*. Northwestern University Studies in Phenomenology and Existential Philosophy. Evanston, IL: Northwestern University Press.

Oksala, Johanna. 2022. The Method of Critical Phenomenology: Simone de Beauvoir as a Phenomenologist. *European Journal of Philosophy* 31(1): 137–50.

Oudshoorn, Nelly. 2020. *Resilient Cyborgs: Living and Dying with Pacemakers and Defibrillators*. Health, Technology and Society. Singapore: Springer Nature / Palgrave Macmillan.

Overgaard, Søren, and Dan Zahavi. 2009. Phenomenological Sociology: The Subjectivity of Everyday Life. In *Encountering the Everyday: An Introduction to the Sociologies of the Unnoticed*, ed. M. Hviid Jacobsen, 93–115. Basingstoke: Palgrave Macmillan.

Parnas, Josef. 2003. Self and Schizophrenia: A Phenomenological Perspective. In *The Self in Neuroscience and Psychiatry*, eds. Tilo Kircher and Anthony David, 217–241. Cambridge, UK: Cambridge University Press.

Parnas, Josef, and Mads Gram Henriksen. 2014. Disordered Self in the Schizophrenia Spectrum: A Clinical and Research Perspective. *Harvard Review of Psychiatry* 22(5): 251–65.

Petitmengin, Claire. 2006. Describing One's Subjective Experience in the Second Person: An Interview Method for the Science of Consciousness. *Phenomenology and the Cognitive Sciences* 5: 229–269.

Petitmengin, Claire, Anne Remillieux, Béatrice Cahour, and Shirley Carter-Thomas. 2013. A Gap in Nisbett and Wilson's Findings? A First-person Access to our Cognitive Processes. *Consciousness and Cognition* 22(2): 654–669.

Petitmengin, C. 1999. The intuitive experience. In The View from Within. First-person approaches to the study of consciousness, eds. F. J. Varela and J. Shear (eds.), pp. 43–77. London: Imprint Academic.

Petitot, Jean, Francisco Varela, Bernard Pachoud, and Jean-Michel Roy, eds. 1999. *Naturalizing Phenomenology: Issues in Contemporary Phenomenology and Cognitive Science*. Writing Science. Stanford: Stanford University Press.

Ratcliffe, Matthew. 2008. *Feelings of Being: Phenomenology, Psychiatry and the Sense of Reality*. International Perspectives in Philosophy and Psychiatry. Oxford: Oxford University Press.

Ratcliffe, Matthew. 2014. *Experiences of Depression: A Study in Phenomenology*. International Perspectives in Philosophy and Psychiatry. Oxford: Oxford University Press.

Ravn, Susanne. 2009. Sensing Movement, Living Spaces: An Investigation of Movement Based on the Lived Experience of 13 Professional Dancers. Saarbrücken: VDM Verlag, Dr. Müller.

Ravn, Susanne. 2017. Dancing practices: Seeing and sensing the moving body. *Body & Society* 23(2): 57–82.

Ravn, Susanne, and Helle P. Hansen. 2013. How to Explore Dancers' Sense Experiences? A Study of How Multi-Sited Fieldwork and Phenomenology can be Combined. *Qualitative Research in Sport, Exercise and Health* 5(2): 196–213.

Ravn, Susanne. 2021. Integrating Qualitative Research Methodologies and Phenomenology—Using Dancers' and Athletes' Experiences for Phenomenological Analysis. *Phenomenology and the Cognitive Sciences* 22: 107–127.

Ricœur, Paul. (1990) 1992. *Oneself as Another*. Trans. Kathleen Blamey. Chicago: The University of Chicago Press.

Romano, Claude. (1998) 2009. *Event and World*. Perspectives in Continental Philosophy. Trans. S. Mackinlay. New York: Fordham University Press.

Ryle, Gilbert. 1946. Knowing How and Knowing That: The Presidential Address. *Proceedings of the Aristotelian Society, New Series* 46(1): 1–16.

Rosen, James C. 1990. Body-image disturbances in eating disorders. In Body images: Development, deviance, and change, eds. T. F. Cash and T. Pruzinsky, pp. 190–214. New York: The Guilford Press.

Rosenberger, Robert. 2013. The Importance of Generalized Bodily Habits for a Future World of Ubiquitous Computing. *AI & Society: Knowledge, Culture and Communication* 28: 289–296.

Rosfort, René. 2019. Phenomenology and Hermeneutics. In *The Oxford Handbook of Phenomenological Psychopathology*, eds. Giovanni Stanghellini, Matthew R. Broome, Anthony Vincent Fernandez, Paolo Fusar-Poli, Andrea Raballo, and René Rosfort, 235–247. Oxford: Oxford University Press.

Sass, Louis A., and Josef Parnas. 2003. Schizophrenia, Consciousness, and the Self. *Schizophrenia Bulletin* 29(3): 427–44.

Sass, L. 2019. Three Dangers: Phenomenological Reflections on the Psychotherapy of Psychosis. *Psychopathology* 52(2):126–134.

Schmitz, Hermann. 1965–1978. *System der Philosophie, Part I-V*. Bonn: Bouvier.

Schmitz, Hermann. 1990. *Der unerschöpfliche Gegenstand: Grundzüge der Philosophie*. Bonn: Bouvier.

Schmitz, Hermann. 2019. *New Phenomenology: A Brief Introduction*. Atmospheric Spaces, n. 6. Trans. R.O. Müllan and M. Bastert. Milan: Mimesis International.

Schnegg, Michael, and Thiemo Breyer. 2022. Empathy Beyond the Human. The Social Construction of a Multispecies World. *Ethnos* 89(5): 848–869.

Schnegg, Michael. 2023a. Phenomenological Anthropology. Philosophical Concepts for Ethnographic Use. *Zeitschrift für Ethnologie/Journal of Social and Cultural Anthropology* 148(1): 59–102.

Schnegg, Michael. 2023b. Eleven Namibian Rains: A Phenomenological Analysis of Experience in Time. *Anthropological Theory* 23(1): 33–55.

Schnegg, Michael. 2025. Collective Loneliness. Theorizing Emotions as Atmospheres. *Current Anthropology* 66(2): 206–231.

Schnegg, Michael. 2024. Rural Boredom: Atmospheres of Blocked Promises. *Journal of the Royal Anthropological Institute* 30(3): 627–645.

Schutz, Alfred. 1962. *The Problem of Social Reality: Collected Papers I*. Phaenomenologica 11. The Hague: Martinus Nijhoff.

Schutz, Alfred. (1932) 1972. *The Phenomenology of the Social World*. Trans. G. Walsh and F. Lehnert. London: Heinemann Educational Publishers.

Schutz, Alfred, and Thomas Luckmann. 1973. *The Structures of the Life World*, Volume 1. Northwestern University Studies in Phenomenology and Existential Philosophy. Trans. R.M. Zaner and T. Engelhardt, Jr. Evanston, IL: Northwestern University Press.

Sergiou, Carmen S., Emiliano Santarnecchi, Ingmar H.A. Franken, and Josanne D.M. van Dongen. 2020. The Effectiveness of Transcranial Direct Current Stimulation as an Intervention to Improve Empathic Abilities and Reduce Violent Behavior: A Literature Review. *Aggression and Violent Behavior* 55. https://doi.org/10.1016/j.avb.2020.101463

Slatman, Jenny. (2008) 2014. *Our Strange Body: Philosophical Reflections on Identity and Medical Interventions*. Amsterdam: Amsterdam University Press.

Sørensen, Jesper B. 2005. The Alien-Hand Experiment. *Phenomenology and the Cognitive Sciences* 4: 73–90.

Stanghellini, Giovanni, Matthew R. Broome, Anthony Vincent Fernandez, Paolo Fusar-Poli, Andrea Raballo, and René Rosfort, eds. 2019. *The Oxford Handbook of Phenomenological Psychopathology*. Oxford: Oxford University Press.

Staudigl, Michael, ed. 2025. *Phänomenologie des Politischen: Konturen, Konstellationen, Kontexte*. Wiesbaden: Springer.

Steinbock, Anthony. 1995. Phenomenological Concepts of Normality and Abnormality. *Man and World* 28: 241–260.

Stephan, Christopher, and C. Jason Throop. 2023. Anthropological Phenomenology and the Eventive Ground. In *Horizons of Phenomenology. Essays on the State of the Field and its Applications*, Contributions to Phenomenology 122, eds. Jeff Yoshimi, Philip Walsh, and Patrick Londen, 337–354. Cham: Springer.

Stoller, Silvia, ed. 2016. *Simone de Beauvoir's Philosophy of Age: Gender, Ethics, and Time*. Berlin: De Gruyter.

Smith, Jonathan A., Paul Flowers, and Michael Larkin. 2009. *Interpretative Phenomenological Analysis: Theory, Method and Research*. London: Sage Publishing.

Stoller, Silvia, and Helmuth Vetter, eds. 1997. *Phänomenologie und Geschlechterdifferenz*. Vienna: WUV-Universitätsverlag.

Stoller, Silvia, Veronica Vasterling, and Linda Fisher, eds. 2005. *Feministische Phänomenologie und Hermeneutik*. Orbis Phaenomenologicus. Würzburg: Königshausen & Neumann.

Svenaeus, Fredrik. 2000. *The Hermeneutics of Medicine and the Phenomenology of Health: Steps Towards a Philosophy of Medical Practice*. International Library of Ethics, Law, and the New Medicine 5. Dordrecht: Springer.

Thoma, Samuel. 2019. Into the Open: On Henri Maldiney's Philosophy of Psychosis. *Philosophy, Psychiatry, and Psychology* 26(4): 281–293.

Thoma, Samuel, Michael Konrad, Lisa C. Fellin, and Laura Galbusera. 2022. Paving the Way for Systemic Phenomenological Psychiatry—The Forgotten Heritage of Wolfgang Blankenburg. *Frontiers in Psychiatry* 22. https://doi.org/10.3389/fpsyt.2022.909488

Thompson, Evan, Antoine Lutz, and Diego Cosmelli. 2005. Neurophenomenology: An Introduction for Neurophilosophers. In *Cognition and the Brain: The Philosophy and Neuroscience Movement*, eds. Andrew Brook and Kathleen Akins, 40–97. Cambridge, UK: Cambridge University Press.

Throop, C. Jason. 2008. On the Problem of Empathy: The Case of Yap, Federated States of Micronesia. *Ethos* 36(4): 402–426.

Throop, C. Jason. 2010. *Suffering and Sentiment: Exploring the Vicissitudes of Experience and Pain in Yap*. Berkeley, CA: University of California Press.

Throop, C. Jason. 2012. On Inaccessibility and Vulnerability: Some Horizons of Compatibility between Phenomenology and Psychoanalysis. *Ethos* 40(1): 75–96.

Throop, C. Jason. 2018. Being Open to the World. *HAU: Journal of Ethnographic Theory*, 8(1/2): 197–210.

Toombs, S. Kay. 1987. The Meaning of Illness: A Phenomenological Approach to the Patient-Physician Relationship. *Journal of Medicine and Philosophy* 12(3): 219–240.

3

Toombs, S. Kay. 1992. *The Meaning of Illness: A Phenomenological Account of the Different Perspectives of Physician and Patient.* Philosophy and Medicine 42. Dordrecht: Kluwer.

Tsakiris, Manos, and Patrick Haggard. 2005. The Rubber Hand Illusion Revisited: Visuotactile Integration and Self-Attribution. *Journal of Experimental Psychology: Human Perception and Performance* 31(1): 80–91.

Van Manen, Max. 1990. *Researching Lived Experience: Human Science for an Action Sensitive Pedagogy.* Albany, NY: SUNY Press.

Van Manen, Max. 2017. Phenomenology in its Original Sense. *Qualitative Health Research* 27(6): 810–825.

Varela, Francisco. 1996. Neurophenomenology: A Methodological Remedy for the Hard Problem. *Journal of Consciousness Studies* 3(4): 330–335.

Varela, Francisco. 1999. Dasein's Brain: Phenomenology Meets Cognitive Science. In *Einstein Meets Magritte: An Interdisciplinary Reflection. The White Book of 'Einstein Meets Magritte'*, eds. Diederik Aerts, Jan Broekaert, and Ernest Mathijs, 185–197. Dordrecht: Kluwer Academic Publishers.

Varela, Francisco, and Jonathan Shear. 1999. First-Person Methodologies: What, Why, How. *Journal of Consciousness Studies* 6(2–3): 1–14.

Vendra, Maria Cristina Clorinda. 2020. Paul Ricœur and Clifford Geertz: The Harmonic Dialogue between Philosophical Hermeneutics and Cultural Anthropology. *Études Ricœuriennes / Ricœur Studies* 11(1): 49–64. https://doi.org/10.5195/errs.2020.488

Verbeek, Peter-Paul. 2000. *What Things Do: Philosophical Reflections on Technology, Agency, and Design.* Trans. R.P. Crease. University Park, PA: Penn State University Press.

Verbeek, Peter Paul. 2008. Cyborg intentionality: Rethinking the Phenomenology of Human–Technology Relations. *Phenomenology and the Cognitive Sciences* 7: 387–395.

Verbeek, Peter-Paul. 2011. *Moralizing Technology: Understanding and Designing the Morality of Things.* Chicago: The University of Chicago Press.

Vermersch, Pierre. 1994. *L'entretien d' explicitation.* Paris: Edition ESF.

Wajcman, Judy. 2004. *TechnoFeminism.* Cambridge, UK: Polity Press.

Waldenfels, Bernhard. 1983. *Phänomenologie in Frankreich.* Frankfurt a.M.: Suhrkamp.

Waldenfels, Bernhard. (1987) 2020. *Order in the Twilight.* Series in Continental Thought 24. Trans. David J. Parent. Athens, OH: Ohio University Press.

Waldenfels, Bernhard. 1990. *Der Stachel des Fremden.* Frankfurt a.M.: Suhrkamp.

Waldenfels, Bernhard. 1994. *Antwortregister.* Frankfurt a.M.: Suhrkamp.

Waldenfels, Bernhard. 1997–1999. *Studien zur Phänomenologie des Fremden, 1–4.* Frankfurt a.M.: Suhrkamp.

Warren de, Nicolas, and Marco Cavallaro (eds.). 2024. Phenomenologies of the Digital Age. The Virtual, the Fictional, the Magical. New York, NY: Routledge.

Wehrle, Maren. 2015. Normality and Normativity in Perception. In *Normativity in Perception, New Directions in Philosophy and Cognitive Science*, eds. Maxime Doyon and Thiemo Breyer, 128–139. London: Palgrave Macmillan.

Wehrle, Maren. 2016. Normative Embodiment. The Role of the Body in Foucault's Genealogy. A Phenomenological Re-Reading. *Journal of the British Society for Phenomenology* 47 (1):56–71.

Wehrle, Maren. 2017. The Normative Body and the Embodiment of Norms. Bridging the Gap between Phenomenological and Foucauldian Approaches. *Yearbook for Eastern and Western Philosophy* (2): 323–337.

Wehrle, Maren. 2020a. Becoming Old. The Gendered Body and the Experience of Aging. In *Aging Human Nature. Perspectives from The Philosophical, Theological, and Historical Anthropology*, eds. Mark Schweda, Michael Coors, and Claudia Bozzaro, 75–95. Cham: Springer.

Wehrle, Maren. 2020b. 'Bodies (that) matter': The Role of Habit Formation for Identity. *Phenomenology and the Cognitive Sciences* 20: 365–386.

Wehrle, Maren. 2021. Situating Normality: The Interrelation of Lived and Represented normality. *Chiasmi International 23*: 99–119.

Wehrle, Maren. 2024. Normality, as a Concept in Phenomenology. In *Encyclopedia of Phenomenology*, eds. N. de Warren and T. Toadvine. Cham: Springer. https://doi.org/10.1007/978-3-030-47253-5_185-1

Weiss, Gail, Ann V. Murphy, and Gayle Salamon, eds. 2020. *Fifty Concepts for a Critical Phenomenology*. Evanston, IL: Northwestern University Press.

Young, Iris Marion. 1980. Throwing like a Girl: A Phenomenology of Feminine Body Comportment Motility and Spatiality. *Human Studies* 3: 137–156.

Young, Iris Marion. 2005. *On Female Body Experience: "Throwing like a Girl" and Other Essays*. Studies in Feminist Philosophy. Oxford: Oxford University Press.

Zahavi, Dan. 1999. *Self-Awareness and Alterity: A Phenomenological Investigation*. Northwestern University Studies in Phenomenology and Existential Philosophy. Evanston, IL: Northwestern University Press.

Zahavi, Dan. 2005. *Subjectivity and Selfhood: Investigating the First-Person Perspective*. Cambridge, MA: The MIT Press.

Zahavi, Dan. 2011. Varieties of Reflection. *Journal of Consciousness Studies* 18(2): 9–19.

Zahavi, Dan. 2015. You, Me and We: The Sharing of Emotional Experiences. *Journal of Consciousness Studies* 22(1–2): 84–101.

Zahavi, Dan. 2018. Getting it Quite Wrong: Van Manen and Smith on Phenomenology. *Qualitative Health Research* 29(6): 900–907. https://doi.org/10.1177/1049732318817547.

Zahavi, Dan. 2021. Applied Phenomenology. Why it is Safe to Ignore the Epoché. *Continental Philosophy Review* 54: 259–273.

Zahavi, Dan. 2020. The Practice of Phenomenology: The Case of Max van Manen. *Nursing Philosophy* 21(2). https://doi.org/10.1111/nup.12276

Zeiler, Kristin. 2020. Why Feminist Technoscience and Feminist Phenomenology Should Engage with Each Other: On Subjectification/Subjectivity. *Feminist Theory* 21(3): 367–390.

Zigon, Jarrett, and C. Jason Throop. 2021. Phenomenology. In *The Open Encyclopedia of Anthropology*, ed. Felix Stein. Facsimile of the 1st edition in *The Cambridge Encyclopedia of Anthropology*. https://doi.org/10.29164/21phenomenology

Index

The manufacturer's authorised representative in the EU is Springer
Nature Customer Service Centre GmbH, Europaplatz 3, 69115 Heidelberg,
Germany. If you have any concerns regarding our products, please
contact ProductSafety@springernature.com

Printed and bound by CPI Group (UK) Ltd, Croydon, CR0 4YY
23/04/2026
02095588-0012